Pelican Books
Astrology

Marc Edmund Jones's wide-ranging activities
have included separate careers as practicing
astrologer, editorial consultant, Protestant
minister, and motion-picture scenarist.
Throughout his adult life he has been
strongly attracted by the occult and by
virtually all the inadequately explored and
divergent outreachings of the human mind.
This growing interest led to his founding of
the Sabian Assembly in 1923. His many books
and other writings have left a permanent
imprint on horoscopic interpretation and have
helped bring to it a more strictly scientific
orientation and a greater accuracy in performance.

Marc Edmund Jones

ASTROLOGY
How and
Why
It Works

Penguin Books Inc, *Baltimore, Maryland*

Penguin Books Inc, 7110 Ambassador Road, Baltimore, Maryland 21207

First published by Sabian Publishing Society 1945
Revised edition published 1969
Published in Pelican Books 1971
Reprinted 1972

Copyright © by Marc Edmund Jones 1945, 1969

Published by special arrangement with
The Sabian Publishing Society and Shambala Publications, Inc.

Printed in the United States of America by
Kingsport Press Inc., Kingsport, Tennessee
Set in Gael

Contents

Nothing is permanent but change.
Character is destiny.

HERACLITUS OF EPHESUS

Foreword

This book has been in the process of writing throughout the more than thirty years during which judicial astrology has been a matter of deep interest. At first a mountain labored, and brought forth a mouse, the experimental pamphlet, *Evolutional Astrology*, rather handsomely illustrated by George Winslow Plummer and published in 1916 by the author as a gift to the *Societas Rosicruciana in America*. A detailed outline of ideas for a volume tentatively titled *Key Principles of Astrology*, and scheduled to follow *Key Truths of Occult Philosophy* (which appeared in 1925), was presented as classwork to a group of California students early in 1924, and this material subsequently became *Temple Astrology* in the mimeographed series. Meanwhile, beginning in 1922, the demonstrated value of a preliminary organization and presentation of subject matter, first orally before various critical groups, and then in the tentative mimeographed form, led to what ultimately became the Sabian project, under which the scheduled total of three thousand lessons or reports will have been completed during the current year.

A new outline for a fundamental text, based on what had been learned from a teaching perspective in many hundreds of class sessions through some fourteen years, was expanded into the mimeographed *Sabian Astrology* lessons, the initial series on the subject issued from December 3, 1928, to June 10, 1929, and these comprise the materials gradually reworked into the contents of the present volume. Dane Rudhyar, the first professional contributor to the popular astrological literature in America, took an interest in the mimeographed expositions from the time they were issued, and an acknowledgment of his part in awakening a more general appreciation for the Sabian presentation has been made in the foreword to *Problem Solving by Horary Astrology*. Mathilde Shapiro and Margaret Morrell were responsible for the actual start of the present text by suggesting that its serialization in abridged form would help in the clarification and refinement of its details. The debt to these young women is very great because, during the time the articles ran in *American Astrology Magazine* from February, 1940, through January, 1941, they gave an evening a month, helping to prepare the installments.

The manuscript in this 1940 draft did not meet the needs of a fundamental text, at least as these were uncovered on several cross-country lecture trips, and so it was withdrawn from the publisher then interested in the series. The smaller *How To Learn Astrology* was written and issued as a trial balloon to determine the acceptability of a general approach which was in no way either fundamentally metaphysical or blindly authoritative. That two further texts have preceded this fourth one, which is logically the first, is due in part to exigencies of publishing and in greater part to the extraordinary difficulties in its preparation. Miss Shapiro has read each of the four drafts completely, as well as galley proofs, and has done yeoman work in checking keywords and delineations on the basis of her experience in using them through several recent years. Mrs. Morrell has read page proofs and checked the mathematics throughout. The author's secretary, Miss Elsie Boyle, who has now lived through her third astrological book, has taken almost entire responsibility for technical typographical and stylistic points.

Astrology, How and Why It Works is dedicated to Paul G. Clancy, primarily in recognition of his outstanding contribution to American horoscopy. He arranged to open the pages of his magazine to the Sabian materials at a luncheon conference in the summer of 1935, long before the author felt his contribution was ready for the general public. Mr. Clancy has created many channels for the New World's revitalization of the stellar art, providing a focus of stimulation in this country not unlike that created by Alan Leo and his *Modern Astrology* a generation ago in London. Ten years of friendship with Paul Clancy have been a happy, rewarding and at times adventuresome experience.

The book is released for publication very reluctantly. The final reading of its pages has been a devastating event because, if the achievement is a compensation for the effort in what it reveals of an ultimate promise, the performance does not call for any excessive pride. The difficulties, largely verbal, remain as nearly insurmountable as they were three decades ago, largely because astrology, in a curious way, is a more refined instrument of analysis than any possible common tongue used for its description. It is virtually impossible to restrict particular words to special horoscopic meanings, simply because the requirements for knowing them in such a fashion would be no different from those for grasping the astrological indicator *per se,* i.e., there would be no communication of idea. Experience, to become astrologically transmissible, has to be carried behind language in a very real sense, and this has made is necessary to write these pages in clichés and formulas, with every reasonable lean upon sheer repetition.

A fundamental vocabulary has grown up with usage, so that some terms can be committed to memory by the newcomer, and thereupon used in his mind as pegs on which to hang the fabric of the new dimension in his thinking. Hence it has been possible to supplement these orientation words to some extent, and to set them apart as keywords. This spares the average person any distress over the very great problems that lie, so to speak, behind the scenes, and that are inherent in the conglomerate of stray materials such as rest in disorder beyond the impressive outer façade of every human science. No effort has been made to compromise a final utility by any superficial pretense to an exactness or unambiguity which not only does not exist, but probably never will. Thus ideas which are co-ordinate astrologically can appear ridiculously dispar-

FOREWORD

ate in everyday language, as in the classification of the three temperaments on page 178. Many horoscopic implications would seem complete *non sequiturs* to the uninitiated, as in details of the microcosmic alphabet commencing on page 190.

The principal source of difficulty, when an effort is made to approach astrology critically, but from the outside and without an adequate preparation through an actual experience with its intellectual mechanism, is that there are an unending host of distinctions which are very sharp in horoscopic analysis, but definitely hazy when expressed in any simple form of words. An illustration is the contrast between will and identity on page 285. When individuality and personality are compared, on the one hand, or personality and emotion, on the other, the word personality is employed in two distinct connotations, as can be observed on pages 287–8. This usage is more convenient for the astrologer than to bring in a new term, since he has no difficulty in seeing personality as a function-in-process in the one case, and as a circumstantial *fait accompli* in the other. It often takes the neophyte a number of years to discover that this overlapping of reference can be a contribution to clarity rather than confusion. In this text, as an example, he will find sagacity as a keyword for Sagittarius on page 232, and also on pages 291 and 292 as a distinguishing mark of Jupiter in contrast with the intelligence of Mercury and the wisdom of Saturn. Again, consciousness is seen on page 48 as a ninth-house matter, and on page 291 as another phase of Jupiter's activity. These apparent inconsistencies are multiplied indefinitely in horoscopic literature.

The least obvious but most serious of the difficulties in astrological writing is the fact that the English language makes no basic separation whatsoever between objects which identify action because they are ends in view, and objects which are merely the potential material of experience. Hence there is no self-identifying vocabulary to keep planetary meanings from slipping off into house or sign significations. In the case of the Venus implications, described beginning on page 297, there is a rulership of money, which is almost the basic second-house meaning, as explained on page 68. Food and clothing, as indicated by the same planet from the activity perspective, are really sixth-house factors, as brought out on page 65. In time, of course, as the horoscopic vocabulary is enriched, these problems will recede more and more into the background.

New York City, March 19, 1945

This book has served the needs of students and friends of astrology for a quarter of a century and I am happy that it will now serve a wider audience as well, through a paperback edition which incorporates all the latest corrections and revisions. I am especially pleased that this popular edition is served by the quality of the new publisher, Penguin Books, and by the company my books finds with theirs.

MARC EDMUND JONES PH.D.
Stanwood, Washington 1970

Horizons

CHAPTER ONE

The Magic of Hemispheres

At the very beginning of things, according to the Biblical account of creation, God began His labors by a series of divisions. There is a word in the Greek for this. It has come down into the English, where it is very useful although not particularly familiar. It is dichotomy, which means cutting in two. Because it is a convenient term, it will be put to work rather often in the following pages.

As a start, a little attention to the dichotomies described in *Genesis* may be of considerable help in seeing just what astrology is, how it works, and what it is able to do.

In the beginning God created the heaven and the earth.

And the earth was without form, and void; and darkness was upon the face of the deep. And the Spirit of God moved upon the face of the waters.

And God said, Let there be light: and there was light.

And God saw the light, that it was good: and God divided the light from the darkness.

And God called the light Day, and the darkness he called Night. And the evening and the morning were the first day.

And God said, Let there be a firmament in the midst of the waters, and let it divide the waters from the waters.

And God made the firmament, and divided the waters which were under the firmament from the waters which were above the firmament: and it was so.

ASTROLOGY: How and Why It Works

And God called the firmament Heaven. And the evening and the morning were the second day.

(Genesis, 1:1–8)

The point here is not that God is the giver of astrology, in any literal fashion. Neither is there any reason for believing that the scholarly Hebrew priests, who worked out this opening section of the Pentateuch, were at all interested in the science of the stars. They had the job of explaining existence and life. The astrologer has exactly the same task. What to a degree was inevitable in the one case is real light upon an equal inevitability in the other. In other words, there is only one possible way for getting at things, as far as the human mind is concerned. The universe must be divided—more and more of it screened off, pushed aside and removed from consideration—until what is left can be grasped, or made the basis of judgment. This dividing, when it becomes an intellectual analysis under rigorous conditions of control and record, is the method of science.

The connection between these Biblical verses and the venerable art of astrology is remote indeed, amounting to little more than the fact that they illustrate conveniently, rather, the psychological method which has had an effective refinement in the horoscope. The dichotomies of *Genesis* begin with a distinction between heaven and earth, and then move on at once to a second division between light and darkness. Irrespective of any other implications, the start of analysis is obviously an orientation in space and time. What is immediately at hand is earth, and what is distant or outside ordinary experience is heaven. The here of it, as distinguished from the there, takes its tangible form in a pattern of progress, or becomes day and night. This distinction in its turn is a realization of the now in events, as against what was and what will be.

A very natural question arises at this point. Are the foregoing observations a correct interpretation of the Bible, in the sense that the original author of the passage sought to make things clear in this way? The matter is unimportant. The basic

4

orientation reveals itself to the investigator because it is a necessity in any thinking about origins, whether this be the beginning of the universe as a whole or, as an example, of Mr. Theophilus Smith of Plymouth, Massachusetts. Astrology capitalizes on the necessity. It is not likely that the learned rabbis, struggling with their cabalistic sentences somewhere around the time of Nebuchadnezzar's Babylon, were conscious of these psychological factors. It is even less probable that the creators of the astrological techniques, through the centuries, have been aware of the scientific elements entering into the perfection of their procedures. Men made bread and alloyed metals long before the advent of chemistry and physics. Understanding always follows experience, even if it happens to contribute to some new experience which, in its turn, can lead to further understanding.

How does astrology build upon the fact that the human mind operates, in general, in a certain inevitable way? The dichotomies at the opening of *Genesis* seem to afford the best of possible clues. God next makes a division between the waters and the waters. This almost seems a matter of tweedledum and tweedledee, but in reality it makes good scientific sense. What appears now is a firmament, to effect the division. There has been endless speculation over the cosmological concepts of ancient Israel, but everything of the sort is beside the point here. The Hebrew word translated "firmament," רָקִיעַ, means an extended surface, since it comes from the verb to "beat out" as applied to malleable metals, and the simple idea is a solid dome separating the waters of space above and below, thus:

Any overliteral notion of a fixed ceiling in the heavens, however, results from a focusing of attention at the wrong place. What God accomplished, so to speak, by arching away the crude substance of creation, was to provide elbowroom for experience upon the flat expanse of everyday reality. It was then possible for dry land to appear—according to this symbolical description of beginnings—and for living creatures to start their functioning upon it. Hence the dichotomy is not dramatized half so well by the vaulted firmament as by the surface made available to man, this is, the ground of personal identity. A more serviceable diagram, adapted to the modern reader's acquaintance with Mother Earth as a globe, and with a universe reaching in all directions, would be like this:

What has been captured in diagrammatic form now is the fundamental concept of the horoscope.[1] The horizontal line

[1] In its representation of a ground for experience upon the earth, the plane of dichotomy belongs on the surface of the sphere, where it would resemble the position of the embryonic layer developed by a chick, on top of the yolk in the egg, thus:

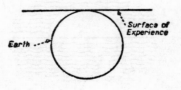

of these diagrams—which, it is necessary to remember always, is a flat surface as seen sidewise—is the ordinary horizon, with every symbolical as well as literal implication to be explained through the chapters to come. In order to permit the representation also, in the most convenient form for analysis, of the relation of the whole heavenly vault around the earth, horoscopic practice conventionalizes the figure. The astrological horizon is shown passing through the center of the globe, in parallel to the true horizon on the surface. The terrestrial ball is placed within the celestial sphere, in the following fashion:

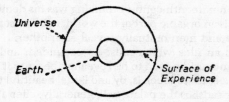

Present-day convention then proceeds to insert axial lines to represent the twelve HOUSES of the heavens. These lines are eliminated as they pass through the smaller circle, purely as a matter of optical clarity, so that the normal horoscopic map, before the insertion of the astrological characters and figures, appears this way:

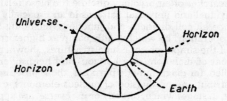

A great deal will be said, in later pages, about the naïve symbolism of astrology. No mastery of the stellar science is possible without understanding the degree to which nature herself has dramatized the essential relations among things in general.[2] It is here that a real horoscopy has its foundations since, from one point of view, astrological judgment might be defined as a scientific naïveté at work. It is an orderly analysis of various relationships through their most simple significance. Indeed, the best of life's insights may be of this primitive sort, even when instinctive and without the blessing of science. Because experience takes place in nature, natural and unconditioned factors supply not only the substance of the experience as such, but also the means for its conscious realization. Hence the real heart of Charles Darwin's contribution to nineteenth-century thinking was his demonstration that man is an organic part of the world, not a prisoner within it. Nature and men mutually reveal each other.

Here is an idea which must be expanded, and clarified. Symbolism must be seen to be revealing because it is natural. What is pleasant to touch is, by and large, beautiful to the eye. Whatever satisfies the palate will, generally, offer a seductive perfume to the nostrils. The norms and values of the mind are grounded of necessity in the gratification of the senses, since these are the individual's link with his world of experience. However, a person who is ugly by abstract standards, but who proves a benefactor in some given circumstance, can radiate a genuine beauty, so that the subjective side of life is no less a part of nature. Man may divide up his universe in everyday

[2] The researches of embryology disclose the close relationship between individual and universal patterns in an especially interesting fashion, since all cell divisions and junctions, including the first intracellular operations by which highly complex higher creatures develop out of the simple protoplasmic structures, show a preliminary establishment of dichotomizing horizons and hemispheres. Slightly oversimplified, for diagrammatic purposes, these processes involve a sorting, distribution and division of nucleus elements, on the fibers of a spindle, in stages which, directly or in reverse, are approximately as follows:

living, but he cannot cancel out the relationships of any one part of it with every other part. The whole remains total or complete. The conscious anchorage of astrology in this one all-important fact is the principal secret of its effectiveness at its best.

The work of the statisticians shows that, all considerations being equal, desirable traits have a positive correlation with each other. This is a mathematical way of saying that the smartest person tends to be the healthiest, the most prosperous, and so on. No one need quarrel with the proposition, even on a first encounter, if he will remember that these qualities are identified through the manifestation of them by the so-called fortunate people of life, i.e., they present a statistical pattern of desirability. Nothing is attractive intrinsically. Its attractiveness, rather, is a symbolization of its meaning in experience. The Greeks well understood this when they made such qualities no more than attributes, or elements put into experience by the meaning which various acts or reactions will have for the individual. The qualities at root result from choices, or natural selection, and are to be charted as distinctions of the mind.

Practical astrology originates in this charting. The zodiacal sign Libra, which describes the sun's location as seen from the earth for an approximate thirty days following the autumnal equinox, is the scales or balance in the astrological symbolism.[3] This is a way of capturing the functional idea of a transition from growth and outreach to harvest and ingathering. A Libra person, in the language of horoscopy, is an affable one, inclined to be pleasant and ever prone to go along in feeling and opinion with whoever is closest at hand for the moment. The symbol emphasizes the instability of this teeter-tottering, which is one point of view, and also the valuable quality of enthusiasm arising out of the capacity for quick alignment to other people and circumstances.

[3] All consideration is of northern-hemisphere ideas. Actually man in the antipodes seems to show little correspondence to the reversed relations there, tending to remain a creature of the north even though he may have settled down under the equator long ago.

The question suggested at once is, what possibly can be the relation between the fall equinox and a Libra person? The answer in any usual sense is, none. The correspondence is all a matter of what can now be identified as a statistical ordering. The new mathematical technique of statistics—developed in the past generation by science, business and government —measures, in precise detail, a phenomenon eternally evident in nature, namely, that like things not only have relationship in their likeness, but that they tend to increase it. The one constant principle in all knowable reality is that anything which has any existence attempts, at it were, to be more of what it is. Not exactly expressed in such a way, this oversimplification—which is convenient for the present analysis—underlies the newly dominant concepts in physics, psychology and the other sciences.

Astrology is an organization of the divisions and distinctions in life on a definitely statistical pattern. Exactly as the best-looking young people are apt to be the most competent, so Libra individuals tend to disclose what will be found to be autumnal-equinox factors in the astrological charting. What are autumnal-equinox factors? Why, naturally, characteristics proving to be constant under a Libra emphasis. Astrology does not create anything. By the same token it reveals nothing that is hidden. Instead, it facilitates the measure and judgment of what is actually encountered in experience. Its method is a controlled exaggeration of some things, for the better recognition and understanding of others, on the pattern of all psychological analysis.

The astrologer starts out by assuming that every individual who is created in the image of God must establish the world of his own experience in the same way that God does. He sets up a firmament, by the very act of being, and so delineates his own personal hemispheres. The fact that the horoscope technique employs an actual heavenly sphere, to measure as well as symbolize them—thereby providing for an outlining of events in certain predictive potentials—is merely item one in the uncompromising naïveté of astrological analysis. It is as though the baby were able to go outdoors at the exact moment of his delivery, to stand there with arms outstretched, and to turn around slowly and actually define an astronomical horizon in the celestial vault. It is in this way, by being born, that the infant symbolically identifies his own or private universe of reality, and charts the psychological ground of his being as a foundation on which, for him, all experience must rest.

The magic of hemispheres, as astrologically established, lies in the illimitability of their capacity to symbolize things. There is not only a basic set given to character at birth, but also a continuous reconstruction of personality throughout life. The individual, for the total of his years—and as often in the course of events as he desires—may project a special firmament through the whole of manifest existence, and thereby create a particular horizon for himself in some one or another pattern of relations. Here is where choice and free will become power, and where horoscopy can help man to become the director of his fate in a very true sense.

CHAPTER TWO

Rhythm
and Reality

When Alponse Karr, in 1848, evolved his happy phrase, "the
more it changes, the more it's the same thing," he gave an
impudent and Gallic lightness to one of the most fundamental
of human insights, to wit, that there is a factor of certainty on
which man may depend, throughout life's shifting confusions.
Francis Bacon, by comparison, is ponderously scientific. "It
is sufficiently clear," he explains in his *De Natura Rerum,* "that
all things are changed, and nothing really perishes, and that
the sum of matter remains absolutely the same."

Closer to the astrologer's heart is the creative imagination
of the early Hebrew mind. It is a singer of Israel who really
gets the concept of stability into words of power. The Psalmist
shows the way for every individual who would get a steadying
hand upon the course of his own destiny.

The heavens declare the glory of God; and the firmament
    sheweth his handywork.
Day unto day uttereth speech, and night unto night sheweth
    knowledge.
There is no speech nor language, where their voice is not
    heard.
Their line is gone out through all the earth, and their words
    to the end of the world. In them hath he set a tabernacle
    for the sun,

Which is as a bridegroom coming out of his chamber, and
rejoiceth as a strong man to run a race.
His going forth is from the end of the heaven, and his circuit
unto the ends of it: and there is nothing hid from the heat
thereof.

(Psalms, 19:1–6)

The hazards of life have always been a persisting nightmare
in human consciousness, despite the dulled sensibility of the
masses, or the thin coating of a rational self-aplomb by which
most cultured individuals seek to insulate themselves from
their primitive apprehensions. The mortality of the young
among both men and beasts in ancient times, together with
the common handicaps and incapacities resulting from accident or disease, and the loss of opportunity or advantage from
simple inability to muster an adequate energy or cleverness,
all dramatized the insecurity of existence. Personal relationships of blood and marriage were no more dependable than
others. Every community faced the chance of onsweeping
war, famine, pestilence, flood and earthquake, often without
warning, and there might be nothing at hand of a physical sort
to which a frightened soul could cling. Man's fears have long
remained the principal ingredient of both his conscious and
subconscious self-awareness.

There were unchanging elements in the midst of all these
things, however, even if they were no more than the certainty
of repetition in calamity's onset. While men were utterly
helpless against the risks of existence, they were yet, curiously
enough, able to reproduce or repeat their own identity in
their children. Moreover, they saw the foliage and creatures
around them survive in this species of metempsycho-
sis—which seems to have been a simpler idea for the savage
than for his learned descendants. It was obvious to primordial
man that life, while characterized by the utmost instability
on the surface of existence, nonetheless presented a pattern
of continuity. Imperfectly as he may have sensed the fact, it
identified a greater reality in his thinking. The human mind

13

felt itself a part of this continuity, especially in the realization whereby the human individual became religious, or began to know God. Here was a divine instinct which established hope and faith as the counteragents for every stark deficiency in self-integration.

The job of identifying the process whereby man gets the inner or subjective side of himself out into the unstable world of phenomena about him, making his understanding objective enough so that he can point to it, and thereupon refine it as knowledge and philosophy, belongs to the anthropologist and the psychological theorist. The astrologer merely observes that the basis for any such transition—in which an elementary creature becomes a social animal—is the discovery of some reference of stability in the everyday world to which a self-assurance can be assimilated. Such a frame of orientation, unless made a matter of imagination, must be found in nature. Out of all possible forms of natural religion in this sense, the worship of the sky—that is, man's ultimate anchorage of his consciousness in the completely dependable vault of heaven—is the most significant in religious history. It is the historical beginning of horoscopy.

The survivals of a primitive animism in astrological practice show how man's self-assimilation to nature can take place on the superstitious side, that is, in an enthronement of the fearful rather than the hopeful and self-reliant aspects of consciousness. There are still those today who go no further than the imitative magic of the savage, seeking to propitiate evil by a species of mental reproduction. They worship it by the abject respect they show it, and by the degree to which they regard it as inevitable. Devotees of astrology on this level always surrender to unfavorable indications. They invite calamity by making no effort at all to utilize the conditions constructively. They expect good things to come to them because Venus smiles or Jupiter chuckles in his beard, so to speak, quite irrespective of anything they may do to cooperate with the happier potentiality. They are the people who carry an ephemeris of the planets' places in their pocket, to make sure they overlook no chance to subject the most trivial details of their living to the guidance of an aspectarian. They make a virtue of their complete inability to act with wisdom or intelligence apart from a conformity to the limitation they accept in every passing moment, and so they regress unsuspectingly to the utterly hazardous world of the savage.

Primordial man himself, in contrast with this degeneracy of modern self-reliance, has left ample testimony to his very clear realization of a steadiness in nature. He often saw, in the cosmos, an order on which anyone could depend in a more mature way, thereby bringing peace and happiness into his own private affairs. He developed the credo to which the Psalmist has given voice. The heavens with their regularity of rise and set, the unimpeachable rhythm of day and night, the unswerving path of the sun and stars—these are reliable things in a context of even the greatest confusion. The heat of the sun becomes a recompense for man after the storm and cold, and there remains no corner of experience where the sustaining power of an ultimate reality cannot be found. The reassurance written in the eternal sky is that the unlimited ongoing can become very personal. This intuition of unquenchable energy, of an inexhaustible creative vitality, is brought out most characteristically by the Old Testament's colorful figure of the bridegroom. The youth, taking on his full adult responsibilities as he has a proved knowledge of his own strength, represents the true cosmic stature of all men and women.

The continual recurrence of phenomena in the heavens, the rhythmic reality of the ages is the firmament, are a prophecy of man in his immortal reality. The subtle assurance here transforms risk into freedom, while chance takes a new form as choice. The individual is established in the sky to symbolize his capacity for mastering every hazard of lesser being, and to dramatize a profound psychological principle which the ancients approximated rather well in their mythology, or their allegorical half-realizations. The analogy between man and the universe became almost a commonplace of thinking with the rise of a conscious philosophy. The doctrine of MICROCOSM and MACROCOSM—popularizing the idea that the individual is the cosmos in miniature, while the greater universe is the total man in his real being—has been traced from the earliest Greeks, as Heraclitus and Empedocles, through Plato and Aristotle, on down into the modern period. The major work of Rudolf Hermann Lotze is entitled *Mikrokosmos,* and the concept has been carried to an interesting extremism in the monads of Gottfried Wilhelm Leibnitz.

Astrology, rather than conventional science or philosophy —or even the occultism which leans most heavily on this correspondence—has put the conception of the heavenly man to work in a practical or everyday fashion. The SIGNS OF THE ZODIAC, as allocated to various parts of the body, beginning with Aries at the head and ending with Pisces as ruler of the feet, enable the astrologer to visualize an actual human organism—in a complete generalization of its powers, of course—stretched around the whole empyrean vault. This zodiacal creature, taken down from the sky, has graced drugstore almanacs and the more blatant sort of astrological publications for generations.

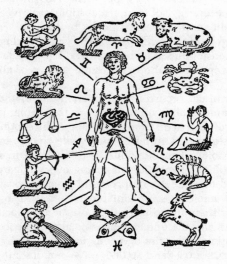

The significance of the heavens in astrology arises from their charting of entirely human relationships, represented by this popular form of anatomical macrocosmos. The celestial indications are developed from two different points of view, however, and the horoscope is created by blending them. First in ordinary public interest is the zodiac. It provides the more general perspective, and delineates the dependable or ordered factors as in contrast with the more individual elements of hazard, risk, chance, choice and free will. The zodiacal circle is the path of the sun, as measured or seen from the surface of the earth, and it is, actually or astronomically, the orbit of that latter body. The annual movement of the sun swings to the north from December to June, and to the south in the other six months, reaching the Tropic of Cancer above the equator and the Tropic of Capricorn below. The schoolmaster's globe usually shows the course of this journey in the following fashion:

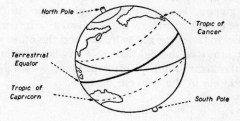

The concern of these opening chapters is the celestial EQUATOR rather than the zodiacal circle (or ECLIPTIC, in more technical designation). The signs of the zodiac, representing the relatively eternal or unchanging features in man's character —as these in their turn are revealed or mirrored in the firmament—are the consideration of Part Two in this text, when the analysis turns to the constants in experience. It must be realized, however, that both these great circles used in astrology—that is, the ecliptic or sun's apparent path, and the terrestrial equator as it is extended out into the celestial sphere—are created by the motions of the earth, and so are phases of the globe's activity in a complex of physical energies. The heavens dramatize the basic relations in man's life, but they are only able to do so because the planet on which he lives is an active participant in the ceaseless and restless balancing of mass against mass in the larger milieu of a solar system. The movements of the earth are the basis of astrology, completely and in every respect, even in connection with the other moving bodies, as will be explained in Part Three.

It has been seen that when the individual has an actual beginning, he is really describing a horizon in the physical cosmos. This represents him as an entity, mathematically, in the special way already indicated. He becomes measurable, astrologically, because he thereby delineates his own personal universe. Thus the baby has been pictured, in a purely symbolical sense, standing outdoors and turning around with outstretched arms to complete the basic dichotomy. Now, in order to get any notion of the horoscopic mechanism, it is necessary to add to the earlier and quite imaginative description. If a gigantic knitting needle could be put in the earth —with one end at its center, perpendicular to its surface and also parallel to the spine of the infant, and the other reaching the outer limits of the celestial sphere—the turning of the globe on its axis through twenty-four hours would describe a complete circle in the heavens, thus:

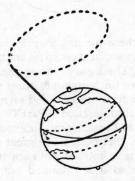

If the birth took place at the equator, shown here by the double line, the needle would simply retrace the extended or celestial equator in which the diurnal or daily motion of the earth is measured. However, both such circles of axial motion are parallel, and in consequence it is quite proper to consider the activity of the one as taking place in the other, mathematically. They show the same movement in the same fashion, which makes them functionally identical. The astrologer, therefore, always employs the latter, where he establishes the houses of the horoscope as shown on page 7. The circle which there defines the universe or heavenly vault is now seen to be the celestial equator (representing all circles parallel to it).

The Measure of Reality by Motion

It is necessary to digress at this point, to emphasize the fact that all astrological symbolism is created by the actual movement, in one phase or another, of whatever may be symbolized. Nothing in equilibrium is ever significant in its motionlessness. In fact, there is no absolute or static reality in any possible substance or relationship, as modern science has begun to make very clear.[1] Objective existence is merely a condition of constancy in a co-operative activity, whether in a simple aggregation of atoms or a complicated social structure. Man himself at all points, physically and psychologically, is a complex of motions. His organism has its continuity in a dynamic economy of chemical changes, supporting the distribution of the energy which facilitates them. Any living animal takes in oxygen and gives off carbon dioxide, consumes proteins and releases nitrogenous waste, and so on. It exists through its unceasing interaction with its total environment. The symbols of astrology, to have any functional effectiveness in the mind, must diagram experience in the terms of the movements which constitute both man and his world, and

[1] The Bohr and Heisenberg concept of uncertainty is an interesting exposition along these lines at the time this text is prepared for publication.

which thereby permit the latter to take on the representation of the former.

The horoscope and its suggestive indications are all derived from the motions of the earth originally, since every other heavenly activity is mediated through the celestial body on which man finds himself. His presence on the globe means that, in his experience, it remains motionless as the ground of is being, and that its movements are necessarily translated elsewhere. Thus its most important daily rotation on its axis causes the entire heavens to turn around, in a very true sense. This establishes the celestial equator, or the circle of the houses, as the foundation for horoscopic delineation. These equatorial divisions present the particular orientation of the individual in the world he has made for himself, and they are the primary mansions of astrology. They, like the earth, remain stationary in man's experience. They are the basis of his private reality, and the entire celestial vault turns through them clockwise—as viewed in the normal diagram—rising in the east and setting in the west every twenty-four hours.

There are twelve houses in the celestial equator, as already indicated in preliminary fashion, and it has been explained that they are established first of all by the individual's original horizon. This basis for the horoscopic figures has been shown on page 7, as follows:

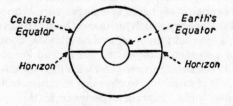

The horizontal line is the horizon seen sidewise, as pointed out before, and it must be remembered that the two hemispheres together comprise the entire cosmos. In other words, the houses are not just geometrical pieshaped divisions of the equatorial circle but are rather sections of the whole heavens, like the segments of an orange when it is peeled. Hence a planet, to be in a given house of the horoscope, does not have to lie in the plane of the equator, but may lean away on either side to a considerable extent. This may be seen by comparing the diagrams on the next page, figure A turning the horoscope to give a sidewise view, and figure B showing the same planetary situation in the normal fashion of representation. Positions *a, b* and *c* in the first instance are all identical with *d* in the second.

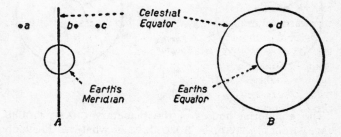

The lean of a planet—that is, more technically, its latitudinal co-ordinate in relation to either the equator or zodiac—has astrological import in certain refinements of technique, but these are beyond the scope of the present text. Therefore its DECLINATION and LATITUDE, or the amount of this lean away from the plane of the equatorial houses and of the zodiacal signs, respectively, are not discussed here. They are always given in an astrologer's ephemeris, but in fundamental horoscopy no attention is paid to anything but the location of the various bodies relative to each other in terms of their situation around the circle of the houses and signs, or their RIGHT ASCENSION and celestial LONGITUDE, respectively. The latter takes care of all the functions of the former in normal practice, so that right ascension may be ignored, as well as declination and latitude, in simple work. The position of a planet in amount of distance away from the earth—the radius vector of the astronomers—is of no astrological significance whatsoever, since all horoscopic delineation stems entirely from celestial movement as interpreted through angles of arc in geometrical relationship. Hence, in the following comparative figures, with A showing distances from the earth and B the astrological convention, the positions x and y in the former case are identical with z in the latter.

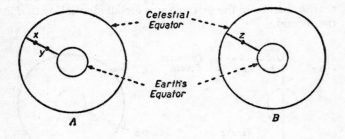

The equatorial houses of the planetary CHART, FIGURE, MAP, WHEEL, NATIVITY or HOROSCOPE of whatever heavenly elements are enlightening to the astrologer. The zodiacal signs are an additional and supplementary means for doing precisely the same thing, giving an added dimension of insight to astrological judgment. Understanding begins with the houses, then passes on to the signs in due course.

With this much made clear, in preliminary form, the next task is to gain some initial understanding of the factors by which the horoscopic wheel becomes a twelvefold screen of indicators. Leaving the zodiac for later analysis, what is the basis for the equatorial mansions? This first circle presents the rhythm of reality in the more intimate outreach of human consciousness to cosmic certainties, leaning upon the "day unto day" which "uttereth speech," and the "night unto night" which "sheweth knowledge." Its houses chart the commonplace situation of normal experience, and the question of present importance is, how do they do so?

The answer has been given in considerable part, as far as

any foundation realization is concerned, through an exposition of the dichotomizing technique, and its demonstration of the necessity that the mind encompass its momentary world—that is, the totality of elements in any context of being—by a progressive sorting out of pertinent relations. The horizon is the beginning in any process of self-realization. It is the actual basis of the individual horoscope, and also of all astrological meanings.

A second great dichotomy arises from practically the same factors that define the horizon. As man stands on the earth's surface, creating the ground of his being, he also divides all the potentials of life, quite literally, into two great hemispheres of (1) the things he faces, or to which he gives conscious attention, and (2) those he puts behind him, or on which he depends more or less subconsciously. What is above or below the earth—to use the astrological terminology in respect to the first great horizontal division—is what life provides by way of a more objective context, on the one hand, as against what constitutes the reservoir of the race, on the other. The distinction between what an individual confronts, and that on which he he turns his back, is a dichotomy of experience on the basis of a real human choice or discrimination, not of a mere immediate situation. Man is symbolized in himself as he faces east—where the heavens rise, and where he reaches out to that which is novel—but is represented by what is essentially other than himself in anything which lies behind him, and which is setting as far as he is concerned, i.e., that which is passing into a consequent or a secondary significance. Hence the new dichotomy creates a sort of up-and-down horizon.

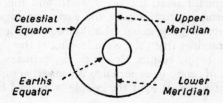

23

Astrology terms the upper point the MIDHEAVEN, or uses the abbreviation M.C. for the Latin *medium coeli*, while the other end of this meridian axis is identified as the NADIR, the I.C. or *imum coeli*.

These two fundamental divisions at the horizon and meridian, in man's total world of experience, complete the physical or astronomical foundation for the symbolism in astrology. They establish the basic axes of the houses. Because they are the most important part of the conventional horoscopic map, they are often emphasized by specially heavy lines in printed horoscope blanks, thus:

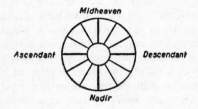

The ASCENDANT and DESCENDANT are the horizon points corresponding to the nadir and midheaven. (The nadir has a logical priority to the midheaven, as will be seen in the next chapter, but it is seldom given first consideration.) These four interceptions of the equatorial circle by the two basic axes are known to astrologers as the ANGLES of the chart. They are also identified rather commonly by the compass directions which —as far as the usual diagram is concerned—reverse the familiar conventions of the map maker. Thus the ascendant is east, the descendant west, the nadir north and the midheaven south. According to tradition, the early astrologers thought that by reversing the geographical directions they would remind themselves that they were looking at the sky, with not altogether happy results. However, the primacy of the east as a point of origin in experience is properly emphasized by its present place, at least for people who read from left to right. The east-west axis, in terms of actual indication of direction, and quite apart from the method of representation on paper, is identical in astrology and geography, but the astrological north and south line is perpendicular to the surface of the earth, on which the geographic north and south are recognized. The midheaven, thus actually upward, lies towards the south for anyone north of the Tropic of Cancer, but this is a matter without astrological significance, and the designation is inept although well-entrenched in usage.

The Fourfold Rhythm of Reality

The two basic dichotomies, expressed in the house axes, have an equal rank in actual astrological practice. Although matters indicated by the horizon have a literal first importance in life, the meridian relations demand as much attention, and are concerned as fully in the development of the more detailed symbolism. What now must be understood is the manner in which the twofold division becomes, first, a functioning fourfold one, and secondly, a twelvefold classification of experience in astrology's very effective categories.

It should be clear that the original dichotomies are entirely overlapping, each creating two complete celestial hemispheres. When the double process is considered, either division may be the initial one, depending on the point of view, whereupon the completion of the other means, in practical fact, a halving of two hemispheres into four quarters. The separation between (1) upper or objective and (2) lower or subjective realms of experience, on the one hand, and between life as (3) initiated or controlled and (4) suffered or utilized, on the other, has only a limited significance, if the analysis does not proceed further.[2] Each of these possibilities

---

[2] A horoscope where the planets lie altogether in one of the four possible hemispheres is quite revealing astrologically, by that fact alone, and such charts have provided a simple case of interpretation for beginners in the author's earlier and smaller text of this series,

properly makes a contribution to the other. Thus, when the universe is divided on the basis of the horizon, there is obviously a functioning intelligence which makes the division. The actual process of dividing represents a facing of life, or of its potentials, and so is fundamentally an expression of the second dichotomy, no matter how much the eastern outlook may be assumed or taken for granted. This means that the one process of hemisphering is really the bisection of a corresponding hemisphere which has already been established by the complementary and similar dichotomizing, and which is not now at the forefront of action, in this way:

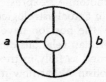

In other words, the horizon at *a* is only completed over to *b* by projection, from the point of view of the meridian's hemisphere in which the horizontal division is taking place. The other half can be said to come into being, symbolically, by an operation of factors described at the descendant. There man leans or depends on things other than those of his own initiation or, in a very true sense, his facing of things has consequences. But the only way he can establish the whole horizon, actually, is by turning around, just as the baby does in a figurative fashion. When he is facing west, he has his back to the east, and so in counting on the fact that what he there described will remain as he has established it, at least until he

---

How to Learn Astrology, Philadelphia, David McKay, 1941. However, not many nativities present this particular arrangement, and its indication is highly general.

can face east again. In a curious psychological way he gives this west the character of an east, momentarily, thus completing the horizon in the following fashion:

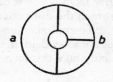

This is the all-important astrological principle of triangulation, now seen in its origin. When something divided into two is redivided in turn, the result is a quartering of the whole, but only two of such quarters are ever significant in relation to the previous division. If the hemispheres of first origin were both to be taken into account, when one of them is subdivided, their original definition would be destroyed or cancelled out, simply because a necessary unlikeness is lost. Referring again to the *Genesis* dichotomy, only one of the hemispheres participates in the subsequent evolution, namely, that claimed from the waters above. Actually any distinction in anything at all must substantiate a difference. Here is a necessity which underlies all logic. The idea is very clear when shown by diagram, figure A producing something which offers no significance to either pair of hemispheres but figure B making the eastern area quite distinct, and so accentuating a practical or actual difference between east and west.

A   B

Astrology, as a mathematical technique of analysis, reveals its logical foundation at this point. All four hemispheres are preserved, but no one of them is ever taken to be of any importance whatsoever except as it (1) ignores, in any special case, that half-universe from which it has been drawn apart, and (2) distributes instead the distinction between the hemispheres of the other and complementary dichotomy. The diagrammatic picture of the ascendant, in any horoscopic charting, would consequently take this form:

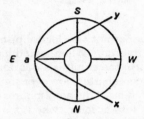

The indication of a is an activity of the east hemisphere, or the facing of things, as primarily a distinction between x or subjective impetus and y or objective conditioning. Thus a, x and y have a continual and special relationship at all times. The ascendant in horoscopy is the over-all indication of personality, and the particular personal equation in life which it represents (a) is always a constant balancing or teetering between inner or free impulses (x) and outer or compelled self-guidance (y), a proposition which will be amplified in detail. There are four ways in which the underlying rhythms of individual existence reveal their ramification throughout everyday living, and these are expressed, as far as the symbolism is concerned, in the following possibilities:

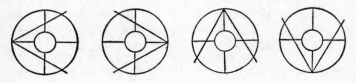

Here is diagrammatic preview are the four worlds of experience to which the next chapter is devoted. When these figures are interlaced, there is, in any given quarter of the whole circle, an emphasis of the basic hemisphere and a secondary influence of each hemisphere of which the quarter is not a part, as follows:

Taking all significance counterclockwise, the more usual direction of astrological relationship, *a.* emphasizes the east hemisphere *per se*, while *b* and *c* in order are the secondary influence of the south hemisphere in the east, and of the west hemisphere in the north. Meanwhile the primary east emphasis is completed at *e* in the north and *i* in the south, balancing the meridian-axis distinctions in terms of east. Similarly, *d* emphasizes north, with *e* and *f* the secondary influence of east in the north and south in the west, while the primary north emphasis is completed at *h* in the west and *l* in the east. The angle at *g* emphasizes west, with *h* and *i* the secondary influence of north in the west and east in the south, while the primary west emphasis is completed at *k* in the south and *c* in the north. Finally, *j* emphasizes south, with *k* and *l* the secondary influence of west in the south and north in the east, while the primary south emphasis is completed at *b* in the east and *f* in the west.

The origin of the houses, as well as the necessity for twelve of them, is thus disclosed on the diagrammatic side. Turning to the astronomical factor, three hundred and sixty degrees of motion in the heavens are divided into equal segments or mansions of thirty degrees, and the point at which each of such mansions begins is known as a CUSP. The houses following the hemisphere divisions or basic axes, counterclockwise, are angles, as already stated. The two other houses linked in each case with the angular one, in the manner shown, constitute, with that angle, an equatorial triad. Each of the four triads takes its name from the point of the astrological compass at which it is focal. The houses themselves are not named, but rather are numbered from the ascendant, *a* in the preceding diagram defining a first house, *b* a second, and so on.

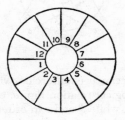

In terms of these numbers, therefore, the fifth and ninth houses derive their meaning from the first, the eleventh and third from the seventh, the eighth and twelfth from the fourth, and the second and sixth from the tenth. The four mansions next counterclockwise from the angles in each instance are the SUCCEDENT houses—the second, fifth, eighth and eleventh—and the four behind the angles, from this point of view, are the CADENT ones—the third, sixth, ninth and twelfth.

The underlying relationship of the houses in the triads has its most simple expression in terms of time. The angles, at the focal points of the circle in a direct symbolization of the basic divisions of experience, have a present implication always. The succedent mansions indicate a future potential. The cadent ones chart factors of the past, or the influence of background and tradition in human relations. The idea of past or future in this connection, however, is not to be taken literally in the sense that anything pertinent is itself remote. Whatever is so designated is, rather, as it has relation to the present. This means some immediate activity of importance more conditioned, limited or endowed, as the case may be, through elements rooted in the remote. Obviously any non-immediacy in astrology is significant through its mediated pertinence. The fact that a man may inherit a large fortune in two years is not now vital beyond the degree to which this posibility has present implication, such as enabling him to borrow money, plan business, consummate marriage, and so on.

The outstanding value of astrology is its persistent emphasis on the reality at hand, that is, on the rhythms of life which may be used to sustain a real fulfillment of human hopes and ideas.

CHAPTER THREE

The Art of Portmanteau Analysis

Charles Lutwidge Dodgson had little reason to suspect that he was immortalizing himself when he took Alice down the rabbit hole, and created his wonderland of strange creatures. The young Oxford profe was making the best known contribution of the mathematical mind to pure symbolism, but he was too much the pedant in his own person to understand this. Lewis Carroll—that is, the fictitious individual of the nom de plume—might have grasped the matter, but the other self of the Reverend Mr. Dodgson never ventured very far beyond the covers of a book.

It is the second narrative, *Through the Looking-Glass,* that presents the astrologer with a truly neat explanation for the process by which his houses, signs and planets acquire what he terms their RULERSHIPS. Alice had been puzzled greatly by some lines of verse, starting off——

> *'Twas brillig, and the slithy toves*
> *Did gyre and gimble in the wabe:*
> *All mimsy were the borogoves,*
> *And the mome raths outgrabe.*

—and Humpty Dumpty didn't hesitate to interpret it for her, with assurance, at a later point in her adventure. "I can explain all the poems that ever were invented," he said, and then proceeded to account for "slithy" as meaning lithe and slimy. " 'Lithe' is the same as 'active,' " he continued. "You see it's like a portmanteau—there are two meanings packed up into one word." Defining "mimsy" as flimsy and miserable, he added, "there's another portmanteau for you."

Astrology is a psychological method for charting or measuring experience. It operates through an analysis of character, and a deduction of the probable consequences of a particular individual's situation under a given set of relations. The astrological delineation of a person has its roots in the astronomical distribution of factors stemming from the moment and place of birth on the earth's surface, as has been explained in the preceding two chapters. Mere mathematical elements have no psychological meaning, however. Hence a technique of correlation is necessary, and it is here that the language of horoscopy comes into being, creating a series of especially inclusive terms. What has been shown, thus far, is the rationale by which the birth of a man is unique in its geometrical patterning, together with the way that mathematics may be used to identify him as an entity in his own right. The next step is to see how the factors of horizon or midheaven—of zodiacal signs or equatorial houses—can yield an actual significance in everyday potentials.

The individual creates and recreates his own world of reality, continually, through the sorting out of its elements in his understanding. The consequent entirely personal dividing up and ordering of experience is an operation of desire and choice, of reaction and self-integration. Since the mathematical mapping of this can go no further than a statistical linking of like things to each other, the evolution of meaning in astrology must come from experience, the limitations and permissions of time and space. Yet success is never more nor less than a matter, in one form or another, of General Forrest's famous getting there first with the most men, exactly as failure is the corresponding inadequate choice, response or act in the given case. Reality is always a convergence of relations, and activity a capitalization upon convenience. This is pretty much a matter of mathematics after all.

ASTROLOGY: How and Why It Works

Astrological indications differ from those of other psychological charting, less deeply rooted in the common world of experience, through their broader spread of relations, their greater coverage of immediate pertinencies. Something akin to the stability of the heavenly vault is gained when reference is to elements persisting in the struggle of man throughout all time, since these cut across all lines of racial or cultural distinction. This is why the stellar art remains unusually naïve, holding close to nature and patterning experience through the initial impulses in which it has its origin. Thus the horizon is the fundamental ground of being, or the underlying constant in self, permitting the most simple definition of character. It is also the special foundation for every detailed ramification of individuality. Mathematically, it provides the original dichotomy of self-existence. Astrology proceeds, in consequence, by comparing all men on the basis of their moments of birth, that is, of the individual origin in each case of this horizontal factor in time and space. The implications are ultimately empirical, of course, because it is what men have done in the past that remains the basis for any intelligent estimation of what they are apt to do in the present or future.

This means that the horizon in astrology is not only the ground of existence for some special person, but for all others as well, at least to the degree in which he shares his various human qualities with them. It is man generalized, with the particular but surprisingly slight modifications which constitute character *per se*. Here is a descriptive facility in sharp contrast with everyday convention. Ordinary language describes people by specific terms, such as carry a minimum of predictive implication. The one child is beautiful and talented, the other morose and ill-dispositioned. John Smith is tall while Larry Brown is short. Mildred is blonde, Mary a brunette, and so on. Horoscopy avoids this superficiality by seeing all men in the person of each, and so presents its immensely broadened reference. To indicate that Mr. X has a Leo ascendant, and Mr. Y an Aquarius sun, is to supply what is well nigh a dossier on each gentleman in question. The astrologer develops terms which compact a host of meanings within themselves. In the apt conceit of the Reverend Mr. Dodgson, he operates with portmanteau ideas and words.

Since the distinctions in horoscopy arise in the horizon and meridian, these primary agents in the sorting of experience must carry an implication which, no matter how abstract or general, maintains a root emphasis on the constants involved, that is, elements of dependability in man's day-by-day living. Astrology indicates this by assuming the operation of two simple lines of symbolic force, or persisting direction of act and response, in all human existence. The first of these expresses the factor of horizon, and is pictured as an electriclike flow of life or animal energies around the surface of the globe, moving principally from east to west. These energies—holding to the symbolism—enter the field of immediate personal reality from the former direction, which is taken as identifying the positive pole of activity, and leave westwardly. By the same token the meridian circle, containing the midheaven and nadir of the horoscope, is imagined as vitalized by a similar stream of spirit, or celestial force, playing upon the earth and through to its center from the heavens. This is seen to reach the periphery of self at the north pole of the chart, or the nadir angle, and to pass out and on towards outer space again at the midheaven.

The two terms LIFE and SPIRIT are portmanteau concepts, carrying a technical astrological reference to the twin dichotomies of experience which, in the first instance, establish the level of events as (1) above or (2) below the threshold of consciousness, and in the second mark the distinction between elements of life (3) held in control and (4) dismissed to the management of other people or agencies. Popular occultism sometimes dramatizes the difference in the frames of reference represented here. When a man is asleep, or resting, the horizontal position of his spine permits the flow of the life energies through him for his refreshment, just as when awake, or active, his erect stand enables spirit to function through his backbone and thereby make him, to the extent of his capacities, a truly creative personality. Astrology sharpens the distinction in this imagery by giving a primary importance to the difference between the positive and negative poles in these theoretical streams of energy. This creates EAST and NORTH as special designations for the potentials of unconditioned impetus, and WEST and SOUTH for the complementary conditioned relationships.

The four equatorial triads can now be delineated, in terms of astrological implication, by adding the derivative houses into the consideration. This is done through the process of triangulation already charted in detail—as far as the mathematical phase of the symbolism is concerned—by the preceding chapter. The three designations angular, succedent and cadent are portmanteau adjectives common in the astrological literature, and it has been seen that they represent, in order and most simply or primatively, the present implication of the house axes (angular), the future potentials shown by the mansions lying on the counterclockwise side (succedent), and the dependence upon past or background elements which are charted by those next to the angles on the clockwise side (cadent). A more suggestive designation of these groups, however is TRANSMUTING, to stress the constancy of change as encountered at the angular or axial houses, and RESULTING and EXCITING, to emphasize the types of interaction revealed by the succedent and cadent groups, respectively. By resulting is meant an individual potentiality, a definite expansion of experience, and so not any mere general consequence of cause, such as is characteristic of everything. By exciting is meant simple encouragement to action, or response to various factors in experience because of the character and conditioning, not necessarily the more specific provocation to emotion or intensity of sensation.

The basic triadic relations, as represented in tabular form, use a past-present-future sequence from left to right to dramatize the actual rhythm of experience. This particular charting summarizes the structure of the houses as a whole, but is somewhat too abstract for any direct employment in horoscopic interpretation. However, the connections exhibited here, with the primary emphasis on the principles behind them, will give additional light upon every rulership of the individual mansions.

TABLE I

The Triadic Relations in the Equator

CADENT: Exciting   ANGULAR: Transmuting   SUCCEDENT: Resulting

IX	Inward Impulse	I	Life Force	V	Life Expression
III	Outward Impulse	VII	Life Relationship	XI	Life Consummation
XII	Inward Compulsion	IV	Spirit Force	VIII	Spirit Expression
VI	Outward Compulsion	X	Spirit Relationship	II	Spirit Consummation

Astrology unquestionably arose, in the beginning, as a wholly empirical science. Man began to observe correspondences between the events in his life and the seasons—or the phases of the moon, and other celestial phenomena—and to organize the correlations to the extent of his intellectual power. By the same token, the individual astrologer today learns his art out of experience, despite the extent to which he may read textbooks, attend classes and study abstract practice. Indeed, this is true no less of the physician, and every other professional of high training who deals with anything as complicated as human nature or the animal organism. The theoretical tabulation of house meanings is of little worth to the person who approaches horoscopy by rational analysis only, or who responds to some dilettante interest. The fundamental terms, no less than the portmanteaus to which they have been likened, must have something put into them before they can have any real value.

The east, west, north and south triads establish the four possible approaches to experience from an astrological point of view. They have been given diagrammatic form on page 31 in connection with their mathematical origin, and now the simple naturalness of this quartering of reality must be recognized within the complex of ordinary everyday living. The four great worlds of man must be understood, not as mutually exclusive domains, but as areas of emphasis in existence. Each is real, and largely self-sufficient, in its own right. No one of them ever interferes with any of the others in even the least detail.

The proposition here should present no great difficulty. Thus a man has a home and a business, as examples of these great worlds. It is possible to say that the interests of the one collide with those of the other, and to document the case, but such a view is quite superficial. Actually, the individual in business disturbed by domestic upheaval is, as far as his money-making is concerned, the type of person he is from a commercial perspective. The simple fact is that the degree to which it is possible for him to neglect his larger affairs, because of home distraction, is a definite factor of his character, and not at all an interference in his money-making by domestic inharmony. This same man, being what he is, could be upset with equal disadvantage by many other things. The disturbance, astrologically, is part of the picture in the great world of trade. The instrumentation of this disturbance by the wife or children is something else, a convenience in the particular instance but always a reality on its own account, measured in its own proper place. Turning to the domestic domain, the fact that he may bring alien relationships into his private life, producing a greater or lesser upset, is again a reflection of temperament. The intruding reality may be the office, or something far removed from business, without effective difference as far as the simple inharmony in his home is concerned.

Thus a principle of real importance is revealed. None of the difficulties in life are a source of trouble because of the specific nature of any one of them, but rather and entirely because of the meaning each will have in some given person's case. The great power of astrology is its continual division or sorting of experience, until every factor of issue or crisis is exhibited primitively or naïvely enough to enable man to change it or direct it as he wills. This possibility of control depends upon carrying everything down to the point where it is detached from all its ramifying involvements in the total pattern of a moment's reality, much as a physician seeks to localize an ailment for treatment.

Of the four great worlds of experience, two have been identified in the preceding paragraphs, namely, the domains of business and of home. The other two are much more primary, however, since the dichotomy of business-home is a social, psychological and exterior more than an individual and interior alignment. Man is of first importance as he exists in and of himself, that is, (1) in the world of his own personality—the self-sufficiency which can be divided off from his co-operative relationships with his fellows—and (2) as he refines himself as a personage in the world of his dependence on others in an individual way, i.e., the domain of the opportunity he gains through his partnerships and immediate or tête-à-tête relations with others. These are the two areas of experience with which existence begins, and with which astrology originates in consequence, as already explained. Hence the consideration starts with them, each in order.

THE WORLD OF SELF

Know then thyself, presume not God to scan;
The proper study of mankind is Man.

Pope, *Essay on Man*

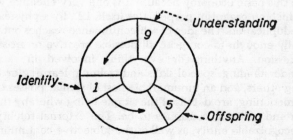

39

The eastern triad consists of the ninth and fifth houses with a focus in the first, and it give the astrological indication of life *per se,* that is, everyday living in its positive phase. The most convenient definition of life, for the purposes of horoscopy, is the fundamental urge of every organism to continue in existence, or to perpetuate itself. An organism, from this point of view, is defined as a fundamentally self-contained, self-renewing and self-perpetuating continuum of energy. Here life force, astrology's portmanteau conception of basic organic activity, is distributed throughout experience, but within the strict periphery of self and its manifestation of itself.

When reality is taken this way, the logical account of it turns out to be somewhat circular, since it begins and ends in a private milieu of circumstances. It is almost solipsistic—that is, completely self-sufficient—but this is its nature in actual, hard and practical fact. Nothing is gained by any metaphysical excursus in this connection. To seek to derive the self from something else which, on its part, would have to be a self in some different aspect ultimately, would call for a further regression towards the supposed source, on and on to infinity. Astrological analysis gains its power from its capacity to operate, effectively and completely, within the confines of the problem or situation at hand.

Life, in its portmanteau positiveness, embraces the many familiar processes necessary to the achievement of a literal self-continuity. Eating, drinking, breathing and elimination in various specializations are all included. Reproduction is a part of this basic economy because it is one very effective way in which an organism perpetuates itself, i.e., by a physical self-reduplication. The idea of self-continuance reaches out, naturally enough, to comprise all possible creative or artistic expression. Anything or everything involved in memory, understanding, special skills and training, learning or teaching others, and an innumerable host of similar phases of self-functioning, are details of the simple living whereby the self, in and of itself, continues to be. The external totality of a recognizable entity, as well as the subjective continuum, is a necessary part of the consideration at the east triangle, so that the focal first house or ascendant rules the general appearance of a person, together with whatever helps to create this or refine it, such as the foundation conditioning which astrologers identify as the early environment.

The word rule or rulership is one of the most important of all terms in the horoscopic lexicon, a portmanteau of a sort somewhat different from those so far presented. It implies measurement or correspondence, of course, but also much more than mere parallel importance or pertinency. Thus the first house rules personality in the sense that any emphases of astrological relationship, occurring in this segment of the heavens, are reflected effectively in matters of self-esteem, of basic self-interest, and the like. This is not a case of cause and effect, although often so taken. Rather, there is a convergence of factors in the actual heavenly stresses and strains which, in statistical language, has a positive correlation with specific types of reality in experience. Rulership identifies those personal areas of potential relationship within which the given probability of act or response is to be identified. An astrological LORD is an alternative term for a specific ruler of this sort.

The Ninth House

The ninth house is the general background of the personality—the inward impulse which preserves the self-fidelity, the inner consistency of identity—and in its simplest aspect the rulership here is over the accumulated experience of the particular person for whom the horoscope is cast. This means the aggregate of everything that has been learned, or those basic resources of consciousness which, normally, are established in the general attitudes of the NATIVE, as astrologers term the individual under analysis. Here is pure intellectual capacity, usually identified as the higher mind in the astrological literature. Most fundamentally, and whether in a broader sense or in the form of some narrowed cult or even private creed, this is a man's religion. It is his conscience, when it comes to his private morality.

41

The house is identified most advantageously by the portmanteau concept UNDERSTANDING, which astrologically becomes its KEYWORD. In the widest possible sense, understanding comprises those fruits of experience by which the personality has succeeded in anchoring itself within itself, consciously or subconsciously. This includes consciousness as such in every phase of ordinary thought and realization, except only the immediate focus of awareness, the point of attention or the act of being one's self, which is charted by the ascendant.

The ninth house rules long journeys, which by definition are those involving more than a day's traveling, i.e., requiring an overnight stay. The essence of the idea here is the generalized but personal significance of remote circumstances. These movements to a distance result from potentials, out of simple or immediate experience, which have become linked to the self, either through direct past activity or else secondary or accompanying ties in other and indirect personal relations. What is indicated fundamentally, in all such cases, is the drawing of the self to some remote actuality brought into present importance.

The house comprises all generalization in actual fact—that is, all bringing of things, otherwise scattered, to an immediate focus in consciousness—and thus includes the operation of the so-called subconscious mind, as in dreams, prophecy, inspiration, and visions, together with the normal expression of the conscious self in humor, perspective, philosophy, and the like. By the same token, its rulership includes knowledge in general, science as an established technique for the acquisition of facts, publications and lectures as certification of human wisdom, law as the codification of experience, and so on. It shows fame as the generally accepted valuation of self, and justice as the impartial adjustment of contributory circumstances to the broad reality of any given situation.

The First House

The first house rules the general focus of life force. This is personality in simple action or reaction as it endeavors, consciously or subconsciously, to continue to be what it is. IDENTITY becomes the principal portmanteau term or keyword for the eastern angle, and this concept comprises the immediate *Gestalt,* or whole impression, by which the native is revealed, whether to himself or others, in any given situation or issue. Most objectively, the identity means the bodily organism, and its general appearance, since these are the outer manifestation of the self's existence. Hence the native's physical type is characteristically modified in correspondence with the division of the zodiac through which the eastern horizon passes, commonly known as the RISING SIGN.

Because the totality of self is essentially borrowed at the outset, or is a convenient utilization or adaptation of materials taken from the general realm of immediate experience, the ascendant shows the early atmosphere in a literal sense, as well as in the case of every specific new phase of experience. This is the general self-revelation, or personality *per se.* The house, therefore, has domain over life itself as such, primarily, or the immediate status of things. It can be said to identify all undistributed experience, or the complete circumstances of existence at any particular point of interest or concern.

The Fifth House

The fifth house, as life expression, shows the direction or projective tendency in any experience of pure selfhood. Balancing the ninth, which is the tradition or background of the personality, this house charts the unlimited potentialities of personal existence, the chance for real adventure. It rules the outreaching, overflowing, self-finding, relatively instinctive or blind and unordered activity of the self ahead of itself, and for all this the keyword is OFF-SPRING. If the corresponding cadent member of the triad, the ninth, is the ordering or generalization of simple selfhood, this succedent emphasis is prodigality, or a particularization of unalloyed self-being through ordinary trial-and-error experiment. In its most usual designation, the fifth house reveals self-expression. This means pleasure and sport of all kinds, from proper satisfaction to utter dissipation, and also the location and occasion for everything of the sort, that is, clubs whether country or town, eating places, athletic arenas and establishments, dance halls and social centers of all kinds, together with gambling places, race tracks, and the financial or commodity exchanges where stocks, securities, grains and various things are bought and sold in the course of speculation.

The house charts all representative or symbolical projection of the self, such as personal adornment, performance in the theater and on down the list to the everyday temperamental release of inhibition, including the varied mischief through which human character tests itself. All spectator amusements are indicated by this house, such as the stage, motion pictures, radio, opera, sports, the circus, carnivals and fairs, together with both amateur and professional participation in such activities as the artist, entertainer, contestant or definitely creative worker.

The projection of self on the succedent side, in the effort towards simple self-perpetuation, necessarily includes everything in connection with any possible reduplication of the identity, such as courtship, its perversion in the form of casual or preliminary intimacy, on to pregnancy and children. It embraces all childlike self-discovery, such as ordinary play in every form, and also the development represented by teachers, schools, the educative techniques and learning *per se*. It should be noted in this connection, parenthetically, that knowledge is placed under the ninth house only after it is gained, that is, put in reserve as part of the native's background or endowment. In the fifth, the rulerships persist through the progressive generalizations of simple self-expression above the animal level, comprising the special courtships, pregnancies and offspring of the emotions and mind, as in artistic creation, formalized art, literaty work and esthetic activity.

The basic idea in all indications of the eastern triad is self-persistence in act or reaction. Thus courtship is a continuance of activity which, in its particular import, marriage terminates. Then the suit as such is ended. Differing from the romantic questing, however, children are a continuance of the self's rhythm in its reduplication, insofar as they have relationship with the parents. They are identified here at all times, even when grown, away from home and married on their own account. The fifth house shows the degree of persisting self-expression in general, and consequently—but in reverse, as far as outward appearance goes—the strength of the personality in declining to act or react, as in the instance of unadulterated resistance.

The portmanteau nature of astrological analysis is nowhere more revealed than in the intermeshing of relationships at all points in the horoscope. This, of course, is a true reflection of life, where nothing exists in isolation. The dichotomies, by which some things are divided off from others for analysis, are a function of the mind, not a charting of any fixed structures in nature. The twelve houses rule various matters because of some immediate, momentary and pertinent implication or emphasis in experience. Hence, what is found under any one of them may be placed under another, or even several others, as the frame of reference changes. The distinction between knowledge in the course of acquisition, and knowledge in reserve or as possessed, has already illustrated this mode of transition.

The fifth house rules the creative dynamic of identity *per se.* In the case of a courtship, when the flow of life force ceases to be a mere projection of self, and is consummated in partnership, the new reality involved is charted by the seventh house. When the art expression, which normally belongs here, is sufficiently alive psychologically to be almost an entity on its own account—or to develop an organic self-determination or a species of immortal existence—the relation to its creator is that of a partner, and another transition to the descendant identifies the fine arts as distinct from the preliminary or relatively dilettante interest shown at the fifth. Moreover, and somewhat conversely, when creative effort becomes the mere manipulation of the esthetic tools for purposes other than the pleasure of doing so—whether these be words or symbols on the one hand, or paper, typewriters, brushes, cameras and what not on the other—the rulership shifts at once to the third. The astrological portmanteaus, therefore, are distinguished not only by what they compact within themselves, but by what they exclude, and by the changes they make in their content as circumstances shift in import.

THE WORLD OF RELATIONSHIPS

There is a tide in the affairs of men,
Which, taken at the flood, leads on to fortune.

Shakespeare, *Julius Caesar*

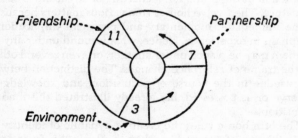

The western triad consists of the third and eleventh houses with a focus in the seventh, and it gives the astrological indication of life in its negative phase, or of everyday living as projected by the self into what psychology identifies, in general, as the other, i.e., not-self as opening new areas of experience to self in a sharing of reality, or an acting by proxy. This is life relationship in contrast with simple life force. Although a continuum, personality has no conscious or real existence except through a constant re-expression of itself. What it is, or does, must be illuminated, or have the co-operation of other being and doing. Mere identity, if established in any sort of a vacuum, is ultimately meaningless. The self is actual in its own experience as it not only continues to be, but as it does so with variation—more negatively, or receptively—by a progressive re-experiencing of its existence. The descendant's triangle charts circumstances in their provision of this continual and changing reassurance to the identity, a distribution of relationship by which self is reflected to itself, variantly and profitably, through its connection with things other than itself in a co-operative chance and hazard. Here is the eastern triad all over again, in a sense, but in an enlarged dimension of true or personal reality.

The Third House

The third house rules the built-up background of these self-in-other relationships of life, establishing its keyword as ENVI-RONMENT. The concept here represents, in the most organic form, the personal ties sufficiently anchored in the fundamental pattern of self to be manifest as blood relations. The specific indication is brothers and sisters, but all family connections are included, except parents or children, whenever they enter a given life pertinently. Because everything shown by this west triangle involves a functional equality, the mother and father are eliminated from any third-house aggregates. They distribute a socially superior reality, to which considerable attention must be given at a proper point in the text. Offspring have been seen to express, astrologically, a reduplication of the self on the creative side, and so must be excluded from classification here as socially subordinate.

The degree to which a shift in circumstantial emphasis will change the house rulership in a special case has been pointed out. Theoretically, of course, a child of the native can become his employer and so be indicated by the midheaven angle, but in such an instance the reference would not be to the blood relationship *per se*, which has become wholly incidental. It is possible to distinguish between particular brothers and sisters —and to trace out the special minutiae of relations here and elsewhere in the interlaced complex of the houses, to an indefinite extent—but this is fundamentally a recourse to HORARY rather than NATAL astrology, even if employed in delineating the horoscope of birth, and so is properly considered separately, although summarized in Chapter Five.[1]

The environment is best understood in its contrast with the intellectual climate ruled by the ninth house and discussed in the preceding section. The third fundamentally charts the outward rather than inward impulse of the native, instrumented not only by blood associations, but all who manifest a fraternal touch of this background sort, such as fellow workers in an office, fellow riders upon a train, fellow delegates at a convention, and so on through every possibility of casual side-by-sideness. By extension, it covers all immediately-at-hand and practical conveniences of normal life, both the use of them and any movement by self for the purpose of putting them to use. Therefore, again in special distinction from the

---

[1] The author's companion volume in this series of seven major astrological textbooks, *Horary Astrology, Problem Solving by,* Philadelphia, David McKay, 1941, devotes better than a hundred pages to more detailed meanings of the twelve houses or to the specific horoscopic orientation of special moments in experience. The natal astrology to which *Astrology, How and Why it Works* provides an introduction is the fundamental science that in the past has usually been termed judicial or genethliac astrology. The solar equilibrium chart is a method of proceeding in a general fashion under the handicap of a lack both of the precise time of birth by hour and minute and of the possibility of rectification by which such preciseness can be established in reasonable supposition. The rectifying procedure together with the three types of progressions or directions and the transits and three forms of horoscopic return constitute the dynamic horoscopy to which another volume of the author's basic textbooks, *The Scope of Astrological Prediction,* is an introduction. Mundane astrology is a popular application of astrological analysis to world affairs and is the concern of a further book of the sevenfold series, *Mundane Perspective in Astrology,* but this is still in preparation.

ninth, this house charts short journeys, or activity where no adjustment in either major consciousness or current routine is involved. Here is utterly simple by-proxy action, or the extreme tendency to dismiss things to automaticity.

The essence of meaning, both here and at the opposite cadent point (i.e. the ninth house) is a definite and often conscious cushioning of the self, in order to establish the set of affairs which might seem the best insurance for a favorable outcome in action. The western triad shows the success any given individual may have in compelling, from the life immediately around him, the ordering which is convenient for him at the moment. Two principal phases of this provide the third-house background in practical experience. One is the artificial structure of civilization itself, comprising all means of communication from language to telephones, and so involving manuscripts, letters, messages and such agencies, together with all the useful skills or arts of which mention has been made, indeed, every ordinary short cut or mechanization in mankind's daily functioning. The other phase of convenience revealed here is the establishment of fixed procedures, grooves of action and standards of response in the general milieu of life, or the common habits and mores of the individual, and of the geographical and ethnical groups to which he belongs.

The astrological rulership includes these things, not only as they are encountered in experience, but as the attempt is made to establish them. Therefore the third house rules change in general, that is, all superficial shifts in environment, and also all minor manipulation of ideas, whether in connection with rumors or with more definitely personal notions as these become infectious and are shared in any way with others. As the ninth describes the deeper attitude toward life—manifest in philosophy, religion or science—the third in contradistinction shows the attempt to order purely transient things—through propaganda, advertising and salesmanship, as an example—as well as immediate impressions and prejudices, or second-hand ideas in general. Astrologers identify this activity as the functioning of a lower mind, and what they mean is the practical comprehension of life's everday opera-tions on a normal or common-sense level.

The Seventh House

The seventh house is the focus of the west triangle, and the center of the process whereby the native continually redis-covers himself in the other self or selves with which he may have equal relationship in joint interest or action. Thus it is the mansion of life-relationship, and it takes the keyword PARTNERSHIP. Nothing can live for itself alone, and man does not even attempt to have any being apart from his fellows. His first learning, as a child, results from imitation, or the process of parallel play, and he tends increasingly, as he ma-tures, to bind himself to others in the convenience of a quite similar parallel living. Here is the whole explanation for mob psychology, and for any man's personal involvement through the group. The descendant, more generally, reveals the de-gree of a native's immediate efficacy, or his capacity for part-nership with a given situation, as in the tide which leads to fortune. For this reason it is the ruler of opportunity, since all the relations it charts have their existence through some end result to be gained—or some idea to be fulfilled—among people who are peers in terms of their right to act. Seventh-house ties, in other words, are never the co-operation of su-perior and inferior in any respect, nor are they the active and passive one-way and almost wholly taken-for-granted conven-ience found at the third.

Partners are as important in business as in marriage, both astrologically and in life. All professional relationship through consultation, or basically public and democratic contact, is indicated by this house, as when advice is given for a fee by a physician, a lawyer or an expert in any particular line of human skill (not excepting the astrologer). In the case of strictly professional services, however, when the analysis is from the horoscope of the professionally trained individual in question, clients or patients are shown by the sixth house. This is not because they are inferior, but because the personal relationship is subordinated to a process of adjustment, of which that particular mansion is ruler. The specialist is involved in a person-to-person contact only as long as a distinctly *vis-à-vis* issue is maintained, a fact with rather curious consequences. Thus the western angle or seventh house charts all the direct suffering as well as the benefit derived from a situation, and includes not only friendly relations with a lawyer, but unfriendly contacts with another person sued or suing. This means direct conflict of any sort, from war to a purely personal scuffle.

The descendant rules what the old books identify as the place of removal. Since it is the focus of the definite other, in the philosophical sense already explained, it obviously is the house of alternatives when this relationship of the other is assumed. In general, it is always the next step ahead, or what the ascendant is just about to be. The third house, in similar fashion, is the just-about-to-be-ness of the ninth, which is a way of saying that the environment—in terms of what it actually is, at any moment—is a continually shifting realization, or objective dramatization, of man's underlying or inner attitude towards life. The eleventh house, to be described next, is therefore the practical or correspondingly externalized stimulus to self-expression, indicated by the fifth, and every house is the detached or immediate alternative to its opposite.

The Eleventh House

The eleventh house in general rules objectives, or that to which the consciousness leans most assiduously. This, seen outwardly, is FRIENDSHIP. The mansion, in common astrological terminology, is the place of hopes and wishes. Here is life consummation in the broadest potentiality of person-to-person relations, including counselors and advice at large, together with the tendency to accept one or another type of counsel. Therefore the eleventh shows preferences, or favorites and favoritism of all sorts, whether these are an active and conscious choice of the self, or are something that has been strengthened or encouraged in consequence of other things. By contrast with the fifth, it indicates not so much a personal or articulate self-expression as, instead, the emphasis in life through which anyone actually reaches out to invite his ever-expanding experience.

Of all twelve equatorial houses, the eleventh is the easiest to describe or understand, a fact which sometimes obscures its real importance. As an extension of the counseling function, it comprises all organization or formalization of advice, especially when this takes form in legislation or enacted law as against that derived from precedent or out of experience (which is ruled by the ninth). Astrology here charts the factor of momentum in life, or of tendency towards the fullest and most instinctive co-operation of self and others, in contradistinction to the simple outspilling of identity. Thus it indicates the statistical drifting or working together of the pertinent elements in reality, the underlying friendliness of whatever accepts and enjoys a common objective. The enriched or fulfilled personality is always that which has its interest centralized in the full flood of events, achieving success through a fellow rather than a separate coherence. The factor of accompanying drive in experience—first encountered in the third house, where necessary co-operation can be taken for granted, and then refined at the seventh in struggle or through the sharpening of self-discovery through others—is brought into the consciousness of the native in tangible fashion at the eleventh, enabling him to gain a genuine personal power through his direct visualization of a life dynamic.

THE WORLD OF CONCERN

Seest thou a man diligent in his business? he shall stand before kings; he shall not stand before mean men.

Proverbs, 22:29

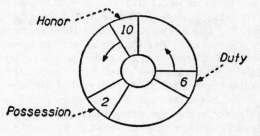

The southern triad consists of the sixth and second houses with a focus in the tenth, and it gives the astrological indications of spirit rather than life relationship, charting the negative experience of the native on the basis of the meridian distinctions. The transition from the horizon, in the astrological schematism, has been given considerable attention in the preceding chapter. There the meridian's function has been seen primarily as the matter of a dichotomy in the experienced materials rather than the time and space situation of self.[2] The developments of true or creative choice requires a plurality of potentials, which demands a social as in contrast with a primitive, one-faceted or largely solipsistic world. The requirement has been reflected, in the rise of human culture, by the division of labor in the community, that is, by the refinement of trading and business, handicrafts and industry, exploitation and public administration. The single-minded adventuring of the self and its special intimates, each of whom is no more than its other psychologically, must give way sooner or later in all experience—and all analysis of the problems faced by man—to the factors comprising a broader association with the many, or the illimitable potentials of the

[2] Readers with a philosophical background will realize that the four triads have a very exact correspondence with Aristotle's four kinds of cause. The ascendant charts efficient cause, and the descendant, final. Material cause is now presented, to be followed by formal at the northern triad.

universe. This introduces a truly objective or impersonal type of activity into astrological judgment. It is the objectivity or impersonality which is emphasized by the negative-positive order of consideration given the two meridian triads, in contrast with the positive-negative order in which the eastern and western groups are presented. A metaphorical eye is applied to the large rather than small end of the telescope.

The portmanteau concept of relationship, as indicating the many rather than the one, comprises personal responsibility as this is socialized in a very real sense, that is, rendered either indeterminate, as far as any necessary reference to a particular individual is concerned, or else communal. At this point the native is seen in his ties with all people together. Whatever person is ever identified in these houses of the southern triad is always revealed not so much as an entity as an officer or lackey, an authority or messenger, a representative in some way of interests which ramify through a whole unit of human society in which the self is participating. The beginning is necessarily negative, arising from the borrowed conveniences of existence at birth, as well as at the inauguration of any special activity. Hence man makes a continual effort, through every detail of these social relations, to gain encourgement for expression. All activity given its pointing at the south triangle is joint action, the self moving in an impersonal and usually unwitting co-operation with other selves, thereby actually creating the materials of experience. Because movement in the midst of the many is negative, the self needs a continual adjustment in its practical, pertinent and everyday association with these materials. Hence its social activity creates the great world of concern, the first domain in which man becomes adult in any real sense. He must now consider others in general, rather than some given other in particular.

The Sixth House

The sixth house represents the total background of social responsibility or concern in the individual's case, charting that broad assumption of value to his fellows by which he demands his place in the world. The keyword DUTY comprises the two-way responsibility which astrologers usually dramatize by making the mansion a ruler of service and servants. The fundamental indication is the activity of an inferior, either self or other, up or down in a social hierarchy. It shows the adjustment rather than the disparity, the reaching across definite lines of difference rather than the maintenance of any artificial distinction. One man must serve another, properly, because the person who is served has a capacity for functioning in some focus of greater social complexity, and so is enabled to distribute the activity of the whole group through the particular instance. Whenever the levels in society are understood in this fashion by all parties concerned, no opprobrium attaches itself to a subordinate positon. The relationship is entirely mutual, and at best is impersonally equated, showing the real nature of this third general dimension in human experience.

Work or labor is revealed in the sixth house, and properly is exalted as movement towards an achievement in social status. When ever effort of the native is outwardly unsuccessful, or obviously misdirected, the situation devolves on background considerations disclosed by the mansion as ruler of misfit occupations. Outward compulsion is then little more than pure negation. A man's struggles, at the worst, will be blind rebellion, a self-surrender of free will to an unfriendly universe, but even the extreme agony charted here may become a creative determination to remake the world of experience by sharpening and expanding every individual skill or capacity.

Sickness, as ultimately a mode of adjustment in experience, is the most familiar instrumentality for the process of social reconstruction. As the degree of interaction between the internal and external energies of life, it includes hunger, fatigue and dissatisfaction as well as the miscellaneous aches and pains of an organism. It is the deviation from normality by which health is knowable on the one hand and useful on the other. In exactly the same way that the house indicates, quite impartially, the service gained from others or given to others, it reveals illness as an agency whereby the efforts at self-expression in some particular social situation are impaired in the one case, or refined in the other. Any constriction of effort is, of course, protective in nature. A man gorging himself with food, continually abusing his digestive system, becomes sick and so momentarily loses interest in his gormandizing. Another person, ruining his eyes or other faculties through over-ambitious self-driving, develops the organic trouble which forces him to check himself. Contrariwise, it is common experience for some individual to rise to the special occasion, under circumstances where a proper mobilization of energy is achieved, and to drive himself to an unbelievable effort without suffering any ill-consequence other than his normal and healthy weariness.

The house represents the physical, commonly available and consciously developed energies of that group of which the individual is a part, as well as of his own animal organism in this social sense, and the consequent service to him, including food and clothing, medicines and the ministrations of a community, together with the smaller domestic animals and cattle, the farms and factories from which he is supplied, the army and navy which defend or conscript him, and so on. An important manifestation of the servant relation is the responsibility of pure custodianship, so that all tenants or stewards are found in the sixth. People served by the professions, the clients of a physician or psychologist, are ruled here, as has been indicated, together with the specific regimen of healing and any sheer drill or discipline.

The Tenth House

The tenth house is the focus of an individul's external situation in human society. It indicates his place in life, as expressed in the keyword HONOR, and as founded upon his concern over human values. Thus the angle reveals the relation between the native and his own total world, but it does not tell anything whatsoever concerning his circumstnces in comparison with the status of others outside his common sphere of activity. A very fine horoscope possessed by a coal miner might indicate his position as a foreman, the same chart among the upper middle class of a small midwest city might account for a person's place as president of a bank, and the same map among the aristocracy of India might identify a maharaja. The mansion essentially delineates man's persisting trueness to his own nature, under the impact of social compulsions. It rules his profession because, after all, a socially dignified activity is a body of special skills bound together in a code of honor, and activated by a group morale. This is the practical meaning of spirit relationship.

The midheaven, in more general fashion, represents authority. This is the power established by the successful individual in building a high degree of personal integrity, or in developing a superior professional place for himself, but it is no less the social compulsion to which the specialist as well as everyone else must submit. The house shows the native's employer, if he has one, and those who are his superiors in the political or business communities to which he must give allegiance, such as the president or governor, the manager or foreman. Here also is the immediate enjoyment of any preferential position in life, or aristocracy as such. The tenth not only rules the fact of all these things, but also charts the effort directed toward their achievement, or their continuous enlargement and fulfillment, thus revealing ambition, advantage, degree of special capacity and the like on the one hand, and credit, stability or administrative competency on the other.

Every house embraces whatever its rulership includes, and in addition the same thing in embryo, as has already been emphasized. There is no basic astrological differentiation between promise and performance, unless a given potential becomes a tangible stimulus with a definitely external impact, as in the just-about-to-be-ness described on page 51. Hence the midheaven charts the self's entirely nascent security, in the world at large, as symbolically represented by the mother. She is the parent who supplies the initial social matrix, in its complete all-sufficiency, through the functioning of her organism. The child remains in her custody after birth, and is only brought into larger and greater social complexes by gradual stages, until able to proceed on its own account in a relatively total independence. There are instances where the father is more a mother than the woman herself, or where a foster mother steps in and is thereupon indicated by the midheaven in her exercise of authority. Recent practice identifies the tenth house as ruler of the close-link parent. It is necessary, however, to be careful in guarding against a superficial assimilation of ideas, as in supposing that because the southern angle indicates business, and that because the father is the one of the parents usually found in the office, he should be described at the upper meridian. Since the child's chart is under consideration, any such correspondence is indirect and inadequate, as the older authorities well understood.

The Second House

The second house reveals the potentials of the native's general social position, or is spirit consummation as best expressed in the values of immediate and personal concern. All this is comprised in the keyword POSSESSION, including financial and similar fluid resources. Of all tangible things, money is probably the most spiritual or social, since it is the most generalized or universal medium of community experience. It can operate successfully as a basis of social linkage between people with the most diverse standards, hence preserving the impersonality of man's third great world. Its basic characteristic is that it distributes inequality in terms of freedom rather than limitation. No man is under compulsion, for instance, to wear a hat of any certain price. He may spend one dollar or ten. Except for quite minor differences, a hat is a hat. The mansion reveals negative social potentiality in this vitally important capture of experience in an almost infinite ramification, giving an individual the greatest possible facility in the use or scattering of pure social reality.

Most inclusively, the second house rules ordinary wealth and prosperity, or its lack, charting loss and gain in general, i.e., freedom to change place in society. The resources shown here comprise not only money but also personal property in the sense of everything which, in one way or another, instruments the simple group activity of self. The wholly generalized nature of the mansion is expressed in the idea of assistance. This means allies, as distinct from partners in a formal alliance, that is, whatever help is received from others at the point where it becomes the native's own, without any particular strings of obligation. The capacity to call forth social aid of this purely impersonal sort is the astrological index of man's liberty. It is the potential of social manifestation, as distinct from freedom or a mere rejection of discipline and restraint, shown at the fifth, and also as in contrast with a more or less subjective self-release in what can easily become fantasy, such as is charted at the eleventh.

THE WORLD OF REWARD

Come unto me, all ye that labour and are
heavy laden, and I will give you rest.
Matthew, 11:28

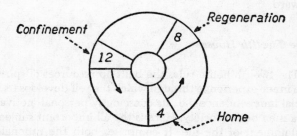

59

The northern triad consists of the twelfth and eighth houses with a focus in the fourth, and it gives the astrological indication of spirit in its positive simple and direct manifestation. Here self achieves a dimension of depth, recovering itself in a sense by its realization of itself in a context, or by its capacity to reach out through the ramifying impersonal potentials of a man's total experience, and so to give definite form of its own choosing to its own complete milieu. Thus the over-all circular logic returns the consideration to its beginning in what occultism dramatizes as an evolution from subconscious existence, or bare identity, into full self-awareness, or an immortal individuality. All these distinctions are symbolical, of course. What is achieved by an analysis of this character is a mental construct, a way of describing reality and charting its relations so that the course of events may be controlled. Taken properly, the circularity comprises a return to center in selfhood, through a continual regrasp and reconstruction of life and its context, and hence it becomes a preservation of the actual without any infinite regression or corresponding metaphysical escapism. Self without depth—or the simple continuum of organic existence—is merely life, but selfhood in an achieved and conscious depth is spirit in the special sense of the astrological portmanteau. As responsibility is individualized through experience, reality becomes private in a very special way. This privacy—as most commonly man's limitation, but more happily his spiritual opportunity—is charted and revealed, in every implication, by his world of reward.

The Twelfth House

The twelfth house rules the built-up resources of spirit, or the inner experience through which the self develops its true social independence, i.e., its consciously personal motivation as a member of society. Here is the all-important subjective sustainment of the life. It comprises both the rationalized flights from reality on the destructive side, with the continual sense of persecution or misunderstanding, and the far more mature and broadened dependence of the cultured individual on his own intuitions. The reflection of the inward compulsion of this mansion, when it comes to everyday relationships, is a tendency to institutionalize the life, and this establishes the keyword as CONFINEMENT. Putting things within artificially ordered bounds can be almost more for the good than the bad, or course, as in subjecting a disordered career to the discipline of an institution, and especially in accepting the kindly services of a hospital.

The house has been emphasized by astrologers in the past as the place of self-undoing, that is, a surrender to the unknown and the imaginary, and they have given much attention to its indiciation of hidden enemies and unexpected calamity. It necessarily comprises prisons and disciplinary institutions, and in the traditonal descriptions of horoscopy shows malice, misery, crime, violence and surprise of every character, or what on the destructive side is every consequence of a completely inadequate subjective sustainment. In contrast with all this, it rules unanticipated help, the gaining or possession of so-called deeper or occult knowledge—the clear or disciplined intuition of the unknown and unknowable—together with a valuable and fundamental sensitiveness to those human relationships which, though below the level of consciousness, yet operate through conscious experience. Here are the immortal inclinations of an individual, as he is able to develop them and respond to their support. In other words, he profits by a self-directed limitation of his efforts to areas in which they are effective, or by a progressive acceptance of some particular cosmic ordering as necessary in his own experience. He makes his personal or essentially secret touch with the cosmos in that true subjective life which is revealed through the northern triad, and in this he knows himself as a microcosmos in a very literal sense.

The mansion charts all things stimulating or disturbing through their seeming size, weight or unmeasurable superiority, and as a result it is the best possible point of mobilization for the true inner spiritual resources of self against the very immensity of the potential as a whole. While it designates, superficially, the great beasts or those of the cattle which are hard to handle—as the representative of the confining factors in nature—it has a much more important rule over the great common realizations which each man must articulate in association with his fellows, to some appreciable extent, if he is not to lose his individuality through the increasing pressure of pure over-all compulsion. It is in this final cadent area of experience that man cradles his own re-embodiment in social potentials.

The Fourth House

The fourth house may be described as the place of soul, or where the self in its own special positiveness, as spirit force, creates an eternal certainty in its HOME, the true estate of the native, both literally and symbolically. Soul is the characteristic act of being, in Aristotle's rather apt definition, or is what an individual becomes in his spiritual right, totally apart from his momentary dependence upon anything exterior to himself. Thus the mansion reveals selfhood in pure abstraction, or charts the end of life at the point where all external and immortal forces merge into the totality of self-existence. What is shown here is the individual's degree of conformity to ultimate expectation, therefore, or the immortality through which he keeps on living, not the termination of some cycle in time. Soul is cumulative, but it is always a present reality.

The total drama of individual existence has often been outlined by astrologers through the transition from the baby's complete dependence upon the external world, charted at the ascendant, to the adult's independent and largely subjective self-fulfillment, which is ruled by the nadir. It is thus that life force is metamorphosed into spirit force. The home, to some extent throughout the process, perpetuates the bondage of early life, but the child actually is able to establish a private reality, one entirely his own, at the very beginning of things, and far more in the home and with his family than anywhere else. In other words, he compels the maximum recognition of his individuality in the intimacy he enjoys with his parents and playmates. The nadir reveals the nascent individuality most importantly in these initial stirrings. They represent the ultimately spiritual impetus in selfhood as this is evident, by the curious circularity of the real, from the very start.

By contrast with the tenth house, the fourth rules the father or remote-link parent. This is the one who articulates for the child, under normal circumstances, the total groping idealism, or outreaching spiritual realization, in which the budding personality moves to establish itself. The father is no more an integral part of the home than the mother, and no less, but he is the very special ambassador, as far as the new entity is concerned, for a great and fascinating world beyond the walls of daily discipline and of ordinary physical limitations.

The Eighth House

The eighth house is the potentiality of the inner or ultimately immortal being. As the twelfth is the place of subjective sustainment, the succedent member of the triad is the point of similar transcendental outspilling or inner self-discovery, establishing the keyword as REGENERATION. This is a psychological rebirth leading continually into the new or fourth dimension in experience. Most importantly and objectively the mansion shows the extent to which the native lives according to the ideas of others. As the completion of his life in the terms of these values, constituting its spirit expression, the eighth is the place of death, or that physical end by means of which the pattern of the given career achieves its set in spiritual continuance (as ruled by the fourth). Here is the unswerving outreach to the hope of reward in the inner sense of a work well done, the inarticulate if not conscious dynamic of human estate, the feeling of fellowship in the invisible company of all who have given good service in the past. It is the day-by-day sense of a need to be pleasing to the established ideals of man, or to have a sense of justification for living, and it is also the occasional self-pandering which can lead to a twelfth-house escapism whenever the anchorage in practical life or relations is inadequate.

The mansion fundamentally indicates the continuing and strengthening realizations of the larger social challenges of life, and presents the point of greatest call to real self-sacrifice. Primarily delineating an approach to the whole of things in pure inner or spiritual potentiality, it indicates fretting or creative concern, such as is manifest in sadness or regret on the one hand and by especially unrestrained delight on the other. The eighth reveals socially, in every respect, what the fifth shows in more personal fashion, and in consequence helps the astrologer in getting at unsuspected depths of possibility for those people who, lacking real ability to rise to the ideals of others, feel themselves defeated and without hope, and so often resort to violent or destructive action. The house rules the termination of all older cycles as essentially the guarantee and foreshadowing of what the new ones may be, and it charts the blind out-groping of personality, or the anarchistic rather than self-indulgent revolt against immediate limitation.

Because the eighth is the second or money house, counting from the descendant or ruler of the basic person-to-person relations, its rulership includes legacies, wills and the money of other people in general. This is technically a detail of horary interpretation, but one which is universally entrenched in the natal tradition, and so properly included in the expositon. It is a good example of the way in which the secondary indications of the twelve mansions are derived; and so a suggestion of the expanded implications which every expert in horary art will have at hand, almost instinctively, to fit any special case he encounters in his practice.

It is now possible to summarize the house rulerships, tabulating them in the common or chronological sequence.

TABLE II
FUNDAMENTAL IMPLICATIONS OF THE HOUSES

I   Identity and its persistence; immediate action and reaction; bodily form; general initiative; personality; early or undistributed experience

II   Possessions as the expansion of social self-establishment; money and its loss or gain; concrete assistance; personal liberty

III   Environment as immediately-at-hand and taken-for-granted relationships; minor skills, instrumentalities and conveniences; brothers and sisters; relatives in general; habitual procedures; communication by any means; local travel and change; simple perception

IV   Home; the permanent estate; final recourse in self and its immortality; spiritual realization or soul; sharable end-results of all experience; father or remote-link parent

V   Self-discovery and self-projection; offspring, literally and figuratively; courtship, experimentation and speculation; pleasure and the chance for pleasure; play and all educative processes; the creative dynamic in personal and esthetic relations

VI   Fundamental sôcial and occupational responsibilities; obligations of service due to or from others; work and sharpening of skills; misfit vocations; army and navy; sickness and healing; food and clothing; domestic animals; adjustment to situations in general

VII   Equal relationship in joint interest; opportunity in general and outcome of act in particular; direct partnership in marriage, business, social enterprise, special consultation, or personal conflict; warfare; unusual achievement in the arts

VIII   Regeneration; challenging self-expectation and fretting; transcendental interests and spiritual self-discovery; death; money of other people and legacies

IX   Understanding as generalization, knowledge, and law; attitudes, religion and conscience; inspiration as self-orientation; personal movement or relation to remote things and places; consciousness generally

X   Place in life; honor and recognition by others; professional capacity; business; authority and superiority in general; mother or close-link parent

XI   Visualized ends of effort and objectives; potentiality in person-to-person relations; partiality in idea and act; advice, friends and friendship; legislation; general momentum in life

XII   Confinement, or experience through institutions, for good or evil; subjective sustainment or built-up spiritual resources; self-accepted limitation in experience, or underlying inclination; touch with the unknown or unexpected, both inimical and friendly

CHAPTER FOUR

Chaos and Order in Partnership

"Chaos often breeds life, when order breeds habit," observes Henry Adams in *The Education of Henry Adams,* thereby reducing the most fundamental of all metaphysical difficulties to an epigram. The average individual goes undisturbed by the fact that some things are inevitable in a relative sense, while others are not. This possibility, which he takes for granted, has greatly disturbed his intellectual superiors. The problem is simple enough in its formulation, but completely beyond resolution by anyone who tries to compact the universe into some special theory, such as can then be compressed in turn into a human mind. To treat the matter on the principle of boxes nesting in a series would merely make the cosmos the most contained or least of the three factors.

It is possible to do things. At the same time, things happen. How can these two processes, which really ought to interfere with each other, manage to get along together as remarkably as they do in everyday life? The answer is that they are cooperative rather than competitive facets of existence, as is well demonstrated by modern discoveries in the mathematical analysis of probability. The contribution of statistics to astrology can be presented, most conveniently, through what is known as the normal or bell-shaped curve.

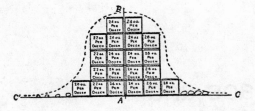

What is shown here, in diagrammatic form, is the commonplace fact that things which are the most usual in their make-up—i.e., are closest to norm—occur the most frequently in experience. Resorting to some oversimplification, the graph above tells the story of eggs produced for the market. These obviously tend to a certain size, which becomes the norm and is represented by the central vertical line, or B-A. Charting the total production on a given poultry farm, during a particular period of time, the eggs which conform exactly to the standard are represented as stacked in cases against the center line. The larger ones are arranged on a scale of increasing size to the right, or towards C, and the smaller ones to the left, or towards C¹. The greater the deviation in size, the less the number of deviate instances, of course, so that there may be, finally, a single huge or freak egg lying by itself at the extreme right, and an exceptionally tiny one equally far away at the left. The dotted line, constituting the statistical curve, shows at a glance how many eggs there are, proportionately, both at norm and in the directions of uniqueness. The scaling up and down is the number of units, and to right or left the degree of departure from the norm.

The point to all this is that the largest number of instances, of anything that can be charted by this one out of many forms of statistical graph, will conform predominantly to expectation, or near enough to it, to establish an order in phenomena, and so make existence predictable in its major lineaments.

The factual constitution of everyday reality is such, however, that there is also a continuing possibility of an unlimited degree of deviation, or of novel development away from whatever may be a normal expectation. In other words, there is a freedom which is in no wise ever cancelled out by the more impressive-looking orderliness of the average. It is to be noted, in the bell-shaped figure, that the curve at no point reaches the base line, or negates the possible instance of greater deviation, even if projected to infinity. The exceptional is never frequent enough, in the cosmic economy, to upset the probability of the norm. Neither disorder, nor favoritism, nor miracle, nor anything else, is a necessary condition of high individuality or creative uniqueness, irrespective of the form this may take. Absolute unorder, or chaos, is actually order's partner and prophet.

The normal curve was discovered first in astronomy, where the deviation in expected performance by stellar bodies can hardly be unrelated to the orderly pattern of stresses and strains in a closed and simple system of energy. The same odd marriage of choice and compulsion was found, subsequently, in a scientific estimation of much less integrated factors—from the point of view of the physicist, at least—in everyday human affairs. The all-embracing orderliness of a universe in its totality does not imply the tight rigidity of a machine, or suggest anything mechanical and exact in nature, but instead reveals the operation of pure convenience, gravitation or the statistical sorting together of like things, as already explained. The reason for a greater degree of exact predictability in the field of the natural sciences—mathematics, physics and chemistry—is the relatively infinite number of discrete units involved in any given measurement. Atoms and molecules, when it comes to inorganic matter, are beyond any possibility of consideration except in the mass. Individual deviations are averaged out, completely, and so do not enter the picture. Hence chemical mixtures can be controlled absolutely, and metallic parts can be manufactured within any desired standard of preciseness.

Human life presents probability at the other extreme of

consideration—that is, where differences are of a primary rather than infinitesimal importance—but this does not mean that the nature of cosmic orderliness has shifted in reference to those deviations, nor that probability itself need be approached in any variant fashion. Chaos and order are still linked together because it is the co-operation of each with the other that makes both possible. The essential change in analysis is understood when it is realized that the deviations from type, in human experience as against atomic phenomena, so to speak, are never lost in the dull averages or norms of huge numbers, but are, instead, the very basis and end of judgment. Astrology might almost be defined as scientific probability turned inside out, or brought to the task of forecasting the exceptional and the possible rather than the usual and the certain. It is here that the statistician is most apt to lose interest, and to dismiss horoscopy as a species of intuitive or psychic analysis, or to assume it to be something which is not scientific at all in the narrower meaning of that term. Indeed, many astrologers themselves have taken this point of view.

The ancient and medieval science of the stars was a real tribute to the synthesizing power of the human mind. Its method was to accept a whole host of indications in the consciousness, one by one, and then to allow the rational processes to bring out the single judgment in their own time, and in their own way. This sort of thinking—unscientific because it cannot be controlled at will—has been used by man since the origin of human society. Beginning as a child, each individual would learn to mark the signs of this and that about him, and to listen for Elijah's still, small voice, to wit: the verdict of the mysterious mental synthesis. It is what psychologists can now identify as a sort of statistical syncopation, such as reveals itself more commonly in ordinary skilled muscular or sensory co-ordinations. The oldsters of the clan, because their awareness had become conditioned thoroughly to all the possible eventualities of simple or tribal life—every one of which must have arisen, or been paralleled, in the half century or so of their own adult experience—would alone be equipped for handling any major issue, or for giving an intelligent decision in the unusual case. Astrologers of a prior generation, equally dependent on this intuitive or introspective method, had to spend most of their lives in preparation for their real work. It is not surprising to find the competent ones rather few in the early days of the stellar art.

The really wonderful things accomplished at times by yesterday's prognosticators because the clue to the true potentials of the horoscope under a modern or rigorously scientific investigation of astrology. Life itself, obviously, had held the illimitable potentialities in which any traditional wisdom of the elders could be conditioned, and here, in planetary divination, was a mechanism which actually reproduced these infinite possibilities of human experience—as they presented themselves in the familiar three dimensions of time and space existence—through a two-dimensional charting on a piece of paper. It was a mode of measurement which could be subjected to intelligent organization, and to an extent which would make it an actual instead of a pseudo science. Because its synthesis was centered in experience rather than in the mind, whether or not the astrologers themselves appreciated the fact, its judgment could be kept under a conscious direction at every step. Business and home, in other words, could be approached in a dichotomized distinction from each other. The examination of man's affairs could be focused at any convenient point of pertinency. What Linnaeus did for living forms in the field of biology by his inauguration of a dynamic or predictive as against a merely descriptive classification, astrology began to do for the reborn psychology which developed with the nineteenth century. It is high drama in man's recent intellectual history that the new science of the soul, under its academic auspices, first chose the way of introspection instead—that is, intuition or the purely mental and ultimately uncontrolled synthesis—under the all-dominant influence of Wilhelm Wundt and his American as well as European disciples.

The preceding chapters have shown how any astrological

inquiry, by a process of dichotomizing, screens out the given unique instance in experience, and then gives it a place in the correspondingly pertinent ordering supplied by the heavenly cycles. The factor of personal difference, and not the cosmic averaging in which it is cancelled out or lost to itself, is the basis of judgment, as has been stated. However, order rather than chaos must be the foundation of the measurement, and there must be a single or fundamental scale by which the ordering is made available for this purpose. Horizons and hemispheres cannot be set up in pure chaos, no matter how universal or unified they may be in metaphysical theory.

Life itself provides man with infinite frames of reference, in each of which there is the compulsion of a norm to be met by the various illimitable potentialities of the self in terms of chance or risk, choice or action. Hence astrology must be accepted, not as the measure of the native's necessary conformity to destiny or fate—or to some outside limitation taken in a metaphysically absolute and false sense—but rather as the estimation of what he may do, because of the fact that he is put together in the particular pattern characterizing him, in choosing from among the many possible ways in which he may constitute his own experience. His freedom persists because he selects the particular order which sustains him. He is the actual creator of his own universe, therefore, in quite a literal fashion.

His manner of doing this is revealed, in the horoscope, by his construction and continuous reconstruction of the various domains or mansions of his own activity, ordered always in respect to the uniqueness of some particular horizon. First to be delimited are the four great worlds of experience, with their interlacing relations diagrammed and made comprehensible, in symbolic fashion, through the cosmos at large. Universal orderliness is charted by this means, and at the same time is individualized also. All things are measured, in other words, as they have existence of necessity, but as they are related in addition to the special experience which some particular choice or act has dictated. There is, in consequence, throughout the horoscopic patterning, a continual distinction between the relatively necessary and the relatively free. What enters experience in the guise of necessity is put to use in the realization of whatever may be projected from self, into this same experience, as the ramification of act or reaction in a free self-discovery.

Thus man establishes himself more or less as he pleases in the four fundamental domains of (1) self and (2) self relationships, and of (3) social concern and (4) social reward. The activities of this self-establishment in the individualized reality are charted by the triangulation which creates the houses. While busy with all this, man also is utilizing a world of external and parallel reality which, willy-nilly, brings the element of necessity into his experience. Here is no restriction, however—no factor that threatens his free will—since the added component in his existence is merely dependability or constancy. Should he select an apple and a glass of milk for his refreshment, and were there no atomic necessities in the case of the substances involved—requiring the fruit to remain a palatable pulp, and the milk to refrain from dissolving into vapor—his action would be meaningless. When an individual starts a business, the enterprise has similar necessities in its make-up, including a reasonable tendency to survival, a pattern of contractual obligations, and so on through the factors making it possible to begin. Astrology charts the potentials both of freedom to act and of expectation upon which to depend, without any superficial distinction between them. Chaos and order in horoscopy are not only partners but bedfellows—or perhaps even a species of Siamese twins—and so altogether indistinguishable in any ultimate view.

Free will or choice represents the dynamic orientation of existence, whereas order identifies its relatively static constitution. The establishment of the equatorial mansions, through the four triads, is the approach to the universe in a self-orientation, primarily. It is this relationship of a geometrical sort which reveals, fundamentally, the principal potentials of an unconditioned act and a deviate self-discovery. What is consequent upon the fact that the twelve equatorial mansions are established in this fashion—and the similar zodiacal divisions likewise, in their turn—is that these mansions are placed in an order of sequence around a celestial circle, and that they have an additional and different sort of relationship because they follow each other in next positions. The circular succession of celestial segments becomes the principal indication of necessity in man's affairs, paralleling and charting the immediate probabilities of direct consequence in everyday experience. Analysis here moves on from the triads to the quarters.

A certain amount of summarization is possible at this point. The astrological patterning represents two extremes in its general relationships, namely, those things which are immediately derived from the native's situation or character, on the one hand, and those which are, by comparison, more anchored in the situation and character of all men. Mother Nature offers her normal lineaments to the observation because all deviations and exceptional factors, for the major part, are averaged out of view. The myriad of individual atoms, particles, special aggregates or organic structures which come to attention are but exceptionally identified in the terms of individual difference. Astrology as a whole, or when taken as the composite of the untold millions of horoscopes which are reflected in each particular one, presents an identical phenomenon. The native is progressively lost in his uniqueness as his nativity is interpreted or given meaning through averaged or stabilized indications, that is, through the elements dependable in all charts. All delineation is a statistical approximation.

The horizon and meridian axes first, and then the initial geometrical relations by which the particular case is given its setting in a twelvefold pattern, comprise the greatest possible extreme of free-will representation. Once any person makes his orientation in life, his relatively unconditioned choice is promptly determined in its consequences, as far as the given chain of relations is concerned. Thus the factor of order in horoscopy shows progressively greater and greater elements of compulsion as the original horizon of pure individuality ramifies in relation through the more detailed implications of the chart. Sequence of connection, which enhances every full and free opportunity before choice is made, immediately thereupon becomes limitation or special conditioning.

Order at the Ascendant

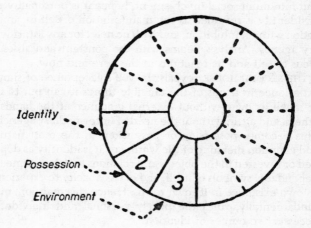

The first, second and third houses together map the development of whatever necessity arises as a consequence of the self's assumption of its selfhood. This quarter fundamentally charts the directness of human action and realization in its original or most simple and everyday phase.

In the analysis of the houses by these quarters—as in contrast with the triads of the preceding chapter—the angular one in every case represents the CONTACT potential in the given distribution of experience. The following or succedent mansion reveals the corresponding ACCEPTANCE potential. The third or cadent one of the three, coming next in order, presents the ORGANIZATION potential. These portmanteau designations correspond to the transmuting, resulting and exciting ideas in the perspective from freedom. Potentiality here represents orderliness as manifest in dependability.

THE FIRST HOUSE or ascendant of the horoscope shows the individual's immediate, wholly natural and unconditioned contact with experience, at the point of maximum self-being and minimum social involvement, hence it is personality *per se*. Identity is revealed as the manifestation of self in simple action without inhibition, and with no need for any intermediary agency. Analysis begins with the constant and absolute focus of self and its reactions in the here and now.

THE SECOND HOUSE reveals the self's acceptance of simple experience in terms of the tangible things it can put to use or make its own, without external guidance at the hands of others, and again without the need of imtermediary agencies. This becomes possession or possessions in the most natural and common meaning of the word, i.e., it is identity as deposited or invested in the objects and relations which become the dependable symbols of itself, and of its capacity to experience its own existence in its own terms. Hence this mansion, most fundamentally, rules the purely personal and individually necessary resources of identity.

THE THIRD HOUSE charts the organizing of self and its affairs in direct personal relationship with everything immediate, other than those special resources or possessions which symbolize its existence to itself. This is general is the ordinary environment, or the totality of the commonly available conveniences through which the identity achieves its unconditioned perspective upon its own existence. Thus the third mansion comprises everything in everyday life that provides a setting for the simple act of being, and which in consequence has the particular quality of at-hand-ness. Here are revealed the relations and functions of living which must be taken for granted, placing the uninhibited reality of selfhood in a necessary context of practical experience.

Order at the Nadir

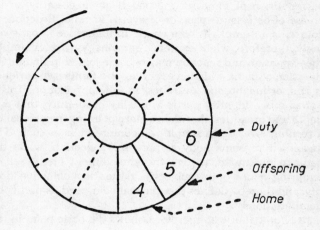

The fourth, fifth and sixth houses together map the development of whatever necessity arises as a consequence of the self's conscious effort to collect and enjoy the rewards of its effort. This quarter fundamentally charts the directness of human action and realization in its terminal and ultimate rather than original or largely solipsistic phase.

In any sequential development of the dimensions in existence generally—as well as in any single or particular experience subjected to astrological analysis—the step forward is a reaction from the preceding stage of things, no less than an actual expansion of the prior condition. In other words, since simple directness is the hallmark of the first quarter, this next group of houses, in their common function, must both add to the original immediacy revealed as the ascendant sequence and react from it. There must be the manifestation of something which is an accentuated immediateness, and also the rejection of a prior adequacy.

The nature of the more in anything is always a reiteration or repetition of some sort, although not necessarily an increase of objects in space or of events in time. Reaction, of course, is an emphasis or increase in difference. Most strikingly, therefore, when existence remains positive or simple, the expansion and reaction may become joined in that intensification of being which in everyday and familiar experience is soul, or heightened awareness in self-appreciation. This is not so much identity *per se* as quality in identity, that is, a depth and breadth rather than a mere pointing in personality, a turning away from simple self-centeredness as such. The ascendant presents body as pure self-collection, while the nadir, contrariwise, reveals the embodiment of the self in enduring values, or in a subjective rather than objective identity, and thereby defines the spiritual being and its particular manifestations.

THE FOURTH HOUSE, therefore, shows the basic point in the self's actual realization of itself in and through an ultimate potentiality. This is the personality's simple and direct refinement of its own existence, a fresh dimension of being represented by the home as contact with a relatively unchanging rather than transient reality. Identity at the ascendant is merely a continuum, while various permanent or enduring elements of experience are here identified as they substantiate man's inner creativeness, providing him with that on which he may rely through all eternity. This primitively is the familiar place or accustomed situation, the home and the community as the passive certainty to which retreat is always possible. By extension the stability takes a more enduring form in monuments or memorials, and so parks and estates, or property when it presents established rather than fluid or negotiable value. The nadir indicates the father in his special responsibility for creating and preserving the family name or reputation.

THE FIFTH HOUSE reveals the acceptance of direct experience on the level of self-evaluation. This most primitively is self-expression, or the necessity that identity attempt various forms of self-outlet without inhibition of any sort, extending or expanding itself in relatively permanent form through offspring. On the unhappier side of life this can be ordinary dissipation, ramifying to include the equally permanent wastage or rejection and elimination of the substance and possessions of self in speculation or gambling. More constructively it is artistic, rhythmic and creative effort of the type identified by men as putting soul into whatever they may be doing, and evident in commonplace or simple sports and pleasures. The activity remains solipsistic, in the sense that the presence or co-operation of others is incidental as far as any particular person is concerned, but it is not the mere self-centeredness of a self continuing to be itself. Thus in organized amusement such as dramatics, when a special role or part is assumed for the moment, or in sports, where the spectator is able to lose himself and thereby gain respite for his soul in a quite artificial reality, the intensification of existence is feeling, or self-evaluation in process. Exactly as the second house indicates whatever inanimate things man makes his own, or constitutes as possessions, the fifth shows what animate or esthetic elements in experience he makes his own likewise, in this special intangible fashion.

THE SIXTH HOUSE charts the organizing of values and rewards in the individual's self-projection, and this becomes the point of transition from the necessities arising in self on the solipsistic side to those consequent upon a direct and consciously personal relationship with others. When analysis is based on the dichotomies which reveal individual free will, and the potentials of unconditioned choice—as in the prior chapters—the distinctions among the axes of the houses are rooted in the horizon as the ground of self-existence, and in the meridian as the conscious squaring of self to its experience. When necessity becomes the consideration, charting the consequence of relationships in sequence, the perspective is no longer geometrical in the former sense. The symbolism makes use, instead, of a single dichotomy, or the one effected by the horizon as not only the indicator of identity but as also the origin of existence in this particular point of view. The six houses so far considered are all beneath the horizontal line. They have been found fundamentally subjective, or wholly self-centered in nature, that is, concerned at all times with the personality in and through its own self-realization. This is in high contrast with the objective side of life, where the self finds a fellow reality in things other than itself.

Hence the sixth house indicates the detailed relations and involvements concerned in this transition from a subjective to an objective realm of experience, or where objects *per se* have a practical reality, and where in consequence the ends in life reach out beyond any naïve selfishness or mere self-sensitiveness. The processes revealed at this point are basically the operation of duty, or of the nascent ties of identity to something other than itself, under conditions where more than caprice, or momentary act and reaction, is required to produce any change. The mansion normally shows the relations of superiors and inferiors, whether as a servant or as served in the given case, and always in a relatively impersonal association insofar as the particular identity of the other person is concerned. The area of experience here comprises all work not particularly enjoyed in its own terms, everything definitely inconvenient or distasteful to do, together with whatever has any tendency to lose its impetus or get out of course the more simple or objective reality of a world which by external circumstances—such as dirt farming, participation in the armed services, and the like, whether self-assumed or under direction—is included, as is all physiological and psychological upset or organic disturbance. The small or ordinary domestic animals are identified at this point through their simple usefulness in service, and the reciprocal care they must have. In all details the rulership of this mansion is really a matter of adjustment, either man's entering into responsibility, or else dropping it in cases where he has no accompanying capacity or opportunity for initiating or controlling the course of events.

Order at the Descendant

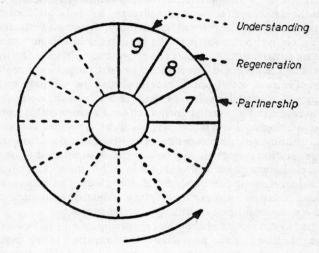

The seventh, eighth and ninth houses together map the development of whatever necessity arises as a consequence of the self's outreaching through its relations with other-than-self factors in the true or conscious world of higher creatures. This quarter fundamentally charts the first or simple and direct form of man's personal touch with others, or of his ability to see himself in them and so to project himself into something greater than himself.

THE SEVENTH HOUSE shows simple and direct response to other personality in terms of a real equality with self, whether friendly or unfriendly, and so is forthright contact with people individually. Most commonly, it indicates partnerships. This means not only regular contractural relations in marriage, and with business associates, but also lawyers, physicians or various specialists as these are consulted in some particular issue. It comprises the possibility as well as the fact of this broad but definite and simple linking of self into the broad relations which, in general, constitute human affairs, and so it is the outcome of any energies directed towards this linking. Thus it becomes the place of opportunity, showing all especial self-mobilization towards public activity as in the fine arts.

THE EIGHTH HOUSE reveals the acceptance phase in the individual's simple and direct move toward these larger realities of human society, and therefore rules the ultimate consummation of all life-values in terms of death, or the necessity to accept a public verdict on any self-achievement. This from the astrological view is the psychological surrender actually constituting any phenomenon of self-termination. It means regeneration or rebirth, and so all turning in interest to new and challenging cycles of relationship within the social milieu. The mansion, in consequence, always charts the degree to which a native must conform to the standards or notions of others, depend upon or utilize their possessions.

THE NINTH HOUSE charts the organizing of any self-awareness of others, or the necessary self-assimilation to the more simple or objective reality of a world which holds self and others in equal regard. This primarily is memory, knowledge and imagination. Here is the native's capacity to give a measure of enduring reality to the projection of personality in something more than the physical body. Man at this point is able to set up relationships with those who are remote in time and space. Consciousness *per se* becomes the ultimate degree of freedom from any momentary or separative situation of the individual identity, and this is reflected in travel or long journeys, on the one hand, and in conscience or the body of religious concepts, on the other, both extending the potentials of partnership towards the infinite ideal. The ninth mansion, in consequence, outlines the higher mind, or the abilities which carry knowledge onward from science, developed at the practical level of life, into prophecy, dreams and every intuitive or mental self-objectification.

Order at the Midheaven

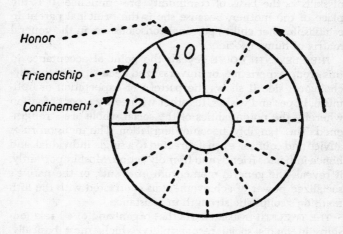

The tenth, eleventh and twelfth houses together map the development of whatever necessity arises as a consequence of the self's concern over the general materials of social experience, or of realities centered primarily in the group as a whole. This quarter fundamentally charts the more complex activity of the individual in his relations with people in the mass, or society at large, i.e., again the transition involving a more, mixed with a difference. Here is where his interest is security rather than reward, and therefore the place where he seeks to dominate others rather than have particular relations with them, whether this be for the better or the worse.

THE TENTH HOUSE shows the general contact of self with life in its total complexity, indicating the individual's social realization or sensitiveness to the group stirrings. It is the focus of honor or reputation as an expression of position in life, showing authority as administered over inferiors or accepted from superiors, and revealing profession or any special body of skills as the basis of community pre-eminence. It is the place of the mother, because she is the principal parent in establishing her child's personal consciousness in the general matrix of human society.

THE ELEVENTH HOUSE reveals the point of acceptance in this group experience, or universalized necessity. On the psychological side it shows the pattern of expectation or optimism, hopes and wishes, together with every aspect of vision whereby the potentialities of the social whole are strengthened. This, tangibly, becomes legislation. The mansion rules advice and counsel, even if directed to a single individual, and hence indicates friends and friendly action. Most importantly, it reveals the general momentum in events, or the native's socialized power of achievement as contrasted with the fifth mansion's solipsistic strength in resistance.

THE TWELFTH HOUSE charts that organizing of all relationships in man's social responsibility which, most basically, becomes the institutionalization of experience, or the ultimate employment of pure necessity. When he cannot make an adequate adjustment in the everyday world about him, the inadequacy gains its psychological ordering in or through the agency of the envy, malice, treachery and other things by which his own private reality is reduced to the degree of inevitable social isolation. When it comes to the extreme instance, he goes to a hospital, a prison and so on, and thus is compelled to retreat to his own bare identity for a fresh start. In the reverse case, however, the process is revealed in that unexpected or broad help from every source which is no less an ordering of his world in response to his own individual development of a genuine social responsibility. The house fundamentally shows the subjective sustainment of tangible achievement which, in due course, permits the transition from objective experience above the horizon, back below for a further self-realization or refinement in the chain of sequence.

Thus the horoscope maps the processes by which the various phases of experience, when once set in motion, are consequent upon each other. It is only as the equatorial mansions establish their relations in a complete circularity of logic or reality that the developments of man's experience are revealed in their distribution of those necessities by which he orders himself, or substantiates his continual self-establishment. There are further possibilities of relation around the circle, showing other sequences of consequence, and an additional chapter will be devoted to these. Now the two fundamental methods by which the astrological significance of the houses is refined—the geometrical and sequential, as summarized diagrammatically in the following figures:

—must be seen to have their ultimate practical or most important synthesis not in mathematical or theoretical considerations, but in day-by-day living. This is illustrated by the common house meanings emphasized in both methods of approach (and so repeated often through these pages). Thus possession (second house) is the present importance of the future potentials developed through a native's social place (tenth) and also the necessary consequence of his act in maintaining his own identity (first). Environment (third) is similarly the immediate contribution of prior direct relations with others of equal rank in pursuance of a given opportunity (seventh) and also the necessity by which whatever the native can take for granted in his immediate living is consequent on the manner in which he utilizes his personal resources (second).

CHAPTER FIVE

The Skein of Convenience

The tumultuous mood which Percy Bysshe Shelley captured in his *Ode to the West Wind* has its final line in the query, if winter comes, can spring be far behind? This provided a title for A. S. M. Hutchinson's best-selling novel of the twenties, and gave popular affirmation to the mind's instinctive faith in what, by and large, is a dependability of existence. Order may be limiting, but it is also most convenient. Tuesday is the sure prediction of Wednesday, and four o'clock a prophecy of five. The observation of Plautus, that there is no smoke without fire, expresses the commonplace realization that life and reality are actually built upon simple consequence. The faulty assumption is merely that existence stands of necessity at one end of the process. Order gives form to chaos, and while this may regiment subservience it also makes free will of use to man.

In the everyday context of choice, chance, risk and uncertainty of every conceivable sort—when taken from a cosmic perspective, or seen as an infinity of potentials—there is an almost absolute certainty of outcome along any one given or immediate line of relationship, provided the special sequence of relations be maintained in its own terms. It is this high predictability of things that supports normal action or reaction. An individual knows that by eating he will satisfy his hunger and, by drinking, his thirst. The average youth well realizes that, if he continues to fling little attentions and objects of thoughtfulness at the head and heart of a happily acquiescent miss of his acquaintance, she will respond with the yes he covets. Experience is put into train continually by the operation of order—a statistical correlation or convenience which is usually dismissed without conscious attention—and man constantly reassumes his identity, or establishes his various horizons of reality, by entering upon or leaving various chains of consequence at will. He is limited simply by the degree to which his act of ingress or egress is oriented properly in the universal economy. His action must be consequential, or a manifestation of order, in its own special frame of reference. Thus the driver of an automobile, who expresses free will in stopping at a railroad crossing to avoid a tragedy, merely sets up new lines of cause.

Consequence is therefore the ramifying context of act or choice—of chaos or freedom—not the compulsion of other and prior act or choice, except as this enters into the given or immediate relationship as a definite convenience. Most metaphysics goes astray at this point, assuming the universe to be static in its basic make-up, and so finding itself driven to one or the other of extreme views in (1) accepting everything in life as foreordained—making man as ineffective as in Coleridge's immortal simile of helplessness, the painted ship upon a painted ocean—or in (2) presuming action to be entirely subjective—that is, largely immune from consequences in any dependable way, and so encouraging the individual to count upon chance, or to echo the remark of Ovid, "to Fortune I commit the rest."

Harry Carr, conducting his column, *The Lancer*, in the *Los Angeles Times* during the early thirties, was fond of explaining that a man who married a Mexican girl thereby married all Mexico. As far as end results were concerned, the groom had established relationship with a set of mores quite different from familiar American standards. He had to be prepared to face the fact, on the ridiculous side, that if he became financially successful the whole body of her relatives—or at least the less fortunate ones—would regard it as quite the thing to come and live with him, or compromise by accepting his support at a distance. This was not a matter of favor, kind-heartedness or penalty, as Carr explained it, but merely the proper procedure, part of the meaning of marriage in Mexico.

Life everywhere is made up of situations which for the principal part, in their background and ramification, are the complex of the shifting cause-and-effect sequences which converge most conveniently in the given reality, whether this be from long acceptance or for any other reason. Free will is gained, not in avoiding these necessities, but in taking advantage of them, that is, using and shaping them to conscious purpose. In other words, man constantly conforms to the consequences of the prior act or reaction about which he does nothing, since these constitute, collectively, the dependability of his own private world. In the same way he creates or re-establishes those to which he gives pertinency, wittingly or otherwise, at the threshold of every move or decision, since they become the continuum which constitutes his being at root. Thus he is sorted out statistically, or made to be what he is in the universal totality of things, precisely as he chooses, directs and selects rather than suffers the events which come in train through his experience. Order modifies him as he modifies order, and this two-way modification is what reality is found to be by any possible definition.

The houses of the horoscope chart the pattern of consequences. What does this mean, in non-technical language? First, they show the probable results of direct act or reaction, both immediately and ultimately. Then, and perhaps much more importantly, they reveal the skein of convenience in any given situation. Here are the everyday probabilities in events, as demanding either activity and decision or else acquiescence, whether witting or otherwise. All this comprises, in human experience, the CIRCUMSTANCES of life. Astrology can be said fundamentally to measure experience as the establishment of sequence, or as the process by which order becomes the manifestation of free will in any immediate relationship.

Sequence as the Measure of Experience

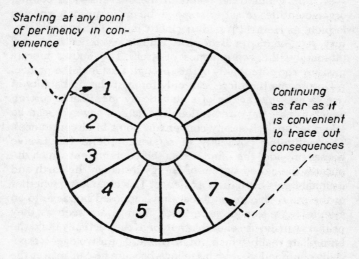

Starting at any point of pertinency in convenience

Continuing as far as it is convenient to trace out consequences

The ascendant is only designated the first house as a matter of convenience, although there is no deviation from this practice in natal horoscopy. Any other one may be the initial mansion in some particular sense, whereupon those that precede are prior, and those that follow are consequent in the terms of the special case, as suggested in the diagram. This possibility is the foundation of horary astrology, a branch of the science to which reference has already been made, and it is of importance here in showing the immediate reference of all sequence.[1] The astronomical and mathematical ele-

[1] Thus it was possible, in meeting the special needs of beginners in *How to Learn Astrology*—the smaller introductory text of this series, to which attention has been drawn in the footnote on page 29—to present the houses in groupings of 12–1–2, 6–7–8, 9–10–11 and

ments charted by astrology do not, of course, actually put the factors of experience into these chains of consequence. There are no causal forces on the order of high-frequency waves or electronic vibrations which radiate from the stars and planets —or from geometrical points in the heavens—and compel organic entities to act or respond, be or do, in some specific fashion. As Heraclitus said succinctly in the fifth or sixth century, B.C., character is destiny. Human existence is always, ultimately, the consequence of itself. The houses merely measure the potentiality of this through a scaling of sequence.

Horoscopy, therefore, can only forecast the probability of events as it has action of a statistically identifiable sort on which to base any predication. The action, however, can be taken for analysis at any convenient point in circumstances. The unlimited possibility of sequence round the twelve houses provides the mind with a self-containment which duplicates the closed system of energy in which the earth and its inhabitants have their existence. This circularity, whether of the mind or nature, defeats any supposed bondage to an infinite regression of experience. Things are seen as they primarily make use of each other, or as they actually build the immediate reality which sustains them. The astrologer is especially equipped to serve his fellows because he can answer the ever-important why of what follows upon what in everyday life.

The first house, of course, is always the occasion for the why, usually a personality struggling to fulfill itself.

(1 TO 2) The second house rules possessions as the simple or first normal consequence of existence. Nothing can continue to be except as it continually assimilates substance to itself. Growth is the condition of life. Man's resources may be largely subjective or spiritual, but his organism still gathers, expends and replaces flesh and bone. The living fact of per-

---

3-4-5 instead of the 1-2-3, 4-5-6, 7-8-9 and 10-11-12 groups, or normal quarters of the equator, used in the prior chapter to dramatize the initial sequence of circumstances in natal astrology.

sonality is the tangibility by which it is evident in its immediate circumstances, or the degree to which it can depend upon external existence. This is marked in the success with which it mobilizes what it needs to substantiate itself.

The sequential relationship represented by the immediate factor of consequence, in the single remove from any mansion to its next, can be understood more effectively by observing the one-step progression in significance as this continues through the twelve houses in order. Each of them in turn, counterclockwise around the equator, is the focus of some certain stage in experience, but only because this represents the possessions, assimilations or accumulations of the one preceding it, both astrologically and in life.

(2 TO 3) The third house, or environment, describes man's effective or genuinely real possession of his resources in a broader ramification of his private reality. In other words, what he may collect or otherwise make representative of himself, constituting it his property in the first or simple sense, will have no meaning or significance, or will retain no value as a possession, except to the extent it fits into the scheme of reality which is pertinent to its being. An individual's personal context is that in which his direct self-substantiation is most definitely convenient, or in which, in a very true fashion, his possessions are able to continue the assimilation of their own practical existence to themselves. This is the taken-for-granted phase of circumstances, such as characterizes the third-house rulerships most fundamentally.

(3 TO 4) The environment in its total potentiality cannot really be experienced, or possessed, in any conscious sense —to continue this one-remove progression in house sequence —until it in its turn is similarly substantiated or made more tangible in some special phase of itself. Man achieves such an end by specializing a part of his private world as more particularly his own, i.e., where his environment has particular resources. This is the fourth house, or home as the truly self-sufficient and highly personal milieu of experience.

(4 TO 5) Home is barren and meaningless, however, unless in turn it has its possessions in the assimilation of the per-

sonality's characteristic actions to the values which constitute its existence, so putting its stamp upon certain special acts or reactions as the self-expression revealed by the fifth house. The creative release of self thus becomes, at all times, the experience through which self, for the moment, is sufficiently at home to act freely and without inhibition.

(5 TO 6) Self-expression on its own account is not adequately representative of any man until it is refined or more definitely possessed through real effort in some disciplining pattern, as ruled by the sixth house. His expressiveness gains its reality in his consciousness when he develops the necessary ties of duty with his fellow participants in a general social adjustment. He must be genuinely stirred within himself to have any true resources in creative activity, and it is his frustration here which becomes sickness.

(6 TO 7) Labor and suffering, the balance in obligations shown at the sixth, is not effectively personal until it has some special focus through the tête-à-tête relations charted by the seventh house. The sense of contractural potentials, or the social vision and capacity for special fellowship with others revealed at this angle, are the most direct resources of human service and effort in the raw adjustments of living.

(7 TO 8) The seventh-house opportunity or enjoyment of genuine partnership, whether in transient relations or through the whole of a life, lacks personal resource or satisfaction unless there is an enduring change in self, such as is disclosed by the eighth house.

(8 TO 9) The regeneration or rebirth of the eighth is meaningless unless it has its fruits or possessions in the ideas or concepts of the ninth house, that is, the inner consciousness of personal achievement, or an enlarged and dependable realization of selfhood.

(9 TO 10) The general attitudes of the ninth—including whatever may be known, reasoned or deduced by the mind—are the resources of thinking, or the possessions of the rational being, only when the personality can place or recognize them, definitely and surely, in the general social reality or pattern of community affairs identified at the tenth house.

(10 TO 11) Place in life, or the gaining of a pertinent realization of social reality as such through some generally recognized achievement, is never actual in personal experience, or sure in everyday living, until confirmed by the resources in objectives and vision shown by the eleventh house, that is, made a matter of true individual concern.

(11 TO 12) The hopes and wishes, or advice and counsel, together with the general momentums of life revealed by the eleventh, have no personal pertinency, and are of little importance to the self, unless they create the special resources of subjective sustainment indicated by the twelfth house. Lacking all inner orientation, or direct relationship to personality otherwise, they often remain little more than dreams, idle words, and external assumptions, and so never become the potent moral dynamic they ought to be.

(12 TO 1) Subjective sustainment, or confinement and institutionalization as the protection of man—however much against his conscious wishes and efforts—are of no direct value to him except as they establish the tangible possessions and resources of pure personality in and of itself, such as are given a focal identity at the ascendant, and are thus preserved in their individual existence.

Sequence in a Regression of Immediateness

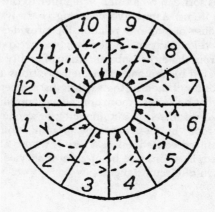

Sequence around the circle is dictated by the nature of the geometrical divisions in which the sequential factors are identified (here the twelvefold scheme of mansions). The simple transition shown by a move from one house to its next provides the nearest possible measure of an immediate or relatively unconditioned consequence in events, while the relations of a more intricate sort, traced out by a pattern of houses separated from each other, is a consideration of the necessities in a progressively greater measure of order, such as is in even sharper contrast with chance, choice or chaos. It has already been suggested that there is an obviously increasing degree of limitation at the hands of other consequence—for better or worse—whenever any given impetus of relationships expands out from its own center in original action, or ramifies into the complex of infinite potentials about it. The skein of convenience reveals the more general no less than the specific necessities in man's everyday affairs.

The next degree of complexity in circle relationships, charting the wider or more involved consequences of free act, is the chain of sequence when each equatorial mansion is taken in connection with the second one following—that is, by skipping one—or in its tie with what in horoscopic language is its own third house. Any possible ambiguity in these number relations can be avoided if it is remembered that ordinal indication of this sort can be a reference either to the additional or the total items. Astrology's counting is always inclusive. The third-house or skip-one relationship provides a forward step in the regression of immediateness in experience by moving on from the direct substantiation of reality around the circle, indicated by the houses in their positions adjacent to each other and outlined in the section just preceding, to an analysis of what becomes a more limited or generalized ordering. Reality is dismissed to automaticity, or anchored in momentary fashion, by an acceptance or utilization of purely taken-for-granted consequences. Here is where attention or effort is freed, in a sense, to be of greater service elsewhere in the pattern of circumstances.

(1 TO 3) Thus the normal third house of the horoscope charts a general environment in which personality can lean upon a host of details in the minutiæ of life relationships, without either interest or concern, and this is almost the sole condition of civilized existence. The infinite regression is defeated by the fact that these taken-for-granted phases in the pilgrimage of man are progressively limiting with the thinning out of vitality in the self. Relatives and neighbors, communication and routine activities of living, all constrict man to the degree he fails in the simple impetus of being himself, just as they multiply every convenience of normal living to the extent he succeeds in continuing alive in any truly positive fashion.

(2 TO 4) Possessions and money affairs show the extent of their foundation in free potentiality on the one hand, or in limitation by any external situation on the other, through the home, that is, the conditions in the fourth house as the third of the second. Man's residence is where he can, at the best, dismiss the cares of worldly possessions to a complete automaticity. Money spent on this personal domain often remains a possession in transformed fashion, or a continuing asset. Indeed, accumulations of property in the form of an estate, or capital funds invested for security and income rather than used in an effort towards their own increase, are ruled by the nadir angle. Here is where the native's resources are actually taken for granted, and where, at the worst, he may be the most financially constricted, since the demands at this point are those from which he is least able to extricate himself.

(3 TO 5) Environment, when properly understood and utilized in the light of its potentials in convenience and community support, yields an ordering in an enlarged, uninhibited and creative individuality, i.e., when man is equipped with a surrounding aura of self-sufficiency. The taken-for-granted complex of life in this phase—the third house of an original third—is revealed ultimately as a culture, a body of self-expressive acts-in-common, a series of characteristic types of

instinctive self-expression, which naturally aggregate men into groups and thereby distribute the genius of the whole through each person according to his own talents or pleasure.

(4 TO 6) Home has its ultimate ordering in the many and various ways it contributes to the balancing of personal effort, or in the happy organization and discharge of duties. It dismisses rest and security to automaticity in the sense of making labor a prerequisite of being, that is, a privilege and an assurance of greater rewards. The spirit which preserves man's residence and retreat becomes actual in a cheerful performance of chores, and in the adjustment of every division of labor—otherwise limitation at the sixth—to the exaltation of individual reality within the family.

(5 TO 7) Offspring and creative artistry, sports and self-expression of every sort, are enhanced, dramatized and given self-maintaining actuality by the opportunity in vis-à-vis contact and partnership, i.e., a limitation or ordering at the seventh house. The relationships at the descendant permit the tentative experience of the fifth to be dismissed to the automaticity of a life-involvement. Courtship, through the serious contemplation of marriage, is forced to direct the projection of self into channels of circumspection, after any preliminary self-discovery through trial and error. Pleasure has its surviving sentiment in an adult responsibility, an acceptance of life as a challenge to individuality.

(6 TO 8) Duty—as the over-all designation of the work, labor and adjustment of the sixth—has its ultimate refinement or permanent limitation in the regeneration and rebirth of the eighth. The relations between inferiors and superiors are exalted and clarified in the dismissal of brute or unordered struggle to the automaticity achieved in distinction. Here is a recognition of a personal importance whereby self-expenditure, or the exercise of individual differences, becomes a spiritual transformation, an immortal self-realization.

(7 TO 9) Partnership and the affairs ruled at the seventh are brought to a genuine individual ordering through the disci-

pline of consciousness in the ninth. The internal development
of a sense of values is a dismissal of tête-à-tête experience to
an automaticity of idea, an escape from the annoyance or
difficulty of loosening or dissolving the direct or immediate
ties of life when they have served their purpose. The limitation of knowledge preserves any relationships of permanent
worth, and facilitates the dissolution of all others.

(8 TO 10) Regeneration or rebirth has its practical ordering
or limitation through the established place in life acquired by
the native at the tenth. The recognition of his self-achievement, in the form of an honoring by others, is the true dismissal to automaticity of his eighth-house self-realization or
social training.

(9 TO 11) Understanding in the ninth, as an individual's
thinking or outreach to norms and standards of judgment,
gains its dependable orientation through his refinement or
establishment of objectives in the eleventh. These may be
evident in his widening circle of friends, or in an ordering of
simple external reality as this shows itself by the irresistible
momentum in his affairs—the dismissal of his progress to automaticity by the cosmos itself—but in every case his hopes
and wishes are the practical limitation of his thoughts, and of
his efforts towards any evaluation of reality.

(10 TO 12) Honor or place in life, and the individual's obedi-
ence to the scheme of authority within which he functions in
any given reference, have their limitation and ultimate ordering in the subjective sustainment ruled by the twelfth. Man
may wear a crown exteriorly, but his dignity will be little
more than a nightmare in experience if he cannot carry the
kingly realization deep within himself. He must dismiss any
exalted position—his social reliability—to the automaticity of
his own subconscious realizations.

(11 TO 1) Friendship, practical ideals or expectation, the
hopes and wishes of the eleventh house, have their end-satis-
faction in the ordering self-awareness of the personality at the
first. The eye of vision is limited by the well-being of self in
its first and simple focus. Man's dynamic ambition for himself

is what he may be, in a total automaticity of self-gathered selfhood, as an individual among his fellows.

(12 TO 2) Confinement, or the self-acceptance of some external frame of reality or convenient institution for basic or inner orientation—the subjective sustainment of life ruled by the twelfth—becomes externalized, ordered and given intelligible form for the conscious mind through the possessions ruled by the second. The dismissal of the inner reactions to automaticity is revealed, outwardly, by the available possessions or practical liberty of life.

Regression in a Cancellation of Difference

It has been pointed out that the movement from the single instance to a statistically adequate number of them is the root of all order in the universe. It has been seen that the exact principles of physical science are only possible because they deal with such an infinite quantity of atoms of phenomena that any individual difference is averaged out completely. The consequences which appear in sequence, when analysis around the astrological circle is in terms of houses removed from each other rather than adjacent, similarly exhibit much less difference among them than when these mansions are taken one after the other directly. The fact that every alternate house represents the dismissal to automaticity and order of things ruled by the prior mansion in this skip-one relation is an illustration of the point, since the taken-for-granted status of things is a definite species of indistinction. Moreover, when the houses are linked in a 1–3–5–7–9–11 group of odd-numbered or positive, and a 2–4–6–8–10–12 combination of even-numbered or negative ones, they are sorted into a group entirely derived from the horizon in the first case, and into one stemming wholly from the meridian in the other.

Here is the basis of astrology's positive and negative mansions in both great circles, and a further example of a regression from distinctiveness to complete generalization, or what in the skein of convenience is an increased limitation, whether utilized or suffered. The transition from one house to its next, the first or most normal consequence of free choice or act, eludes this later phase of consequence, and gains an added significance through that fact. The relation in adjacency, from one point of view, is the effective basis in any astrological patterning of life. It not only yields much vital detail in the horoscopic techniques, but provides a simple if uncritical explanation for the art as a whole. When man remains creatively alive, and is truly individual to the maximum extent of his own desire and interest, he is very active in the world about him. He blends, continually, the positive and negative elements screened ut by the special sequence of negation and automaticity which comes next in order. When he surrenders to his destiny, however, and tries to make a bargain of acquiescence with his world of reality, the limitation of mounting complexity then tends to crowd in upon him, leading ultimately to a complete frustration and self-degeneration.

The greatest of all cancellation of difference in experience is represented by mere repetition, or by the following along in chain of those things whose distinctions are significant only in a re-emphasized regression of relationship. Astrology as a result finds the skip-a-house sequence around the equator very valuable in identifying the members in any succession of relations which are more important in likeness than difference. This is a particular detail of horary practice, but one often useful in natal delineation. Thus the third house rules brothers and sisters, in general, and also the first or eldest one, with each alternate mansion then representing the others in the order of their priority in the native's experience (usually chronological age). By the same token, the fifth house indicates all children, and also gives a more specific charting for the first of them as his life is reflected in the parental economy, with a second child identified in the seventh, a third in the ninth and so on. Parenthetically, adopted children are treated the same as natural ones, and no distinctions are made between the offspring by various marriages. Miscarried or stillborn infants are taken in their proper place if accepted as individuals in the consciousness of the mother.

Subjective Sequence as Clockwise Relationship

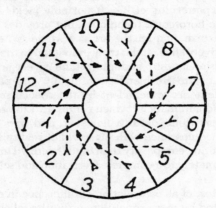

There are not only the possibilities of sequence counterclockwise around the circle, but also the same relationships in the opposite direction, with a reversed implication. This mode of analysis has little value except in the simple house-to-house progression, however, since all the more ordered relations of life and experience are essentially reversible ideas, as will be increasingly evident. Whereas free will and choice tend to establish straight lines of consequence, reaching out towards an illimitable potentiality, order at all points seeks to restore a balance in nature, or to defeat any regression towards infinity and so bring reality back to center. When it comes to mansions in simple adjacency, the forward or counterclockwise implication in any move from the domain of one to the other is a substantiation or validation of the first by the second, as has been demonstrated. It is in this positive direction, to use the astronomer's language, that man proves himself to himself. His backward lean, contrariwise, is not upon the consequences of act and choice, or even upon their potentials, but rather on whatever may sustain the stirring or impulsion to act or choice as this exists entirely within his own economy. Thus the relation of the first house to the second is transitive, or tending to set up sequence, but of the first to the twelfth by contrast, intransitive or inclined to encourage self-impetus. What is charted by the clockwise sequence, therefore, is what might be termed—at least as seen outwardly, or as evident objectively—the moral dynamic, or the inner stimulus to act.

(1 TO 2) Personal identity has its urge to be itself in the subjective sustainment of the twelfth house, or is motivated in all things by a desire to emerge from its confinement and feel that it is what it is.

(2 TO 1) Money affairs or possessions are subjectively dependent upon the continuing outreach of the personality towards its own self-discovery, i.e., its self-establishment through some one or another form of expenditure.

(3 TO 2) Man's environmental situation, his capacity to take more and more things for granted, is due to the dynamic resident in his possessions, or in his self-confidence as instrumented by tangible and expendable resources.

(4 TO 3) The home in its psychological adequacy, or similar poverty as the case may be, depends subjectively upon the environment in which it comes to be established, or upon the number of things that can be taken for granted.

(5 TO 4) Self-expression or offspring, as the most spontaneous outspilling of individual existence, is stimulated by home encouragement, and has its moral dynamic even more importantly in the enduring values the native is able to anchor permanently in his own experience.

(6 TO 5) Duty or labor as an expenditure of effort, whether compelled or given freely, obviously must depend for inner dynamic or sustaining capacity upon the nature and degree of the native's development of a genuine self-expression. He works as he is able or willing to let himself go.

(7 TO 6) Partnerships and tête-à-tête relations are depend-

ent subjectively upon an ability to work hard, or a gift for the adjustment of self to the external demands of others as well as to the individual or organic economy. The dynamic is in a sense of preparedness through real effort.

(8 TO 7) Regeneration or rebirth has it psychological lean upon a native's development of his active and changing relations with his fellows in the terms of a practical and functioning equality, a capacity to rise to opportunity. He recreates himself to the degree he is able to respect others.

(9 TO 8) Understanding and the higher mind depend ultimately, when it comes to subjective motivation, upon the individual's continual reconstruction of himself as a socially competent organism, or as he is moved to realization by the ideals he builds into his own being.

(10 TO 9) Honor, or place in life, is dependent upon a personal consciousness of reality, and any such achievement is motivated by the development of values which can be used to measure self and society, or which demand continual employment for their broadening reference.

(11 TO 10) Friends and the forward expectation or momentum in events depend subjectively upon whatever social position the individual has been able to make manifest among his fellows, thus encouraging him to seek new dimensions in human relationship.

(12 TO 11) Subjective sustainment, in its all-important inner organization of man's potentials for self-realization, leans psychologically upon the external momentums in life, the practical demonstration of any validity in the deeper reactions.

The Further Regressions to Order

The sequence among the houses set up by skipping over two of them in each case is an emphasis of the fundamental axes, as in the groupings 1–4–7–10, 2–5–8–11 and 3–6–9–12. This is the basis of the angular, succedent and cadent distinction, respectively, to which much attention has been given.

When the sequence is created by passing over three mansions, or the fifth-house relationship in its application to the whole skein of convenience, the groups thereby established, 1–5–9, 2–6–10, 3–7–11, and 4–8–12, are the triads created in the original intrahemisphere distribution. They are the foundation for the entire derivation of house meanings. A sequence of sixth-house intervals (or by jumping over four mansions in each instance) is significant in the fact that it returns the arrangement to the fundamental series of next relations, at least to the extent that all twelve houses are included and that a twelfth move arrives back at the starting place. The principal value of this grouping is its demonstration of the logical circularity or ultimate order which the equatorial houses chart for life as a whole.

Thus identity continues to be what it is, ultimately, through duty (1 to 6), which in its turn is strengthened through hopes and wishes (6 to 11), confirmed by the permanent values established in this process (11 to 4), and built into the fiber of self as understanding (4 to 9), thereupon making possessions possible in a truly responsible sense (9 to 2), equipping the native to meet others in co-operation and as an equal (2 to 7), and helping him to gain a subjective sustainment from any limitation or institutionalizing of life (7 to 12), so that his self-expression remains conditioned by his own inner reality (12 to 5), and thereby becomes competent to substantiate itself in a recognition of his own intrinsic worth among men (5 to 10), permitting him to dismiss the lesser things of his experience to automaticity (10 to 3), and to concentrate on his own self-refinement (3 to 8), in this continuous reconstruction of his own experience, or circular confirmation of his own identity (8 to 1).

Eighth-house intervals produce the same sequence, but in reverse order, showing the identical process in more intransitive form. The ninth-house sequence duplicates the fifth-house triads similarly. The tenth-house relations reverse the fourth-house axial ones. This reversibilty of astrological indication has its principal significance, however, through the houses which lie opposite each other, or which constitute what is hardly to be taken as a sequence in the ordinary meaning of that word, namely, six groups of two each, created by seventh-house intervals (skipping over five mansions). Here is a most important relationship in astrological order, used first of all to chart the succession of things which, in experience, can only follow each other by a process of elimination and reconstruction. Thus new parents or marriage partners (other than where polygamy is practiced) are possible only after the death or legal removal of their predecessors. Hence the seventh house indicates all partners of any given category, such as marriage or business, and then shows, in addition, the particular significance of the initial one. The ascendant identifies a second partner particularly, the descendant again a third, and so on. Foster parents are treated in the same fashion at the midheaven and nadir.

Every house has a particularly active relationship with its opposite, a fact which has been very evident in connection with the house axes, and which provides a real starting point for horary analysis. There are twelve of these polarities, as they are known to astrologers, although only six actual pairs can exist in the heavens. In order to indicate the considerable difference when a polarity is taken from one side, as in contrast with the other, each house is given an additional keyword. The ones emphasized in the preceding chapter serve to identify the more positive facet of experience, and the new designations will show the significance of each mansion in the same circumstantial connection, but from the alternative perspective. Here is sequence in its closest approach to absolute order, producing relationship around the circle in a double fashion, or in a continual reconstruction of the balancing stimulus upon which all phenomena must depend ultimately.

The Balance of Stimulus in Convenience

(1 TO 7) The beginning of all perspective on man is his identity at the first house. This is the center of his being, and it

at once creates a necessity that he reach out to the periphery of his being, or know himself in wholeness. Here is the balancing of mere existence with a definite OPPORTUNITY in the seventh.

(2 TO 8) The initial step creates a necessity for discrimination or choice in the individual's experience, so that he must retain certain selected materials of his activity as a basis for his further self-unfoldment. The establishment of possessions in the second house in this way at once develops the need for a complementing release or surrender of accumulated but unused realities, which ultimately is a final accounting, a discarding of things, or DEATH, at the eighth.

(3 TO 9) Holding some things to self, and putting others aside, requires a context in which to act, or the environment at the third house. This promptly creates the need for some sort of a balancing and synthetic realization, or a capacity to arrange things in generalization, which is CONSCIOUSNESS or the corresponding indirect contact of the ninth.

(4 TO 10) With the developed sense of selfhood, resulting from the process at this point in the symbolical description, man's effort takes on the color of private interest. Therefore he has a home in the fourth house. The resulting responsibility immediately pushes him into BUSINESS at the tenth, the corresponding public interest in which he balances his existence at this stage of its development.

(5 TO 11) His private interest demands a continual and compensatory contribution of self to the outer world at large, setting up the phenomenon of offspring at the fifth house, or the definitely creative act of selfhood. This immediately has its balance in the symbolical act of creation on the higher level through imagination, or the projection of self through OBJECTIVES in the eleventh.

(6 TO 12) Self cannot continue to give of itself without a context of necessity, ordering and supply, and the manifestation of this is duty in the sixth house. This may be service to others, or the capacity to compel service, together with the organization and distribution of self-effort. In any case, the

TABLE III

The Polarities of the Houses

I	IDENTITY Center of being	VII	OPPORTUNITY Periphery of being
II	POSSESSION Utilization of reality	VIII	DEATH Surrender of reality
III	ENVIRONMENT Direct contact	IX	CONSCIOUSNESS Indirect contact
IV	HOME Private interest	X	BUSINESS Public Interest
V	OFFSPRING Act of self	XI	OBJECTIVES Purpose of self
VI	DUTY Practical adjustment	XII	PREDILECTION Psychical adjustment
VII	PARTNERSHIP Relation to others	I	PERSONALITY Relation to self
VIII	REGENERATION Life reconstruction	II	LOSS AND GAIN Life manipulation
IX	UNDERSTANDING Reality at a distance	III	PERCEPTION Reality at hand
X	HONOR Present recognition	IV	IMMORTALITY Final recognition
XI	FRIENDSHIP Potentiality sought	V	PLEASURE Potentiality claimed
XII	CONFINEMENT Limitation used	VI	SICKNESS Limitation refined

result is the beginning of a distinction among people, which calls forth the balancing PREDILECTION at the twelfth, that is, the psychical adjustment by which the individual is able to bring about different responses from various other people, or to adjust himself in mood or attitude.

(7 TO 1) The discrimination of act towards others is responsible for a changing relation to them, and an equalization with them, or the reality of partnership at the seventh house ultimately, and this is balanced by the many-faceted self known as PERSONALITY in the first, that is, the social identity which only exists in order that all the shades of difference typified by these others may be unified in itself.

(8 TO 2) Partnership promptly sets up the need for a fluid co-operation with non-partners in its activity, which requires a regeneration of self in the eighth house, or a reconstruction of life to make use of the resources of others. This is balanced, of course, by the consequent necessity that the self also reconstruct the values and symbols which reveal the actuality of its own experience through LOSS AND GAIN at the second.

(9 TO 3) The social reconstruction of self is the whole basis for any organization of ideas—any relating of the self to reality at a distance—through the intellectual activity and understanding at the ninth house. This is balanced by PERCEPTION in the third, i.e., the practical and creative insight into the immediate usefulness of all things on their own account, or as they become available close at hand.

(10 TO 4) Understanding is the basis of all realization of worth in its personal or individual phase, and this puts down the foundation for the honor in the tenth house which, as balanced in the skein of convenience, becomes the fixation of achievement through an IMMORTALITY or wholeness of the conscious self at the fourth.

(11 TO 5) Honor calls to its own, and this has expression in the relation of friendship at the eleventh house, or the continual encouragment and enlargement of potential relationships for the self. The balance of the impulse to momentum in the more formal fashion is that PLEASURE in the fifth by

which conscious individuality enhances its reality in a creative fulfillment of itself.

(12 TO 6) The self's driving determination to uncover potentialities in life leads it to establish a total reality which it can never really substantiate, and the result is a confinement of the conscious identity in the twelfth house by the transient boundaries it thus sets up. This is balanced by an employment of all such constriction in a creative self-mobilization, a figurative if not literal SICKNESS in the sixth, and the principal agency through which any limitation is faced or defeated.

The acceptance of a reality beyond the immediate possibilities of its substantiation makes it necessary for the self to reaffirm itself in its own identity, and this becomes a refocusing of its center of being on some new level of realization. It is then ready to begin the whole process over again, as often as is convenient or profitable.

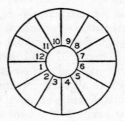

Thus the diagram of life's circumstances charts a continual interweaving of free choice and ramifying consequences in experience. The analysis so far has concerned itself with the single individual, however, taken almost solipsistically in the pattern of his own potentials, or in his relations to other persons or groups as these are centered in himself. Now he must be linked to his fellows in a much more tangible way, because he does not inhabit this world of his alone, even if he does create it for himself, and does do so entirely according to his own convenience.

Characteristics

CHAPTER SIX

The Magic of Human Nature

Unless you can muse in a crowd all day
On the absent face that fixed you;
Unless you can love, as the angels may,
With the breadth of heaven betwixt you;
Unless you can dream that his faith is fast,
Through behoving and unbehoving;
Unless you can die when the dream is past—
Oh, never call it loving!

ELIZABETH BARRETT BROWNING,
A Woman's Shortcomings

Milord is an important executive, and his day at the office has been a particularly difficult one. Leaving early, he makes his way in weariness to his castle, which is a series of rooms in one among a cluster of tall apartment buildings. In clinging tightly to these special cells, by a long-term lease, he reveals a certain affinity to the bee, and his mood of the moment finds his world constricted, if not wholly boxed up by a technical civilization.

When milord enters his castle, however, the whole aspect

of reality is changed. There at the twin windows of her bed-chamber, in the flooding warmth of an afternoon sun coming low across the park and its bordering mass of trees, is the lady of his life. She wears a yellow house-dress of no pretension, merely clean, and starched. Her hair, which holds its youth so strangely, is taken up off her face and ears in a style born of her insouciant happiness. She radiates a fullness of living with which an entire universe has come to endow her, in co-operation with her own special attitude. Occupying the little rocking chair he has had cut down and freshly uphol-stered, for the fine needlework which is her relaxation, she looks up to greet him with the smile which has long been her embarrassment because of its prodigality.

A day's weariness is lifted from the soul of the man. The daily apprehension on her part—a haunting fear that this might be a dream after all, with nothing left but to follow Mrs. Browning's suggestion, and die—evaporates completely. An alchemy is at work. It is legerdemain, miracle, occult inter-vention, not something to be put under a label, merely, or dismissed with an identifying word. What is it? Is it genuine, or only a phenomenon of the mind?

The executive would unquestionably sacrifice his own life for this bond in understanding, if the call upon him were direct and clear enough. He knows that an indis-soluble com-panionship has become the very fiber of his conscious being. Wholly apart from the psychological factors which may have cradled the beginnings of the tie—irrespective of whatever may have constituted a private little symphony of moonlight and music, or of whatever form the age-old mysteries of Aphrodite may have taken in lace and lusciousness, in scent and special sympathy of soul and spirit—the cold, hard and statistical fact, to which all idealization must not altogether blind itself if it wishes to preserve its values, is that two in-dividuals, with a persistent and slow care of which they proba-bly were totally unaware, step by step and point by point through every variety of external experience, have found each other consistently unchanging in a basic mutuality of interest.

There have unquestionably been side issues, the continual distraction of individuality as it moved in and out of center in its necessary and unceasing reconstruction of its own world. There were quarrels, without doubt, and occasional periods of sharp emotional wrench, or the distraught agony of feelings when twisted out of the underlying at-one-ment. What alone was important, however, was the unswerving continuance of that which constituted the relationship. This is an otherwise unidentifiable something which exists for the simple reason, no more and no less, that it has persisted in its existence. There have been many threats to its being, but these have only strengthened it in the terms of what it is, all because it has continued to be, despite every one of them.

Here in simple essence is character, in one phase of itself as called forth and shared by two people in close contact with each other. It is the greatest of all possible intangibles, yet can anything else be cited of equal objectivity in human experience? Milord of the business world and his lady, in the high magic of their comaraderie, exhibit a commonplace of nature as far as usual description goes, since it is merely the mating instinct dignified by a seventh-house formalization. Their universally normal impulses have effected a graduation from the trial-and-error acquaintance at the fifth mansion. On his part, he is creating a sure place in life, such as has its measurement at the midheaven. Her little chair and the yellow dress are a symbol to him of what the two of them together have made their own at the nadir. The twelve houses of a horoscope, however, give no inkling of this new dimension in the constants of human existence. There are a million marriages without the particular alchemy of her Cheshire smile, or of his persistently prankish and original ways of showing her that his faith is fast indeed. By the same token, there are a myriad other ties between men and women where the mutual development or sustainment of genuine personal worth is no less marked, although identified by far different symbols and manifest under every variety of situation.

Characteristics are the measure of identity in what must be recognized as its complete transcendence of ordinary circumstances. The approach to an understanding of them must be from an entirely different point of view, and for this Thomas Carlyle, in his *Heroes and Hero-Worship,* provides a convenient starting point with a most epigrammatic and yet most accurate insight into human progress. "The history of the world," remarks the caustic Scotsman, "is but the biography of great men." Behind this fairly obvious fact lies the important principle recognized by Epictetus in his *Discourses.* "Nothing great comes into being all at once," explains the famous slave, "not even the grape or the fig." Character is consistently cumulative, gathering its own fiber out of what has proved of value to the race through its survival. Thus it constitutes and supports the species of living things, as Charles Darwin saw perhaps more clearly than anyone else in recent times.

Personality in its continual refinement is the hope of civilization because the outstanding individuals, in any context of time and place, always become the mainstay of their fellows. They are more able and eager to draw the constants of experience to a center in themselves, and thus to dramatize them, and facilitate a selection of the best potentials of human nature for support and emulation. This process creates a higher or psychological species as a sure matrix, ultimately, for themselves as well as everyone else. Every man, whether on a greater scale or lesser, is a type in social reality, and he serves his fellows in precisely the same way that they serve him, namely, through the statistical sorting out of the mutual conveniences, or circumstances, to which the first part of this text has been devoted. The superficial divisions of labor among men reflect the individual's special capacity in each case, and it is here that characteristics become personal distinctiveness, revealing life in the dimension above situation *per se.*

Individual differences, whereby personality becomes distinct in this manner, are very slight in primitive or tribal living. Courtship takes place, measured by the fifth house, and marriage has its indication at the descendant. There is a patriarch to grace the midheaven, exactly as there are thatched huts or tents of skin to give as much implication to the nadir as the city tower of steel and cement. When shoes become useful there is a cobbler—to use the illustration employed by Socrates in Plato's *Republic*—but the men are fighters for most of their days, and the women are held to a primitive non-distinctiveness by the exactions of carding, weaving, milling and a host of home crafts and chores. Each individual of the clan has character, naturally, but it has relatively few facets. There is little scope for one of them to assimilate himself into the person of another through vicarious experience, and so but a minimal substance for the cultural complexity which establishes civilization with its literal cities, its immensely ramifying communities of mental interests and spiritual insights. The beginning of a true human evolution is in the rise of a personal identity capable of expanding the horizons of the group, and enabling the masses to visualize themselves in a larger potential through the dramatization of their characteristics by the great ones of their own blood.

The exaltation of character is the positive dynamic in all self-realization, and in all social progress. Human beings gain stature, or acquire power, as they are able to establish a reality through which they can feel themselves reassured. This may be either an inspiration by greatness, or else a successful calling forth of exceptional effort from others. Thus simple people look for a savior, while those of greater capacity champion the less fortunate about them. No individual can be everything in and of himself, but must instead complete his own existence by his fellowship with others. Human nature becomes the act of being one's self on the practical as against that relatively solipsistic side of things which, in astrology, is measured by the houses. This presents the factor of FUNCTION, in contrast with circumstances, and introduces the zodiacal signs as differentiated from the equatorial mansions.

Character is Destiny

The problem in an estimation of character is not a charting of the possible co-operation between an antithetical free will and order—as is the case in any analysis of circumstances—

but rather is the recognition of a somewhat parallel interaction between (1) purely organic and (2) wholly social potentials. The manner or nature of act in a particular frame of reference must be viewed in the light of the personal specialization or individual preparation for participation in the given experience. The initial perspective in the horoscope, provided by the houses, measures man through the total complex of affairs in which he is found, using various dichotomies to isolate everything of pertinence in a single point of time and space. The basic procedure through the signs is almost exactly contrary, since each relevant phase of personality is taken as the culmination of the native's entire past and present reality, as well as that of the race which lives through him. The world is centered in this individual according to various illimitable characteristics. These enable him to assimilate, into his own nature, everything of importance to himself. Thus character is destiny, as Heraclitus long ago claimed. Human nature is not merely something that has being, it is also the living personality which can do things.

No one lives for himself alone, however. Destiny is social, inherent in the characteristics of high and low alike. The most exalted men and women must of necessity look to others for their personal self-certification. William Hazlitt in consequence, in his *Table Talk,* is able to affirm that "no really great man ever thought himself so." Probably the most dramatic example of this projection of self into others who may, for the moment, typify certain desired potentials of the race, was provided by the usually quite self-sufficient Bonaparte at Erfurt, a story which Emil Ludwig tells graphically in his *Napoleon.* The Corsican was seated at breakfast when he looked up and saw Goethe in the doorway. Viewing the sexagenarian poet for the first time, he was unable to speak for the moment. Then, more to himself than his companions, he exclaimed, "Voilà un homme!"

Superlative personality, which Ludwig terms the "godlike kinship of a genius with his fellow genius," provides the strongly knit warp of constancies on which the filling threads

116

of history have been woven through all the ages. Life in its everyday channeling, however, does not reach to these outstanding people, except most remotely. The catalysis of character operates on a practical plane, even though the principles are always best exhibited in the extraordinary instance. Mr. Downstreet extends himself a little in order to match the example of Mr. Upstreet, and the community thereby is bettered, although both these men may be quite obscure. When it comes to an estimation of personal worth in normal affairs, custom decrees an examination of actual performance in a commonplace community, and it is here that the real integration of human individuality is best observed. Fundamentally the idea is that nature tends to repeat itself, and that a man will usually act in the future as he has in the past. When his recommendations show him honest and conscientious for many years back, it is presumed that he will continue to be just that. His functioning, as in contrast with his circumstances, is his general persistence in certain ways of acting. Character is cumulative in every way. What it develops is an organic and psychological constancy.

The question might be asked, why does a kitten lick herself? From the day of her birth the little creature has been cleaned in this way by a solicitous mother cat, and the process in time inevitably engenders an appetite which, like the habits of all higher creatures, demands its satisfaction. When the day comes for the feline youngster to do her own grooming, the developing *psyche* is at the point where the fur hurts, in a sense, unless it is stroked by the loving if filelike surface of the tiny tongue, and so Miss Felis takes over the function herself. Through all her later life this care becomes a necessity which only the most dire of calamity will drive out of consideration. So ingrained into the very fiber of her being is the Narcissus-like self-stroking that it becomes almost a matter of instinct, perhaps an actual inheritance of acquired characteristics. Functions are these necessities of being.

Why does man have personality? Because, like the kitten, he must give expression to the necessary narcissism of his own nature. He is useful to himself and his fellows, superficially in the terms of the general circumstances to which attention has already been given, but more importantly on the basis of what he makes of himself in his development of enduring characteristics, as already suggested. The scope of his influence may be great or small, the distinction of his personality much or little, but he smooths his own fur in this way, psychologically speaking, whenever and as ever he can, and thereby continues to be what he is. Moreover, he does this in many different areas of experience, and with highly varying degrees of import to his own identity and to the place he makes for himself in the world.

Here as an example is the gum-chewing stenographer whose hair needs attention, and whose suit should go to the cleaner, but she has a voice which conjures orders over the telephone, and a gay spirit which creates an exceptional morale in the office. She ungrudgingly shoulders the support of a helpless parent while her sister, who smells only of Shalimar, has not been home for a month, nor brought in a dime towards its support for six. And here is Old Man Forester, a periodical drunkard who has put his wife in the hospital some four or five times, but who in fifty years has never failed to get his bills paid somehow, and to see to it that his brace of boys got a better chance than any of the dead-enders with whom they were raised. These illustrations can be multiplied, endlessly.

People have recognized the ridiculous admixture of traits in themselves for centuries, and have sought to screen out whatever characteristics might be the most significant in any general scheme of things. In trying to identify each other in terms of their most promising potentials, they have facilitated human co-operation and understanding. While the obvious classifications of family and clan, race and nation, have served in part, these have always been lines of division or separation. The problem demands a deeper analysis. What human temperaments will work together across all superficial lines? What types of people can best co-operate with each other for their common interest? What are the most universal elements of affinity among men, and how can they be recognized other than by trial and error?

Such considerations have given rise to the most popular if most shallow form of astrology, dealing with the sun signs and the twelve groups of people created by the zodiacal months of birth. The general public has realized that there are simple or fundamental sets of character which ought to be taken into account in everyday human relations, and this has been one way to identify them. Fortune-tellers have capitalized on the solar indications to warn Aries people from marrying Capricorn natives, and to suggest that Gemini individuals fraternize with the children of Aquarius. A very deep truth is expressed, by and large, but with great weight upon too weak a straw. Exactly as each horoscope has a dozen houses, despite the difference of emphasis upon various ones through the circumstances of life, so every man has all twelve signs in his make-up, irrespective of what may turn out to be the greater importance of one or more among them. The next and necessary step in this presentation, therefore, is to get behind mere superficiality, and to see how the zodiacal symbolism arises, and how each of these ecliptical divisions gains its fundamental relation to the native and his horoscope. To chart the functional role of characteristics in everyday experience will be the task for several following chapters.

CHAPTER SEVEN

Perspective and Reality

It is not impossible to claim Ralph Waldo Emerson as the first American astrologer of consequence. This does not mean he practiced horoscopy, although it is on record that he gave some thought to the art (*Conduct of Life: Beauty*). Rather he seems to have understood the proper implication of any relationship between a man and his stars, and to have seen that the heavens and history, alike, hold up a mirror to human nature. There is a curious observation, found in his *Essays, First Series: History*. "As crabs, goats, scorpions, the balance and the waterpot lose their meanness when hung as signs in the zodiac, so can I see my own vices without heat in the distant persons of Solomon, Alcibiades, and Catiline." Perspective is the basis of any enduring reality, according to the suggestion here, because the transient focus of circumstances is transcended, and individual differences are helped to refine themselves into genuine constants of character.

Astrology, of course, has no absolute way to chart the affinities between a native and those of greater prominence to whom he might be liked. Moreover, the procedure might be entirely meaningless. How many clients would remember enough about Solomon to gain any dynamic stimulus from a comparison with him, if the practitioner were able to make it? Would many of them know that Alcibiades and Catiline are not to be dismissed as mere unscrupulous politicians, that Napoleon is of least importance for the battles he fought, and that Goethe was primarily concerned with much more than *Faust?* The particular characteristics which became the basis of selection from great lives by the astrologer might not be obvious to the person consulting him. Human nature presents as many paradoxical blends of its elements in the perspective of history as in the individual horoscopic analysis.

When a man becomes outstanding among his fellows he may seem simple, and highly consistent, largely because attention is limited to his achievements—to the special traits brought forward by his dramatic focus in the public eye—but he will be found no different from anyone else in the fact that he continues a member of his species, both for better and worse. Human characteristics must be generalized in a much more fruitful fashion than in these broad comparisons. Any intelligent recognition of them must contribute to the conscious refinement of personality, and also to a definite control of individual destiny. An effective first step is through hanging them in the zodiac, as Emerson aptly describes the procedure.

PERSPECTIVE HUNG IN THE SKY

Nature, in her most dazzling aspects or stupendous parts, is but the background and theatre of the tragedy of man.

John Morley, *Critical Miscellanies: Byron*

Astrology reveals human characteristics effectively because nature provides the ground for analysis, precisely as in the case of the horizons through which a perspective in circumstances has been gained. The measurement is in the heavens because a relative simplicity of relation is thereby used to map out what would otherwise remain a hopeless interweaving of the factors in any individual's make-up. What must now be seen is just how the signs of the zodiac can chart the generalizations of human traits. Here is the major obstacle to many a brilliant mind, leading to an almost off-hand dismissal of astrology's claims. There is, actually, a close correspondence between the apparent path of the sun, created by the earth's orbit, and those conditions on the globe's surface which have been responsible, throughout the ages, for sorting out individual differences, and so making human characteristics the source of the various psychological species. What is its nature?

The correspondence rests, first of all, on certain mathematical considerations, and these will give a clue to the total pattern of relations. The connection of the ecliptic with the celestial equator, in which the houses are identified, has already been shown on page 17, as follows:

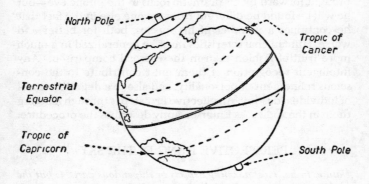

Tropics of Cancer and Capricorn are established around the sphere, showing the extreme points at which the sun can be found directly overhead, from its northernmost position in midsummer to the corresponding most southern one at Christmas time. The swing of the luminary back and forth across the equator in this fashion represents, geographically, the annual journey of the earth around the zodiac, while the daily rotation of the planet carries each degree of Sol's inching sidewise crawl, up and down in terrestrial latitude as it thus marks out the seasons, all the way around the globe daily. The ecliptic in consequence, is indicated on its surface rather arbitrarily. The interception of the two great circles actually takes

place in the heavens, and they are perhaps better diagrammed in this style:

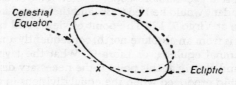

Celestial
Equator

y

x

Ecliptic

The celestial equator is indicated by the dotted line, the
ecliptic by the solid one, and the points of interception are
at x and y. Because the astrologer employs both these circles
simultaneously, he must have a means for representing their
common relations, that is, for showing the factors of either in
the particular ground for measurement provided by the
other. His chart, in other words, must represent the signs of
the zodiac as well as the houses, and usage no less than necessity has established the latter as fundamental in analysis. Since
the equatorial mansions are diagrammed directly, by drawing
the circle and its segments to scale, the signs are indicated by
a notation at the cusp of each house in the equator, showing
which one of the ecliptical mansions—and also which of the
thirty degrees that comprise it—have astrological correspondence to the segment in what then becomes the basic horoscopic circle. Equal divisions of thirty degrees in diurnal motion are projected over into the ecliptic, as shown in two of
the twelve instances, thus:

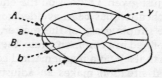

A

y

a

B

b

x

The notches *A* and *B* on the zodiacal circle represent the points projected from the cusps of the ascendant and second house on the plane of the equator (i.e., *a* and *b*, respectively). If this were an actual horoscope, erected for Quito, Ecuador, the ascendant would be Leo 6° 36′ and the second-house cusp would lie at Virgo 7° 17′. The point of view in all horoscopic charting is from an absolute north, consequently *x* represents the autumnal equinox, or Libra 0°. What the layman must understand clearly at this point is the necessary distortion in relationship produced when the equal divisions in one circle are carried over into another, the plane of which has a different slanting. This is obvious to the eye if the simple angles involved are placed in a separate diagram:

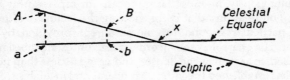

The distance from *A* to *B* is obviously greater than from *a* to *b*, judged by observation alone, in this case 30° 41′ against 30° 0′. As it happens, however, this is only half of a total proposition which, more than anything else, comes up to plague the young student. The equatorial mansions are equal thirty-degree divisions of the heavens in their own circle, the plane of which, parallel the equator, passes through the birthplace, and lies towards the north or south pole as the case may be. In the example just given, Quito is on the equator and so the additional complication has been avoided for the sake of an initial and more simple grasp of the matter. The equatorial houses can be defined in a common circle, the center of which is that of the earth itself, as a mathematical convenience, but the geographical situation makes an adjustment necessary when it comes to the correspondences in the zodiac.[1]

Actually what is measured in a horoscope is motion. The eastern horizon at the moment of birth, as described from the place of that event, is the ascendant in fact, no matter how it may be represented. The definition of the houses in the earth's literal equator does not alter their basic nature, since the diurnal turning of the sphere is revealed identically in both the equator and any circle parallel to it, but there is an extra distortion in the correspondence of the equatorial mansions to those of the ecliptic whenever the place of birth is located towards either pole. The simple case diagrammed for Quito at the equator can be corrected for a birth at New York City where, with Libra 0° in the same relative position before the third cusp, the ascendant would be Leo 20° 35′ and the second-house cusp Virgo 12° 35′. In comparison with the preceding diagram, the angles would appear thus:

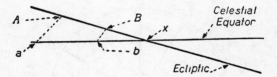

The situation first charted at Quito is greatly exaggerated at New York because, at 40° 43′ north latitude, twenty-two zodiacal degrees correspond to nearly thirty-one at the equator, both representing the normal thirty in the house circle. The practicing astrologer, most fortunately, does not have to make the intricate computations involved in charting these

[1] All consideration in this text is on the basis of the Placidian system for determining zodiacal correspondences to the house cusps, the one of several (as those of Regiomontanus, Campanus and others) now having practically universal acceptance by astrologers, and the one justified theoretically because it really divides diurnal motion. Thus the divisions of the houses are never even thirty-degree segments in right ascension, except at the equator, due to the spherical (really spheroid) shape of the earth.

relations between the two great systems. They are available to any degree of accuracy desired in various Tables of Houses. Similarly, all the other technical information he needs is ready for him, prepared conveniently in the form he must employ, either in an ephemeris or else in supplementary publications, such as those which give the kinds of time used in various parts of the world at certain periods. The newcomer only needs to set himself in mind for the fact that he will never encounter an instance where there is an even-degree correspondence of all signs and houses in a horoscope.

If the equinoctial points Aries 0° or Libra 0° are found on the ascendant, the distortion is at a minimum. Thus a case taken for Washington, D. C., as an example, shows the twelve equatorial cusps, as identified in their zodiacal correspondences, as follows:

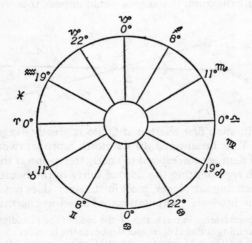

As in contrast with the houses of the horoscope, which are merely numbered, and represented in the modern diagram quite simply by the actual spokes of the astrological wheel, the signs of the zodiac are named, and have their special symbols in addition. What the astronomer knows more coldly and impersonally as degrees of celestial longitude, ranging from 0° to 360°, have a much more definite character in astrology through the twelve thirty-degree spans. This means that a stranger to horoscopy, wishing to proceed in his investigation, will have to stop to familiarize himself, in at least a general fashion, with a species of alphabet.

TABLE IV

The Zodiacal Alphabet

♈	ARIES	Ram	♎	LIBRA	Balance
♉	TAURUS	Bull	♏	SCORPIO	Scorpion
♊	GEMINI	Twins	♐	SAGITTARIUS	Archer
♋	CANCER	Crab	♑	CAPRICORN	Goat
♌	LEO	Lion	♒	AQUARIUS	Water carrier
♍	VIRGO	Virgin	♓	PISCES	Fishes

These names are little more than the Anglicized form of the Latin descriptive term given above in English.[2] It will be noted, in the horoscope for the city of Washington, that Cancer and Capricorn each occupy the cusps of two houses, and that Virgo and Pisces do not lie on any. These two latter signs are said to be intercepted, and INTERCEPTION in astrology indicates that whatever is ruled in such a case is either less strong, or else in not as outwardly manifest as normal expectation would suggest.

[2] Many mispronunciations are common in 1945. Aries is a three-syllable word, AYE-ree-eeze or AIR-ee-eeze. TAW-russ, GEM-uh-nigh, LIE-bra, Saj-ee-TAY-ree-us, and Ah-KWAIR-ee-us offer some difficulties. PISS-eeze alone is correct, as far as dictionary authority goes, but PIE-sees is almost universally preferred by astrologers. The symbols are ancient representations of the zodiacal creatures, quite obvious on the whole. The ones for Leo, Virgo and Capricorn may come from Greek initials or ligatures. Straight uprights often indicated Castor and Pollux. Aquarius is identified by waves, and Pisces by curves for the fishes.

ASTROLOGY: How and Why It Works

The Evolution of Zodiacal Correspondences

Just how do the signs of the zodiac chart human characteristics? The primary factor, of course, is a statistical correlation, as has been suggested at the very beginning of this text, on page 9. Now it is necessary to return to the mathematical relationships through which Libra, in the zodiac, and the autumnal season, on the earth's surface north of the equator, actually come into being. The swing of the sun's meridian angle, back and forth from north to south, is the basis for the seasonal changes, as every school child knows, and the corresponding potentialities of human character—those which have statistical concordance with an astrological emphasis of the sign Libra—have their origin in a very similar possibility of deviation from norm.

Men are distinguishable from each other because it is possible for them to lean away, in either direction, from every plane of the dead average in which all distinction, or all individual existence, tends to disappear. The evolution of personal differences from the indistinctiveness of tribal life has already been sketched, in broad terms, in the preceding chapter. Elements of experience are not real because they exist, but because human individuals assimilate them to themselves, in the process which has been illustrated by the underlying transition from ascendant to descendant on page 47. Here is the commonplace of human relations *per se*, transcending the boundaries of time and space, as well as all lines of class or situation, and so creating function as an enlarged dimension of living.

Life itself dramatizes experience as this dimensional outreach of self, continuously and in a host of ways. Thus a group of artists were summering one year in a relatively isolated rural area. Existence in this district was hard, superficially uneventful enough to hold the farmers to a very limited norm of values. Reality for them was primitive in a true sense, that is, indistinct. They had few resources in the social or transcendental perspective which the signs of the zodiac delineate at root. One of the visiting families, with two little children, had employed a local daughter to look after them. When a number of the painters gathered on a knoll to watch, with urban ecstasy, an exceptionally spectacular setting of the sun, this nursemaid trailed along, leading her charges. After some four or five minutes, she pulled the mother of the youngsters down to earth with a timid touch.

"Please, may I run and tell Ma and Pa to look?"

"Why, they'll see it themselves!"

"No, ma'am, we never see sunsets here."

Human nature develops only with the greatest difficulty at the equator, where a persisting sameness tends to stultify any individuality. Humanity has found and refined itself, principally, in areas ranging back towards the poles, as in temperate zones where higher life has a stimulating interaction with the four seasons, or at least on high plateaus where the contrast in day and night defeats any lush stagnation of the tropics. The variety in nature is always a prophecy of the potential distinctions in man, and these are what astrology measures in the horoscope by reduplicating, in a sense, the original excitations and co-operations of nature. Character is destiny because, while the circumstances in which a given personality is found are responsible for the distribution of its special traits across its own private ground of experience, its particular capacities are the basis of its functioning in its own unique fashion. Characteristics give a personal implication to every event in existence, and this fact is the origin of zodiacal meaning.

The equator establishes the mansions in the ecliptic, and then creates their significance in every particular case, thus measuring man's individualization. The exact geographical location of a horizon, in its tilting towards one or the other of the poles—while not in any way modifying the equatorial or ecliptical mansions of astrology in their own circles— greatly changes the zodiacal correspondences to the house cusps, and this potential of mathematical difference is the very core of horoscopy. It produces the individuality of an astrological wheel, and thus charts the particular co-operation of function and circumstances in the given native's case. The two circles are linked to each other permanently because they arise in the two fundamental motions of the same body, and so measure an experience which exists only through the interaction between an entity and its situation in a statistically parallel fashion. The actual measurement begins in both circles where they intercept each other, or at the equinoxes, and by agreement at that one of the two points which represents the spring rather than the autumn season in the terrestrial hemisphere where man's present civilization has developed. The equator establishes the ecliptical signs mathematically because it determines these equinoxes.

The zodiac consists of the twelve mansions or segments in the ecliptic, containing thirty degrees of celestial longitude each. There is a slow clockwise movement of the equinoctial points against the pattern of the stars seen behind them, a slipping back of perhaps fifty seconds of arc a year and known as the PRECESSION OF THE EQUINOXES. This fact has encouraged a rather common criticism of horoscopy's claims, rooted in the assumption that the zodiacal signs are star-groups rather than geometrical divisions in a circle of motion. What happened, at about the time of Hipparchus, is that some unknown genius devised or rearranged a mnemonic and mensural device to help astrologers in a day when there were neither books nor tables in any modern sense. He symbolized the ecliptical mansions by arbitrary but generally rather happy patterns, such as could be fixed in the mind as well as in the heavens, and represented them by lines traced from various of the more prominent or brighter stars to others seen as nearby from the earth's perspective. Thus Cancer, which on the whole requires the least imagination to recognize in terms of what the star-group is supposed to indicate, is put together as follows:[3]

[3] The arrangement at the left is sketched by permission from *Webster's New International Dictionary, Second Edition*, Springfield, G. & C. Merriam, 1934, 1939, and that at the right is the one adopted by William Tyler Olcott in his *Field Book of the Stars*, G. P. Putnam, 1907.

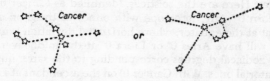

The Great Bear is more familiar to the average person, but it is not one of the zodiacal twelve and, moreover, it is only known commonly through a part of its whole, since most people see nothing but the Big Dipper. Symbolism of this sort is entirely artificial, of course, but it can be exceedingly useful if not permitted to become more than an aid to the eye, or a mental construct to help the imaginative faculties. These CONSTELLATIONS of the ecliptic, often termed the natural zodiac to distinguish them from the mansions defined by the equinoxes, have moved along the full span of a sign since they were established—or last realigned with the ecliptical divisions of equal thirty degrees—hence when the sun on March 21st appears at the vernal equinox in the heavens it is also, approximately, at the point dividing Pisces and Aquarius in the constellations. This leads to the definition of an Aquarian Age in popular occult writings, and permits the astrologer's critics to suppose that Aries is in Pisces, and that horoscopy is thereby invalidated.

The equinoxes are an obviously primary factor in the development of sign meanings. The points of pause to the north or south in the pendulum swing of the sun during the course of its annual pilgrimage around the earth's orbit, in contrast to the equinoctial points, are of equal significance. They represent the extreme emphases, not of personal insouciance as charted by the individualizing equator through its first definition of the zodiacal generalities at Aries and Libra, but rather of the broadest possible personal completeness of particular sort. The sharp differentiations of summer and winter, in a sense, are distortion *per se,* or a heightening of experience in its lean away from all dependence on mean values or mere averages. Here are the solstices, identified as Cancer 0° and Capricorn 0°. Any horoscope with either of these on an ascendant at the equator, where horizontal deviation is nonexistent, will have Aries 0° or Libra 0° at the midheaven, the ninety zodiacal degrees corresponding to the same number of equatorial ones. With Cancer 0° on the ascendant at Leningrad—as an example of high northern latitude on the earth's surface—the midheaven would be Aquarius 9°. This distortion of fifty-one zodiacal degrees in equatorial correspondence supports the astrological implication given the solstitial signs. They chart the maximum possible rejection of the mean in the mass, or the largest possible amount of self-completion in human nature. They reveal the characteristics which enable man, progressively, to create his own private universe.

The thirty-degree divisions in the zodiac originate in exactly the same fashion as the equatorial houses. Two initial dichotomies create the quarters, and the process of tri-section produces the twelve. The root elements in human character are delineated by the four quarters. Each has its own emphasis, first as focal between the distinctions made by the alternative dichotomy, and then by the twofold cooperation with it, the precise relationship analyzed at length in connection with the equatorial houses.[4] The four great worlds of experience, identified fundamentally by the angles in the equatorial measure of circumstances, are paralleled by the four primitive facets of individuality in a corresponding astrological anatomy of the zodiac. These differentiations of basic character have been so obvious to man through the ages, and have had such consistent importance in his earlier attempts to understand his world of potentials, that horoscopy has long been provided with a set of terms ready-made for its purpose, namely, the so-called elements of fire, water, air and earth. In astrology they are the TRIPLICITIES. The word arose because each of them comprises three signs, but it must be remembered that there are four of such groups. They correspond to the triads in the equator.

[4] Summarized diagrammatically on page 29.

PERSPECTIVE ANCHORED TO EARTH

Hidden talent counts for nothing.
Suetonius, *Lives: Nero*

When it became time to begin the writing of this book in its present form, the problem was to find a point of attack. Experience has its rhythms, on the probabilities of which all divination is based, but just why do these operate variously in the lives of different people? Was there a hen-and-egg impasse in a necessity to find either events or characteristics the consequence of each other?

One day two kindred spirits stood at a New York window, watching a group of men and boys. "Well, it's baseball now, isn't it?" remarked the senior spectator. Of course! There it was, the needed springboard to exposition! Ball playing comes in season, so does marbles, so does everything else. Life is a game. Business is cyclic, as are romance and war, happiness and frustration. Here is no fate or destiny, but rather the flow of events in a universal gravitation. As the sun swings north or south, so to speak, a statistical sorting of life and its relations in facilitated. Man acts, and is acted upon.

This was something which had been illustrated, quite dramatically, some years before. On a high-school sand lot in a very small California town a number of adults were helping get the spring baseball practice under way. One youngster batted well out into center field, where an older man seemed much too far back for his position, at least in the light of any hitting so far. The ball in consequence took quite a few moments bounding to the individual in question. Undisturbed, and with extraordinary ease, he threw it straight home, into the catcher's glove, to put out the runner from third. The throw would have been good in professional play, and in this corner of nowhere—as far as sports were concerned—it was remarkable. Who was the chap? Some big-leaguer hanging around?

"That's Jim Bolger, rancher out south of here. Always wanted to be a ball player, but his father made him raise hogs instead. Then he got married and had to settle down, but he's still got the itch. He used to sneak off from work any time he could—"

Returning to mind, the incident became a key idea for explaining human nature. A somewhat frustrated man, a not overly successful farmer, was indulging himself on a warm spring afternoon. Circumstances had made no use of this sportsworthy characteristic, because others had proved of more immediate value. An inadequate perspective had established an inferior reality in normal channels, however. This was the way of life, disclosing the prodigal wastage which becomes the sure promise of free will and its fruits for those who wish to claim them, and the equally thorough support of defeat for all others.

The great miracle of astrology is that it can identify the traits which might otherwise be lost—and so go unused—and can encourage any native to find some better groove for those facets of himself which he may have been nurturing psychologically, if not practically. The charting of personal function by the signs of the zodiac is most valuable in everyday experience because these twelve mansions show not only how the given elements in self are oriented circumstantially, but also how the actual potentials of the functioning itself may be developed.

Every zodiacal sign must be seen in two ways. First is its rulership over definite and necessary functions of self-existence, charting the manner in which the simple act of selfhood must be carried out. Most superficially, this establishes the great zodiacal man in the sky, to which preliminary reference has been made and to which a later and more particular consideration must be given. From this initial ecliptical perspective, Aries rules the head. Everyone has a cranium, and uses it. Hence the sign must be taken into account in every natal chart. It is in such a fashion that a native's characteristics are seen most simply, or organically, in the light of their circumstantial responsibility.

The second way in which the mansions of the zodiac must be considered is through the particular emphasis given to certain ones of them, over and above the others, thus providing the general description of an individual in social terms. The sun-sign indications are an example of this, as is the insight into the nataure of personality afforded by the rising sign to which preliminary reference was made on page 43. It is in this manner that a native's place among his fellows may be estimated, finding it typical of a certain character and temperament. The perspective in reality is here a zodiacal pointing which reveals each human being in the terms of his fundamental fellowship with some particular group, or as an Aries person, or a Taurus one, and so on in various stresses or combinations of character.

The twelve zodiacal types represent the perspective which is hung in the sky and then anchored to earth. The implication of each is collective, as in contrast with the distributive import of the equatorial mansions, and this is the fundamental difference between circumstances and function *per se*. While analysis through the houses brings everything into lines or chains of relationship in time and space, the estimation of character through the signs reveals the converging relations or togetherness of things which, in its totality, maintains a functioning selfhood. The first approach to understanding from this point of view is a recognition of character as a mode of cumulation, with its roots in a definite and really quite literal alchemy.

THE ALCHEMY OF FIRE

Behold, how great a matter a little fire kindleth!
James, 3:5

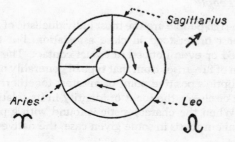

The three signs of the zodiac defined by the vernal equinox are Aries, or that one of them comprising the thirty degrees of celestial longitude measured counterclockwise from the equinox itself, and Sagittarius and Leo, the two mansions which express the alchemy of fire in a subordinate and solstitial distinction. The meaning of FIRE, as both an element of the ancient alchemists and a broad generalization of human character, may be summed up as pure self-sufficiency. The vernal equinox describes man's nature at that point where he is least conditioned or influenced by anything exterior to his own organism, and symbolizes a springlike potentiality which is always an essential part of his make-up. Here an individual's self-integration is at the initial point of focus in the reaction of all existence to human characteristics. He is revealed in his ability to act wholly in and of himself, reflecting the actual development of life and culture in its geographical migration to the north and away from the mean of basic non-distinction.

The fire signs gather into a simple function of individual existence, out of the whole circle or cycle of experience, those elements of selfhood which constitute an illimitable reserve or dynamic naïveté. They indicate, in every horoscope, the innermost genius of personality for being itself in general, or for maintaining its particular distinctiveness apart from all special definition. Here is the astrologer's key to the truly basic characteristics of selfhood. Aries, Sagittarius and Leo are the source, in horoscopy, of all information concerning the well-being of identity as such.

The Fire People

The fire-sign people are the most individualistic of all. They are the best understood in close association, but the least appreciated or even noticed in casual contact. The zodiacal distinction of fire arises from that type of generality expressed by the ecliptic's positive point of greatest togetherness with the house circle, or the focus of identity in its relative absoluteness. When the characteristic is found with a particular astrological emphasis in some given case, the native tends to become engrossed in his own being above everything else, and to find his own selfhood completely adequate or satisfactory in a way that can be very annoying to others. This does not mean that the fire person is selfish, necessarily, but that he is ultimately oblivious to things outside his own private reality. He is conscious enough of the people around him, in the kaleidoscope of circumstances which the houses delineate, but he is so completely self-centered in a psychological sense that he is seldom aware of any other individuality in its own terms. He is inclined to accept his fellows in the precise superficial characterization they present to him through the immediate situation, without either realization of human struggle or appreciation for the growth that may be taking place within their own special worlds. He often seems callous because he is definitely unaware, most of the time, that anything other than himself is alive on its own account.

The dominantly fire native is an utter realist in this sense, with little interest in the possibilities of personal relations. Those who do not co-operate with him are practically nonexistent, as far as he is concerned. The ones who do so are accepted or recognized, but only in the degree of their co-operation, and for its duration in the particular frame of reference. He is not disturbed by enmity because he cannot put himself in any other person's point of view enough to understand its occasion, and thus anticipate its menace. He carries no animus, therefore, and nurses no grudges, although by the same token he may demonstrate an exceedingly long memory, always recognizing the opponent who once has proved a threat to his interests. The fire type ends up a law unto himself. The everyday world is valuable to him when he may use it for his own purposes, and he does so to the full degree of his convenience and capacity. Whatever declines to fit into his scheme is disregarded, if that is possible. Otherwise he seeks to eliminate or, if necessary, to destroy it. This means he is totally dispassionate in the true sense of that word. He feels himself to be all there is of life. To this fact everything else must give tribute, if he is to recognize any living experience as real. Hence he is able to uncover magnificent resources in himself, but when blocked he is baffled most thoroughly because there is no other greater source to which he can turn. What at times is a magnificent aplomb can become an almost childlike helplessness.

THE ALCHEMY OF WATER

The world turns softly
Not to spill its lakes and rivers,
The water is held in its arms . . .
—Hilda Conkling, *Water*

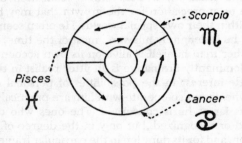

The three signs of the zodiac defined by the summer solstice are Cancer, at the solstitial point, and Pisces and Scorpio, the two mansions which express the alchemy of water in a subordinate and equinoctial distinction. The meaning of WATER, as both an element of the ancient alchemists and a broad generalization of human character, may be summed up as pure self-completeness. It was accepted by Thales, first of the philosophers and scientists among the Greeks, as the original substances of everything else. This is a hypothesis with some literal if superficial support in the almost complete and primary dependence of chemistry, and all organic forms, on the familiar liquid. The solstices have been seen to identity the symbolical point of pause and fulfillment, or where the sun turns in its semi-annual swing from south to north, and back again. They serve, in astrology's natural or naïve representation of reality, to show the consummation of life, or a basic all-completeness in the temperate zones where man maintains his personal constants in a seasonal milieu. The Tropics of Cancer and Capricorn symbolize the extent of greatest possible deviate existence, or movement away from the equatorial mean of simple non-distinctiveness, and this lean to a social self-consistency has a statistical correlation with man's greatest capitalization upon the achievements of all his fellows, through a sort of assimilation to them *in toto*.

The water signs, therefore, have come to represent the most universal generalization of human experience, or the largest possible participation in the undifferentiated wholeness of existence, such as is shared by everyone. They are the source, in any chart, of all information concerning the well-being of the total realm of experience within which a particular native functions. They reveal reality in a fashion exactly the opposite of fire's presentation. In the sense that the first of the four elements finds nothing in existence but itself ultimately, water contrariwise grants reality to everything else in an equal degree with itself. Universality thereby becomes a variant form of absoluteness. Water as an element represents this universal inclusiveness in its tendency to deny the separation of anything from the whole, and gives a clue in the horoscope to those characteristics by which anyone may act in a complete disappearance of himself in the group, becoming its representative. These signs delineate the personal touch with that underlying sustainment by which experience as such is made possible. The personality is not dissipated into the whole by this universalization of the self, but rather the whole is realized and found of use through a personal completeness. The water signs reveal whatever enables the individual to embrace all possible extremes within his own private periphery of reality.

The Water People

The water-sign people are the most expansive or smooth of all. They constitute the type which requires the least understanding in close association, and hence they are the ones most noticed or appreciated in casual contact. Water as an element, like fire, is absolute and primary, but in a reversal of emphasis, so that the individual of this classification accepts everything as existing wholly within himself in a psychological sense, rather than feeling that nothing wholly exterior to himself is of any import in his life. This native includes rather than excludes whatever is of no immediate pertinence in his experience, and is as dispassionate as the fire person in an entirely different way. Exactly as it never occurs to the latter that anything might have any reality apart from his contact with it, so it never enters the head of a man described predominantly by water signs that anything can function aside from that totality which he knows and assimilates into himself. The positive solstitial type enfolds all existence without the slightest reservation, in the nearest possible approach to universal completeness, precisely as the primary equinoctial individuality tends to eliminate everything but the bare solipsistic potentials of selfhood. The complete extremes of personality in this contrast do not and cannot exist literally, of course, but the nature of the zodiacal mansions is best realized by dramatizing the various distinctions they emphasize. The fire group delineates the ultimate of self-contained individuality, irrespective of the actual degree in which it may be encountered, and the water triplicity presents the complementary potential of a sheer universality, again only as approximated in actual society.

The water natives assume that everyone is readily assimilable, and they are distinguished by a strong and at times overwhelming and perhaps distinctly unwelcome solicitude for their fellows. They are like the fire-sign individuals in their inability to recognize the personal distinctiveness of associates and intimates but, whereas the latter will more often push these others aside, the water men and women will seek to enfold them in entire accordance with purely private and personal notions. It is quite incomprehensible to one of this type that his ministrations should be objectionable to someone else. The two primary groups are identical in their essentially naïve intolerance of everything alien to their own nature and experience. They differ only in the fact that, while the equinoctial natives make everything other than self unimportantly discrete, the solstitial triplicity cannot conceive existence apart from itself, even in a rejection or disregard of some troublesome or utterly minor detail of experience. Water knows reality only as it becomes all-embracing in an immediate fashion. The world is a whole in this alchemy of character, and this is a functional fact to which these people must give a continuous and everyday expression.

THE ALCHEMY OF AIR

For they have sown the wind, and
they shall reap the whirlwind.

Hosea, 8:7

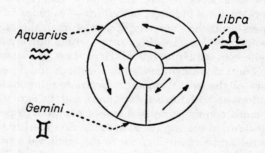

The three signs of the zodiac defined by the autumnal equinox are Libra, at the equinox itself, and Gemini and Aquarius, the two mansions which express the alchemy of air in a subordinate and solstitial distinction. The difference between the two equinoctial points, at Aries and Libra, is one of emphasis on the direction of deviation, that is, towards the north as the positive effort of the self to establish itself through its simple or primitive act of self, and towards the south as its corresponding and negative attempt to have confirmation of itself and its values through both (1) its own characteristic reaction to the external world and (2) the common or typical response of that world to its own desires. In the classification by astrological triplicities, the elements of fire and water are original or PRIMARY, and the characteristics they show are fundamentally primitive or without necessary external relationships. Air and earth by contrast are DERIVATIVE or dependent in the sense that they reveal facets of self which, as functionally insufficient in their own nature, are essentially complex. Function becomes more immediately personal, or directly co-operative, through these secondary types in the four psychological genera.

The meaning of AIR, as both an element of the ancient alchemists and a broad generalization of human character, may be summed up as the pure outreach of self. The original implication of the term is rather lost in English, as against Hebrew and Greek, where the same word (רוח or ruach, πνεῦμα or pneuma) indicates both spirit—i.e., inner or eternal livingness—and the everyday breath of man, thereby identifying not only the activating caprice within him but also the atmosphere in which he moves. Here is not the simple self-assertiveness of fire, symbolized by the sheer undifferentiated integrity of the vernal equinox, but rather the continuing inspiration—in both the basic or literal, and the figurative and much more common implication—of everyday experience, The air signs, in consequence, became the superficial indication of thought and intelligence to the medieval astrologers, but what they show is not so much a circumstantial wisdom as a rational orientation, a continual attempt to validate existence. This permits a step beyond simple self-cognition, and is the generalization of experience through a common participation in human norms and values. These signs in the horoscope are the source of all information concerning the well-being of the conditioned or consciously refined selfhood, that is, the more superficial personality. The alchemy of air is best understood when the element is identified as fire in the process of formation or disintegration. This is pure individuality in that state where it is not certain within itself, and so seeks a continual reassurance, often and of necessity at the expense of others.

The Air People

The air-sign people are the most tenative or uncertain of all. They constitute the group which is the most easily understood or appreciated in any given or conventional reference but which, nonetheless, is the most baffling of the four in general, because it is superficially the most changeable or non-reliable. More than anything else, these individuals are characterized by (1) their effort to participate in whatever goes on around them, (2) their joyous reaction, whenever there is a chance to do something of a tangible nature, and (3) their consistent effort to find a better place for themselves in the world at large. They are fundamentally enthusiastic, as well as partisan. Hence, while the fire and water types are essentially dispassionate, the natives with dominant air indications are very much the reverse, a particular distinction they share with the earth triplicity. The air individual is the most superficially willing and helpful, or else officious and upsetting, of the basic groups. He has the greatest gift for articulation and self-promotion. He is exceedingly adroit in dealing with meaning, significance and implication, as might well be expected of one fundamentally seeking to contribute a reality to relationships which in themselves usually lack enduring qualities.

Differing from the two primitive types, the air and earth people are more transient in their influence on others, as well as in the emphasized pointing of their own being. This characteristic is a necessity, of course, if they are to be as effective in change as the other two groups are in what, by contrast, is always changelessness. The air and earth temperaments are essentially focused in the moment, therefore, and inclined to be more concerned with immediate circumstances than remote and abstract generalizations. Fire and water natives accomplish things, for the major part, by remaining relatively unmoved in a given situation, despite any superficial activity masking their psychological impassivity. Air and earth individuals function by a self-movement or reaction which makes the exterior and transient realities, by comparison, relatively motionless. These latter types, in consequence, are usually most insistent upon having their own way in the passing and trivial details of everyday living. They can become psychologically distressed to an unhealthy extent when the world around them refuses to stay put.

THE ALCHEMY OF EARTH

So simple is the earth we tread,
So quick with love and life her frame:
Ten thousand years have dawned and fled,
And still her magic is the same.

Stopford A. Brooke, *The Earth and Man*

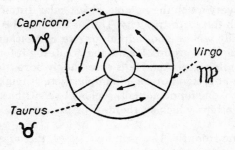

The three signs of the zodiac described by the winter solstice are Capricorn, at the solstice itself, and Virgo and Taurus, the two mansions which express the alchemy of earth in a subordinate and equinoctial distinction. The difference between the two solstitial points lies in the emphasis on the type of fullness which selfhood achieves, following upon the direction of its deviation from the equator. The north, positive and water-sign stress is upon completeness in practical life, or an exterior wholeness, and the south or negative fulfillment of character must be visualized as an inner or spiritual reality. This is utterly contradictory to the usual and material concept of earth as representing inertia, the mere clod among men. Stopford Brooke, in the lines just quoted, catches the basic idea with true insight, as did the ancients in their myths of Gaea, Ceres and Demeter. Earth is the great matrix which, as each individual assimilates himself into its awe-inspiring and illimitable expanse, constitutes him a spiritual entity in his own right. Then he is able to heal and help his fellows, or lift them up, wherever he goes. The meaning of EARTH, as both an element of the ancient alchemists and a broad generalization of human character, may be summed up as pure self-realization. It is the completely personal substance of all things, as embraced in the popular phrase, Mother Earth. Here is where spirituality is ritualized through nature as the needed reassurance of fullness for all living creatures. The magic of ultimate sustainment, as when the perennials yield their testimony to a creative or functional reality year after year, gives man his needed certification of an individual totality. This is far from the equatorial and equinoctial mean of fire and air where he gains his identity, it is true, but merely gets ready to live. Here he knows the fruits of his effort.

The triplicity represents the most comprehensive generalization possible in any real experience, and in any chart is the source of all information concerning the ultimate and practical sensitivity of the native as a responsible animal. A strong emphasis of the triplicity will often indicate a high intuitive ability, as well as a fine gift for the passing fulfillment of self in all others. Hence these signs are a vital clue to the appetites and surface emotions of the being. The doubt by self of its own universality, which provides the psychological origin of the earth alchemy, has its expression not only in the effort to fold all existence into self through the senses, but also in whatever there may be of a pseudo-experience, as the exercise of sensation through an imperfect or incomplete reference. Here is the indication in horoscopy of tendencies toward hallucination and fantasy, or the function of compensation by which the self rejects whatever threatens its own sense of wholeness, that is, denies its need to feel necessary to something other than itself. Personality is revealed in pure objectivity by the earth signs because they indicate the effort of everyone to demonstrate the practical warmth of universality. They chart the self in those phases of itself encountered most directly by others, presenting the self in its attempt to shape the world to its own private potential.

The Earth People

The earth-sign people are the most critical or exacting of all. They are the most responsive to practical relations, but they are inclined to pre-empt more than their own fair share of things, and they are interesting to others only in some special milieu where they can be compelled to make adequate contribution to the joint relationship. Hence, of the types, they are the most dependent on exterior experience as a needed and compulsive dynamic. Because the element is like water in its universality—of which however, it requires constant reassurance—the problem of natives with this predominant emphasis is fundamentally one of interior strengthening, such as facilitates the fullness of an outer consummation. Unlike air, this self-mobilization must obviously be centered more largely in literal than vicarious experimentation, and must be carried on until it has its fruits in an actual realization. Indeed, the earth person must feel everything, whether correctly or as a matter of wishful thinking, wholly complete within some practical and definite frame of reference which he knows or can test. Air individuals may dance around the edge of external reality with considerable success, but those who belong to the earth triplicity must struggle continually to get into everything they do with all of themselves, head and feet, clothes and all.

This means that these individuals are more acutely sensitive about themselves than in any other group. They do not have the agonizing self-awareness of air, but are apt to be on the defensive continually in a very real way, always seeking a justification of themselves to others, indirectly if not otherwise. Their extraordinary gift of sustained participation in experience, when manifest in the realm of feeling, gives them a real passion. They are sentimental instead of enthusiastic, as in the case of their air-sign cousins. Because they are forced to a constant self-mobilization within themselves, of a more personal and less rational sort than air, they are under necessity to instrument or articulate their struggle towards their self-realization by an exaggerated outer symbolism, and as a consequence they are, more than any other group, concerned with the most minute and exact placing and arrangement of things about them. Although emotionally, like water, they feel the whole world has its existence within them, they find the most immediate and effective way to be sure of this is to dictate the petty details of life for others in every possible respect. The earth people in consequence are most characteristically fussy, and are apt to be caught up in a multitude of minor concerns.

147

CHAPTER EIGHT

The Divinity
of Difference

"I would rather sit on a pumpkin and have it all to myself," confesses Henry Thoreau in *Walden,* "than be crowded on a velvet cushion." In his remark he gives voice to the dominantly recalcitrant spirit of man. This is the divinity in humankind, although people are inclined to see it with horns, or to repudiate it as satanic, whenever they encounter it too directly or with any end result in personal disadvantage. Everyone is well aware that his situation is framed in a milieu of circumstances, on the one hand—the everyday reality charted, in astrology, by the equatorial houses—and that his lot is determined for better or worse, on the other hand, by its roots in his character—the more personal reality mapped in its initial facets by the triplicities, among the zodiacal groupings—but he will kick over the traces at the slightest encouragement.

What this may cost him, in loss or inconvenience, does not matter much. It is a necessity of his existence. His wants, as an infant, have been entirely anticipated. As a child, a youth and an adult, he has learned that his desires must be other than those met in advance, to a varying degree, by agencies exterior to himself. To become and remain an individual he must sit upon a private pumpkin, at least part of the time. If he accepts any real definition of himself from life as a whole, without somehow giving it a twist in the process, he is apt to sink back into cosmic order. Then he will disappear as anything other than a clump of protoplasmic substance. He learns this by very hard experience.

The nature of an individual's self-realization, through his instinctive rebelliousness, is shown astrologically by the signs of the zodiac. These are the same ones which delineate the convenient interaction of simple character with the general matrix it integrates in connection with itself. The measurement is through a further zodiacal distinction, however, revealing the traits of human nature on a more dynamic level of functioning. Here is something quite aside from the relatively static aggregation of characteristics in the four psychological genera. The linking together of three signs in a triplicity, to map the alchemy of a native's self-refinement, shows the basic type of his experience in an entirely social sense. His potentials of recalcitrance make it possible for him to enter or leave any given situation in a far more organic fashion—that is, in any one of several different ways—and this possibility constitutes the dynamics of function.

In each of the threefold groupings of the zodiacal mansions there is one which is focal in the equinoctial or solstitial relationship, and in consequence there are four signs which thereby have a special correspondence with each other by this very different criterion. They chart function on the level of direct or immediate response, presenting the zodiac at its points of closest dependence upon the equator, and constitute the first of three QUADRATURES in astrological practice. They are somewhat analogous to the angular houses, and the other two quadratures have a similar correspondence to the succedent and cadent distinctions in the equator.[1]

---

[1] They are the qualities of the signs, in the technical language of horoscopy—as the triplicity distinctions are the elements—but there is a considerable tendency to use both words loosely, the former to indicate any special characteristics indicated by a zodiacal sign, and the latter to comprise the triplicities, the quadratures and the distinctions of angular, succedent and cadent houses in the equatorial circle.

Individual difference are important because they provide the variety upon which experience builds, or through which character becomes possible, not because of what any one of them may be in any absolute way. While it is true that a person of one sort may be handicapped over another in a given set of circumstances—as a tall man in a low basement, or a little woman in a kitchen with high shelves—these factors are of little ultimate importance. The lengthy gentleman can stoop. The diminutive lady may acquire a folding ladder, which in passing can be quite ornamental. What must be understood is that conditions are never worse nor better than each other in any metaphysical sense, but are merely less or more useful, and that what they are, on their own account, is quite incidental in this connection. Thus the excellence of Jim Bolger's baseball arm was virtually meaningless.

The origin of individual difference is in a deviation from a norm within a given complex of constants. The static factors in these human characteristics have their fundamental correspondence with the seasons or cyclic repetitions of experience which, in astrological symbolism, are charted through the triplicities. Hence the four zodiacal elements are of primary importance in horoscopic delineation, even above the circumstantial indication of the houses, because they reveal the special ground of total reality against which the highly self-willed personality is outlined. What the quadratures bring to the foreground of analysis, by contrast, is the wholly individualistic way in which the given person stands up to experience in being himself, or the level upon which he characteristically enters upon or leaves a particular milieu of relationship, as suggested. The cardinal, common and fixed groupings of the signs—in their geometrical correspondence to the angular, cadent and succedent houses in that order—reveal the fundamentally dynamic recalcitrance of temperament, through the rather simple distinction between those men and women who (1) find the things at hand most interesting, (2) approach experience in mutual act or response with other people, and (3) meet the issues of their existence by following their own inner leading.

THE AMBITIOUS TEMPERAMENT

Ambiton has its disappointments to sour us,
but never the good fortune to satisfy us.
BENJAMIN FRANKLIN, *On True Happiness*

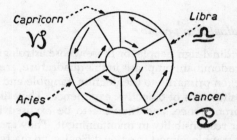

The four CARDINAL or movable signs of the zodiac—Aries, Cancer, Libra and Capricorn—are those established at the equinoctial and solstitial points, there giving definition in each case to one particular triplicity. Because of the consistently close relationship here with the house circle, these divisions of the ecliptic indicate the facets in character which are most fundamentally aligned with immediate and passing reality, or which have the simplest or most direct pattern in the organization of the self's normal functioning. This means self-assertion through a most practical and everyday interest, with the greatest possible balance of awareness or interaction between the inner integration of character and the outer alignment of the personality in a practical world. The native's dependence is upon the crises of life as the agencies by which he may best know himself, and so it is through these signs, in every horoscope, that characteristics tend to embody themselves in circumstances, and that the zodiacal distinctions are apt to lose themselves in the houses. Ambition is indicated as the effort of human nature to put itself on trial and thus gain a continual

151

refinement in experience. Hence the cardinal mansions indicate an individual's most unconditioned reaction to simple situation. They give a special clue, in every chart, to any particular capacity and desire to work with the general potentials of growth and achievement. Also they, in all cases, the functions which are emphasized by the organism as it does so.

The Cardinal-Sign people

The cardinal-sign people, or those whose astrological maps have a predominant emphasis in this quadrature, are the ones who quicken primarily to the definite, tangible and most immediate situations of objective experience. They like a position of prominence, and they ask to be excused from any particular responsibility in maintaining it. They are inclined to accept trouble, almost to enjoy difficulty, no matter to what degree they feel they must protest against their own circumstantial involvements. They are ambitious in the sense of wishing to become increasingly free to act without need for supervision on the part of anyone else. This is the one temperament best equipped to meet emergencies, and those who have it are inclined to invite upset, or even create turmoil, as their most obvious justification for being. They are at once superb in rising to a crisis, and vicious in stirring up in harmony of no value to anyone but themselves. Their prodigal energy furthers growth, and encourages progress as well as wrangling, but in their occasional overfondness for excitement, their obsession with problems, these people defeat as well as accomplish their ends.

THE HUMANISTIC TEMPERAMENT

For I remember stopping by the way
To watch a Potter thumbing his wet Clay:
*   And with its all-obliterated Tongue*
It murmured—"Gently, Brother, gently, pray!"
    OMAR KHAYYÁM, *Rubáiyát* (FITZGERALD)

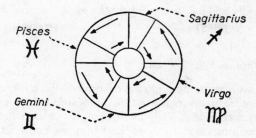

The four COMMON or mutable signs of the zodiac—Gemini, Virgo, Sagittarius and Pisces—are those lying next to the cardinal ones clockwise, or those which, from the point of view established in the houses, back up to the equinoctial and solstitial points. They represent a direction of initiative in exact reverse to whatever seems the usual trend, and reveal the facets of character of basic recalcitrance which seek, primarily, to run counter to ordinary expectation. Here is self-assertion by reversal, contradiction and a curious form of positive negation (arising, in the geometrical symbolism, from the fact that individuality, in the swirl from its own center, here tends contrariwise to the counterclockwise twist natural, because of gravitation, in northern hemispheres). More than anything else the quadrature shows a fellow or proxy activity, since this direction of act cannot maintain itself. A consistent attempt is made, when it is emphasized, to delegate responsibility, to enlist others in whatever is essayed, and even to exploit people. It reveals, in every chart, the tendencies of self to lean upon particular good nature and upon mankind in general as well. In contrast with the frontal and ambitious attack on the potentials of life through the cardinal group, these mansions disclose the facets of any native's personal interest, such as his desire for the welfare of others, in addition to any determination that the efforts on their part shall be a contribution to his own well-being. Here the horoscope charts any effective self-mobilization for normal personal contacts.

This is commonness as the level of action where men most consistently and habitually collect the experience of their fellows into the fiber of self.

The Common-Sign People

The common-sign people are described effectively as those whose interests are centered in direct and highly personal relations with others. They like the places in life which have been recommended to them, and they welcome situations which they know to possess a special merit. These natives are often obsessed with matters of personality. They seek unusually intimate relationships, although not necessarily covert ones, and they have a tendency to center all reality of the moment in some definite individual. They are inclined to view the world around them as activated by definite purpose or animus of one sort or another, and to believe themselves somehow concerned in everything that happens. The humanistic type is highly sensitive to group evaluation of any sort, and in consequence he carries the whole weight of his own being around with him, wherever he goes. Indeed, he will interrupt the process of almost anything until he can, so to speak, pile his own baggage aboard. He is the great joiner and follower in life, always desiring to be a definite part of things. Whereas the cardinal tendency is to recognize an issue, solve it, and then forget it, the common-sign mode of function is to make everything in life as personal as possible, and to keep experience in a state of flux, or pliability of the sort that calls for continued attention, as long as interest holds.

THE TENACIOUS TEMPERAMENT

Endure and persist,
this pain will turn to your good by and by.

OVID, *Amores*

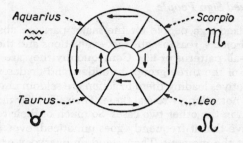

The four FIXED or foundation signs of the zodiac—Taurus,
Leo, Scorpio and Aquarius—are those lying between the cardinal and common ones. Hence this is the one of the three
groups with no touch, either at the cusp or other side of each
segment, with the equinoctial or solstitial points. Its mansions
reveal, most importantly, the greatest possible degree of social detachment in self-stirring or conscious self-activity. Any
temperamental emphasis here, in its freedom from direct
limitation by the equatorial circumstances, is the zodiacal
generalization of true perspective, that is, a form of subjective
function which is primarily self-consistent, and fundamentally
concerned with ideas, values and norms as the materials for
a creative sustainment of self. Here is man's ultimate divinity
of difference in a simple capacity to learn from doing—or
from a resolution of outer to inner reality—and so his gift for
ordering his effective relations in life through a conscious and
uninhibited judgment. The four signs are badly named when
fixity is taken as implying superficial inertness. They are fixing
or establishing, and so foundational or uncompromising. They
indicate a depth of personal reference rather than any blind
resistance to change. They show a width of realization, and
a purposed rather than instinctive stubbornness. Thus these
mansions reveal, in any horoscope, the degree to which the
native may develop his interior approach to life, thereby
quickening the self-confidence by which he is able to move
to the gratest ultimate advantage in any given situation.

The Fixed-Sign People

The fixed sign people for the major part are absorbed in plans, projects, reasons, abstract evaluations and the general or over-all patterns of life. Consequently they are the most difficult of the three groups to understand or describe. The basic motives leading them to action are seldom obvious, and they do not willingly reveal these. Their life is far more internal then in the other two cases. So much of their reaction is subjective that it frequently goes unnoticed, even by themselves at the moment. Their stand on everyday or practical things is firm, and their presence in any situation is far from shrinking. Because their struggle in a persistent self-evolution is not always recognized by others on normal contact, they may appear lazy of dull, and therefore uninteresting. When not analyzed in the light of the ideas they hold, they may seem extraordinarily stubborn in a superficial way, but they are fundamentally open-minded because they are uninfluenced by other than their own judgments, and are able to change their point of view with complete opportunism when it pleases them to do so. Ultimately the most self-consistent of the three types, they are hardly ever understood, unless unusually articulate in some individual case. By contrast with the facility by which common-sign natives will take everyone into their own private universe on all occasions, the tenacious temperament finds mere people unimportant. Compared with the capacity of cardinal-sign individuals for rising to every issue, and for watching the world at large with a zealous interest, the fixed type is inclined to stand apart in a reality of its own and hence, perhaps unwittingly, seeming to be inhuman or unfeeling. These people do not bother to make many close ties, and they miss out on many an adventure, but they cling tightly to the selected few individuals or groups who become the embodiment of their ideas, and they usually find very concentrated and fascinating outlets for their talents.

CHAPTER NINE

Twelve Tribes
of Individuality

Vicki Baum gives a modern twist to Heraclitus when, in her *And Life Goes On,* she remarks, "To be a Jew is a destiny." The twelve basic composites of character, in astrological charting, have a certain correspondence to the traditional even dozen tribes of the early Hebrews, although they do not provide a case of physical demarcation, such as can be inherited or identified apart from racial and family lines. The astrologer merely knows that all people are stiff-necked, in the Biblical phrase, and that the stubbornness which was responsible for the blessings and afflictions of the chosen people, in equal degree, is revealed no less dramatically by the astrological tribes than the lazy Issachar and treacherous Dan of long ago. It is the strength, primarily, rather than the particular nature of any characteristic, that is responsible for its value. This was the fact which had its emphasis in the original account of Jacob's commission, leading to the establishment of the biological lines through his twelve sons.

The zodiacal signs, when taken separately, chart special distinctions in self-persistence which in a sense parallel the colorful uniqueness developed by the progeny of the ancient patriarch. This younger of Isaac's twins, after depriving Esau of his brithright, fled to Laban, his uncle at Haran, where he spent fourteen years in an attempt to master the world by cleverness alone. Ultimately he had to confront his brother, who had by then become the most powerful potentate in that corner of the world. Jacob was thoroughly scared. During the night, alone at Peniel, he wrestled with God in person. However, he clung to his mysterious opponent with an unwavering stubbornness, refusing to let go although crippled by the magic touch upon a tendon of his leg, until vouchsafed the blessing he craved. This audaciousness rechristened him, and as Israel he became the symbolical prototype for those tribes of individuality upon which astrology builds in its analysis of character.

The ultimate foundation of delineation in horoscopy is a competent identification of the twelve psychological species, together with a realization of the practical advantages and disadvantages they face in everyday living. A newcomer makes his best beginning in an actual application of astrology to life by singling out men from their fellows—identifying them astrologically as essentially or predominately representative of one rather than any other of the twelve signs— through the sun positions of known individuals according to the following table:

TABLE V

Approximate Dates When the Sun Enters the Zodiacal Signs

March 21st:	ARIES		September 23d:	LIBRA
April 20th:	TAURUS		October 23d:	SCORPIO
May 21st:	GEMINI		November 22d:	SAGITTARIUS
June 21st:	CANCER		December 22d:	CAPRICORN
July 23d:	LEO		January 20th:	AQUARIUS
August 23d:	VIRGO		February 19th:	PISCES

This can be a very effective introduction to the types, although some individuals correspond to the indications more closely than others. The dates given in the table will vary within narrow limits from year to year, and in case to case, because there is not only an intercalary day each fourth February, but also because the luminary seldom enters a new zodiacal mansion exactly at midnight. Moreover, the sun sign may be overshadowed completely by the ascendant in a particular instance, or by the moon and other planets, especially in the lives of those more than normally involved in the complexities and psychological confusions of modern living. However, the birthday signatures of the zodiac can usually be recognized by the most amateur observer.

THE TRIBES OF COMBUSTION

ARIES

God, give me hills to climb,
And strength for climbing!
ARTHUR GUITERMAN, *Hills*

Aries is the cardinal sign in the fire group, and this means that it reveals, in every horoscope, the characteristic way in which the native meets various crises as essentially a challenge to express himself more positively. The keyword for this mode of action is ASPIRATION. Every person seeks in some way, continually and consistently, to experience a simple fullness of well-being. This is not a matter of option as in the case of the equatorial houses, in the consideration of circumstances— where a man may or may not have money, and can work or decline to do so—but is a basic identity as such. There may be illuminating differences in man's aspiring spirit, as in the degree of its srength and the social level of its effectiveness, but all conscious creatures are characterized by a definite sense that they are going somewhere or are frustrated in their efforts to get under way. The lowest of living forms exhibits a marked excitement in the face of danger. The barnyard fowl, which will run with its head amputated, has become a common symbol for the self's primary recourse to movement in an emergency. Here is the symbolical outreach of personality as the very basis for its existence.

Thus Aries indicates the fundamental psychological drive by which a man remains what he is, both initially and ultimately. It is the unconditioned ambition of his being in every respect, or his simple self-stubbornness as evident without doubt of any sort. It is the place in the horoscope where he remains absolutely and utterly confident within himself. The sign shows how any native will recover or maintain his self-assurance, therefore, even after he is shaken to the depths of himself by some crisis in his affairs. It charts the general pattern of his functioning in a rejection of those situations which are without creative interest to him. Here is the necessarily deep indomitability of all selfhood at root, or individuality as most absolutely itself, and so beyond temporizing. It is the point in the zodiac where the least of superficial definition is possible. Aspiration is the protecting shield of human character, and the cover for its complexity, as well as an identification of its primary stirrings in its own and unsupported behalf.

The Aries Type

The Aries individual—in the case where this sign is rising or contains the sun, moon or an unusual concentration of planets—is the personal epitome of the fire and cardinal characteristics. He stands as personality exalted in its representation of one out of the twelve divine tribes of individuality, in sharp contrast of varying degree with other natives who reveal, in similar fashion, differing dramatizations of functional emphasis to which the signs as a whole give a measure. This highly interesting personage never forgets the fact that it is his privilege to lead the procession, whether or not he chooses to do so. At his worst he is primarily cocksure. At his best he is exceptionally able to inspire confidence in others, and so at times privileged to offer very competent guidance to his fellows. It never occurs to him that anything contrary to his own notion has any validity, or is in any way pertinent, and he can be wrong in spectacular fashion because he is always too apt to see a particular emergency in isolation from all the contributory factors. It seldom enters his head to approach things in any manner other than realistically, and impersonally, and so he may involve himself or his associates without compunction. He is inclined to use any convenient means to solve a problem, and will proceed along immature lines whenever he is unable to recognize and employ the means which might seem more legitimate to people generally. His answer to any issue is action, so that sometimes he stumbles over his own toes.

Empty intellection, idle speculation and ideal considerations are all tiresome to him unless in some way the exploitation of ideas will offer an identification or clarification of some wholly immediate issue, whereupon he may show flashes of great brilliance. This type is not drawn to philosophical synthesis, broad-scale planning, research in the form of prolonged trial and error, and so on. People to him are no different from things, and in consequence they are nothing apart from the context in which they are encountered. Hence he may seem quite heartless to anyone who does not understand his particular psychology. The combination of characteristics here reveals the absolute extreme of freedom from social conditioning of the superficial sort. Hence the Aries tribe produces pioneers, leaders and individualists of high order. They provide a supreme example of the process by which a man will become less and less a person, with the more common human attributes, to be more and more a personage, that is, an incarnation of some special group destiny.

SAGITTARIUS

No one knows what he can do till he tries.
PUBLILIUS SYRUS, *Sententiae*

Sagittarius is the common sign in the fire group, and this means that it reveals, in every horoscope, the characteristic way in which the native is challenged to some essential development of himself by the people around him. The keyword for this mode of action is ADMINISTRATION. It is here that the race as a whole has an effective pointing through the particular personality, and that the individual makes his most immediate contact with his cultural pattern, whether of the ethnic stock, the nation or the family. Sagittarius shows the basic identity of self in its utter obliviousness to the abstract rights of anything other than itself, but in its most direct acceptance of all human expression in real equality. Here is where the native grasps his opportunities for relationships which will amplify and reproduce the traits and potentialities of particular significance in his own economy. It is the extreme point of the me-too spirit in an astrological chart, showing the potential degree of both a naïve companionability and a lack of real discrimination.

Thus Sagittarius reveals the expression, in the most personal manner possible, of whatever facets of reality have come to identify the various species of human kind to each other. It charts the capacity for simple movement *per se,* and the ability to give this meaning. Man, in his relations with anybody else, articulates them through his use of gestures, mannerisms, words and the vast complex of cultural and racial characteristics which have acquired particular implication in revealing the individual intent and background, and this sign indicates his competency in employing them. It rules the native's skill in sports, games and every sort of casual contact with others. It gives an insight into his social pliability, which is usually an unrestrained friendliness, but which can be a complete tactlessness. Here is no departure from the manifestation of pure identity because, in all these relationships, the self is only projecting itself in and through its associates. This fundamentally is the point in the horoscope which indicates how a given nature ramifies most simply but infinitely from its own center, expanding through its self-discovery and holdng itself unalloyed or unimpeded through all the external functions of normal social intercourse.

The Sagittarius Type

The Sagittarius individual—in the case where this sign is rising or contains the sun, moon or an unusual concentration of planets—is the personal epitome of the fire and common characteristics. This means that, from one point of view, he is almost completely the reverse of the Aries type. Rather than the lonely leader, or pioneer individualist, he is the coach, the promoter and wholly conventional administrator. He is affability personified, possessing an exceptional ease in social contact and a fine sense of sportsmanship or superficial fair play. However, he has no sustained or deeper interest in the people with whom he deals, but reacts to them as fellow-participants in the various situations in which he is active, or the organizational activities in which he is concerned, i.e., convenient contributors to common effort in a manifestation of life and its functions. He is perhaps the easiest of all the types with which to have casual touch, but most disappointing to those more interested in enduring ties. He simply dismisses the existence of anyone who will not co-operate in the special manifestations of his own identity—the operation of the fire alchemy on the personal level of temperament—but in consequence he harbors no ill-will and is in no wise revengeful. When others are co-operative his manner is smooth, friendly and even affectionate, and he can be the most completely at ease or naturally and directly human of all twelve types, and so often the most popular.

He is not at all particular, unfortunately, and as a born democrat he may seem to lack ordinary good judgments in personal relations. He is in no wise an intellectual, but he has a capacity for highly intelligent act or decision, always able to recognize the potential usefulness to him of the various factors he encounters in human experience. His realism may take unpleasant form, in a philandering abuse of human confidence, but at his worst he is unmoral rather than degenerate. His sense of obligation simply does not go beyond his own convenience. He has a long and accurate memory for things of vital concern to him, a weak and short one otherwise. Hence he may have extreme difficulty recalling anything of detached reference, while responding with immediate joyousness to some old tie upon any renewal of contact, even though the person in question may have been forgotten for years. He is intensely interested whenever he can have a personal part in events, but otherwise he does not bestir himself to any extent.

LEO

Ay, every inch a king.
SHAKSPEARE, *King Lear*

Leo is the fixed sign in the fire group, and this means that it reveals, in every horoscope, the characteristic way in which the native reacts to ideas, values and generalizations of relationship as essentially a challenge to the competence of his own identity. It also shows his capacity to determine the worthiness of the projects in which he interests himself. The keyword for this mode of action is ASSURANCE. Here is where the bringing of facts into a simple conformity to the ideals held for them is a necessity of personal existence. Life is ordered on the basis of a broad realization in which self must remain unimpeachably central. Whatever refuses to help the native enthrone himself in his total situation, in the sense of contributing to his conception of its justification and ends, must be brought under conscious control, or else eliminated, with a regal ruthlessness. Here is the emphasis of personal purpose in the zodiac. Most primitively it is the cry-baby point in the chart, showing how an individual will make any direct complaint about his role in some particular situation.

Thus Leo is the place of extreme sensitiveness to any threat against self-dignity, and it delineates the extreme possibility of concern over the interests of pure selfhood. This at its worst is utter selfishness, but at its best a complete exaltation of individuality. The discovery or recovery of self through a realization of values develops the capacity of everyone for simple rationalization, and so both self-pity and self-justification are indicated by this sign. Here is no intellection, no creative or true mental process, but rather the almost cut-and-dried employment of ideas or norms as channels through which the identity may expand and enjoy itself. As the fundamental function by which the being is certified within itself, Leo's rationalizing establishes the roots for a supreme and immutable faith, and this sometimes degenerates into a sheer personal stubbornness. Man's ability to conform to his own conscious ideas about himself is his means for definite operation on any high plane of self-realization, and so this sign becomes the point of pride in the chart. It also discloses the self's underlying timidity, or its realization that it needs a further self-establishment in a definite personal identity.

The Leo Type

The Leo individual—in the case where this sign is rising, or contains the sun, moon, or an unusual concentration of planets—is the personal epitome of the fire and fixed characteristics. He is the ruler or supreme magistrate in general temperament because he insists upon becoming, in his own person, the essence of all values held by people around him. Under happy circumstances he may become a genuine blessing to his fellows, and to the age in which he lives. Because he tends to exclude others from his own reality, in any terms of their separate existence, he is content to dwell apart from everyone else, psychologically at least, and this facilitates an appreciation of the values he has chosen to exemplify. He thrives on adulation, and at his best seeks earnestly to justify it by giving a stability to human character *per se*. On lesser levels he becomes exceedingly petty, even spoiled in a childish fashion, and so inclined to great displays of temperament. Because he is consciously dependent upon a constant realization of his own worth, he will, if necessary to this end, distort any ideas about himself. Hence he may be the most creatively imaginative of individuals, and also the most successful prevaricator of the zodiac. Devoid of any deep human sympathy—as unable to accept as to give it because he is spiritually alone among men—he may be driven by his hunger for praise to very noble efforts.

He has an extraordinary dramatic sense because his special gift is a capacity for bringing ideas to life. Rather than express himself, he attempts to give manifestation to these, becoming perhaps the least personally articulate of the twelve types. He seems self-complacent when his concept of things is not accepted by others, since he is inclined then to withdraw altogether from the immediate activity, or to remain quietly aloof. When he talks, he must hold the floor, and when he acts he must be watched and applauded. He is ever superb in the proper situation, but lacking in all capacity for social adjustment. Essentially the conservative, he dignifies a world without making any contribution to its content of dignity. His influence, therefore, is destructive in too small a compass, or in too outworn a set of relations. The Leo type must have a real place in a dynamic scheme of living, where he can be an example to all on his own idea-level, if he is not to be completely disruptive in his efforts to compel recognition from others.

THE TRIBES OF SATURATION

CANCER

God made thee perfect, not immutable.
MILTON, *Paradise Lost*

Cancer is the cardinal sign in the water group, and this means that it reveals, in every horoscope, the characteristic way in which the native meets various crises as essentially a challenge to re-establish his world of reality. The keyword for this mode of action is EXPANSION. The degree of anyone's self-awakening to the simple wholeness of things is indicated here. The sign shows the normal pattern of growth in life. It gives a principal clue to any individual's capacity for learning or teaching, as well as a measure of the extent to which he will be able to maintain his center of aplomb without any adjustment to the broadening context in which he is functioning. When Cancer is emphasized in a chart the native may be so filled with a sense of his own completeness, or naïve adequacy, that he will instinctively embrace everything in sight within his own consciousness. It is a characteristic obstinacy associated with the summer solstice from the most ancient of times. This point in the zodiac dramatizes man's power in clutching, collecting or clinging to whatever happens to interest him at any given moment.

Thus Cancer indicates an individual's maximum capacity for bringing problems or issues to immediate consideration or solution. He may accomplish this directly by an expanding consciousness, a psychological self-mobilization with its heavy impact upon others, or else by reaching out beyond the given milieu in which the issue has arisen, and thereby creating a matrix of greater relations in which selfhood can be central in a more effective fashion, as in the appeal to authority in religion or science. Here is where the inherent abilities of the self are revealed in their entirely latent potentials, consituting simple educability. To the degree a person is unable to bring out the whole actuality of a given situation, he will usually have recourse to a pseudo-reality, a tendency to fantasy or an unhealthy solipsism, which is also indicated at this point of the zodiac. The distinction between actual and phantasmal remains academic, however, since the dreamer of dreams often makes very solid reality out of the substance of his imagining. The sign merely reveals the ultimate and often quite subjective or intangible world in which the native continually completes himself.

The Cancer Type

The Cancer individual—in the case where this sign is rising or contains the sun, moon or an unusual concentration of planets—is the personal epitome of the water and cardinal characteristics. He is like the Aries type in that he is exceedingly sure of himself, but his sense of possession, in every situation where he may find himself, completely overshadows the fundamental and untrammeled individuality which these two signs share rather exclusively between themselves. The Cancer person is willful in his way, but almost wholly unpredictable in the particular stubbornness he may adopt, or in the length of time he may hold to it. He is always limited by his sense of the wholeness in which any reality must rest, and by his need to find or confirm his dynamic place at its exact center. He is neither hurried nor changed by the normal passing of events. Since he speaks out of a complete orientation within his own feelings, whether instinctive or rational, he continually offers the world an explanation, however imaginative it may have to be, of the unresolved elements in human progress. This may include a fullblown plan for the future, also. Hence he is the ideal teacher, and he may become a true prophet. He has the surface placidity of ordinary water but, like any lake or sea, he can rise to turbulence and gather an immense force against opposition. He frequently resorts to tantrums in facing any exceptional difficulty. He often becomes a protector of the weak, and exceptionally sentimental.

Abstract matters are of little interest to him. He echoes the Nazarene's "Sufficient unto the day is the evil thereof," making this the philosophy of his life. He presents an all-inclusive simplicity in everything he does, and is extraordinarily adaptable in outer superficialities. However, he is totally the reverse of this within his own conscious experience, or in connection with whatever may take on any special significance in his mind. He is emotional rather than intellectual, undisciplined rather than conditioned, practical rather than politically minded. Usually a conservative, he may become the driving wedge of some new urge in the racial unfoldment, but even then he is clannish. He is the most essentially religious of the types, and often an effective agitator or stimulating malcontent because of his exceptional power for establishing the imaginative as the real, or for engineering change without surrendering his notions of completeness.

PISCES

One good turn deserves another.
PETRONIUS, *Satyricon*

Pisces is the common sign in the water group, and this means that it reveals, in every horoscope, the characteristic way in which the native seeks to enlarge or unify his rapport with everyone who has any place in his own immediate world. The keyword for this mode of action is SYMPATHY. Here is the point of maximum personal touch with humanity in general, or with people in the mass. It is where human rapport becomes a necessity of conscious selfhood, and where all feeling or emotion gains its greatest emphasis as a part of everyday experience. This is the mansion of the zodiac which shows how far a man is inclined to depend upon others rather than himself, or is led to exalt social relations and to do everything possible to encourage the ordinary graces of life, both his own and those he can call forth in people around him. The sign rules poetic sensitivity and spiritual understanding, and indicates the degree to which anyone can enter into the consciousness of others in a truly creative way, hence developing their confidence and an inner and often unsuspected faith in him and his works. The universal potentials of human relationship, uncovered here, are the basis of fellowship in its most spontaneous form, making it possible to unite the most diverse of individuals in a joint experience.

Thus Pisces presents life at its most impressionable and least self-seeking point, where the being is not only divorced from all real apprehension but where it is able to assimilate itself to almost any eventuality. The self remains exceedingly firm in its own inner convictions, under any particular emphasis of this sign, because it holds no connection in experience unless it proves to be reciprocal in some way. It meets the world in the terms of an immediate convenience, and works towards a unification of group or community effort by seeing both sides of every possible difference of opinion, quite impartially. Here is the discursive reasoning by which men explain their neighbors, usually making excuses for them, and in consequence it is the point of extreme tolerance in the horoscope, charting the basic willingness of the self to accommodate itself to every phase of reality. Pisces shows the capacity of the native to accept any unusual or highly divergent human expression, and to make it very difinitely his own.

The Pisces Type

The Pisces individual—in the case where this sign is rising or contains the sun, moon or an unusual concentration of planets—is the personal epitome of the water and common characteristics. The Pisces native is utterly sure of himself, ultimately, because of his great power of adjustment to others in superficial things, together with his ability to enter into the actual feeling of those about him. However, he has purposes of his own in any move he makes, and his very proprietary fondness for his fellows depends upon the degree they are willing to accept the general wholeness in which he has oriented his own life. They must be content with the subordinate place he may assign to them in his own scheme of reality. He is seldom interested in particular individuals, only in what they mean to him in the terms of a very practical co-operation, but he yet attempts to enfold everyone in his circle of special friends. When encountered in this extremely opportunistic expression of the wholeness in which he lives, he may seem selfish, but he will share everything he has with those who become a part of his private universe. He is exceedingly responsive to suggestion, often revealing a complete acquiescence and non-resistance, but only in the consummation of something he has made real within himself through some process of his highly creative imagination.

He is inclined to develop a mystical temperament because of his extraordinary sense of affinity for the deeper strains of character he uncovers in his fellows, whether this be something of which they are aware or not. Hence he may become the poet, that is, one who articulates the general race experience for those less articulate or imaginative than himself. The Pisces individual is always one by whom all men can be brought to the greatest possible degree of common understanding, since he gives so little importance to family, class and other such distinctions among them. His voice as an artist, whether a leader in his community or just an ordinary person, is universal in its scope. It is always seated in his instinctive recognition of some ultimate wholeness in existence, and yet he may appear to be concerned in some definitely personal interest or project, often awakening a suspicion of his motives by his quiet methods. He is the most essentially intimate of people, because so completely uninhibited by any sense of anything alien in his own nature, but for that very reason it is very difficult for those closest to him to be themselves in the association.

SCORPIO

Skill and confidence are an unconquered army.
GEORGE HERBERT, *Jacula Prudentum*

Scorpio is the fixed sign in the water group, and this means that it reveals, in every horoscope, the characteristic way in which the native reacts to ideas, values and generalizations of relationship, as essentially a challenge to the competence of life in general and of himself as responsible for maintaining it. The keyword for this mode of action is CREATIVITY. This one of the zodiacal divisions shows the greatest potentials for actual good or evil in experience. It brings psychological intensification to its maximum, hence any exceptional emphasis of the mansion was long dreaded by astrologers. The earlier literature of horoscopy—reflecting ages in which the flesh as such was regarded as vile, inherently, and moral doubt or inquiry was thought to be inspired by the devil—actually identified it as the accursed sign, thus hopelessly concealing its vital indication for any normal living. Creative ability is no more and no less than the individual's power (1) to establish a basic whole idea of his own choosing as the frame of reference in which to carry on his business of being himself, and (2) to refrain from operating within any context which he merely inherits or permits to be forced upon him. The ultimate capacity of anyone to shape his own life according to his own private values, whether for better or worse, is here disclosed at root.

Thus Scorpio indicates the moral dynamic, or the directive conceptions developed by any native to meet various necessities arising in his life, and this is the background of all possible finesse in living. Since any distinction between actual and phantasmal disappears in the realm of ideas and values, creativity is always single-minded, or practical in an inner or psychological way, and this mansion is therefore the zodiacal point where the greatest concentration of self in its own interest is to be identified. Here is naïve self-conservation, but also, and much more importantly, the transcendence of physical limitation through a self-discipline in imagination. Scorpio must also be seen as the point of maximum self-consistency in existence, which subjectively is the broadest possible freedom from extraneous ideas, and objectively is the least possible bondage to inadequate relations in the workaday world. It shows the degree of moral courage, or the willingness of the individual to take the consequences of persisting in his own ideas. It also charts the creative rationalization in any flight from reality, or any repudiation of responsibility.

The Scorpio Type

The Scorpio individual—in the case where this sign is rising or contains the sun, moon or an unusual concentration of planets—is the personal epitome of the water and fixed characteristics. He is always the author of his own destiny, or at least he strives to be, and so he plays a self-schooled part in life, even down to the most minute of everyday details. He has a reason for everything, but is himself inscrutable, or impossible to understand, if any effort is made to uncover or analyze his inner processes of self-orientation in an abstract way, that is, as generalized and divorced from his own special personality. Without perhaps visualizing it that way in his thinking, he is always subjecting life to some one or another test of his own devising, constantly putting experience under the microscope in a lesser if not greater degree. He delights in bringing things to a conclusion, or in picking up the strands of relation left loose by others, in order to weave them into a fabric of his own, and he will often tear things down in order to reconstruct them more efficiently. If he is taken on his own terms, or according to the consistency he establishes by his really creative talents, he is the most simple or obvious of all types. However, he is elusive if he is asked to be something in particular, no matter what it is. He is wholly beyond comprehension if interrupted seriously in his favorite game of making it his business to be busy, or conversely, seeing how far he can refrain from all activity except in connection with some entirely private enterprise.

Here is, without exception, the most self-intent of the twelve types. He always possesses inner, idealistic and wholly unlimited resources of motivation and judgment. Anything coming from the exterior and narrowed world of less-introspective people seems thin, transitory and inadequate to him. He is wholly generous and co-operative when others meet him on his own basis, but he can be rigorously unswerving in his course, or downright cruel, when thwarted or forced to act in any way that leaves him divided in his own mind. He is possessive in an utter disregard for everything but himself, since his inner sense of completeness makes it impossible for him to realize that anyone else might be emotionally dependent or psychologically helpless. He is strangely adult from infancy, and assumes all his fellows to be equally able and willing to look after themselves. He has a curious capacity for fighting without enmity, and expects others to understand it. He is exceptionally fair-dealing in a sense of strict equity, but he sets his own standards and will not have them questioned.

THE TRIBES OF INGENUOUSNESS
LIBRA

There is a melancholy which accompanies all enthusiasm.
LORD SHAFTESBURY, *Characteristics*

Libra is the cardinal sign in the air group, and this means that it reveals, in every horoscope, the characteristic way in which the native anticipates various crises in his efforts to establish himself more definitely in everyday affairs. The keyword for this mode of action is EQUIVALENCE. Here is where man struggles continually, and often with a psychological desperation, to resolve his doubts of himself, or to achieve and maintain a balance in normal experience. His very uncertainty sustains his existence, since it makes effort necessary, and creates needs which can be recognized in consciousness. The general potentiality charted here tends to separate reality from the self, and to encourage everyone to seek his own true destiny as the sort of self-fulfillment society at large will certify. Any appreciable emphasis of the autumnal equinox shows a surging sweep of moodiness which can take the native, now high and now low in spirit, to the scene of every passing excitement. This is the point where man develops his greatest inner turmoil. The balancing capacity symbolizes the process whereby he gains validation for himself as a link between things, or as a reconciler among them. In these coupling efforts he betrays the extent to which he seeks recognition, or desires to be noticed, consulted and otherwise helped to feel important.

Thus Libra is the point of simple or unconditioned quickening to experience, not only as a capacity for stirring to definite action or interest, but also as a proneness to interior upset, whether this be exaltation or black depression. Here is the focus of primitive spirituality, since man's transcendental realization is ultimately his ability to maintain a special state of consciousness in more than the usual degree. By the same token, therefore, this area of the horoscope is the seat of love or affection in its functional sense, that is, the excess and especial concentration of feeling in some one given reference. It shows the real mobilization of self-discovery, as reflected in outer experience, and is the indicator of whatever there may be of charm and chivalry in the being, or of the power to establish an immortal aliveness in personality. Any pettiness in a life of lesser achievement is disclosed as fundamentally a sense of falling short, with a desire for compensation in more trivial excitation.

The Libra Type

The Libra individual—in the case where this sign is rising or contains the sun, moon or an unusual concentration of planets—is the personal epitome of the air and cardinal characteristics. Above everything else, the member of this psychological tribe is an enthusiast, seeking with every ounce of his strength to ingratiate himself with all concerned in any momentary situation. Thus he is the ideal politician or statesman, and is always inclined to agree with the person nearest at hand. He is a successful manager because of his capacity to make pleasant contacts with everyone in any given grouping, but a bad planner or ultimate executive because of his weather-vane temperament. He may be as down in spirits as up, and with equal energy, hence of all twelve types the Libra individual is blackest and most anarchistic in disattunement. Ruthless beyond all measure at his worst, he is indefatigable in a mobilization of constructive energy at his best. He is utterly opportunistic, or non-dependable, because he is always obsessed with what confronts him in the immediate milieu. He will hold to the consequences of his moment's allegiance with an indomitability which can be as magnificent as it is, more often, rather wasteful and even tragic.

He is highly partisan rather than loyal, since his attachments are apt to be superficial. He never responds to people or ideas according to their intrinsic worth, but only on the basis of their significance to the issue in which he seeks to establish a balance. He has no patience with things out of context, or in remote reference. In consequence he may be faithless as a friend, although quite delightful as a companion. He is often inconsistent in his thinking, his mind darting from one association to another, but he is usually stimulating in mental contact. He appreciates beauty, splendor and all the high qualities of esthetic values, so that any fellowship with him is warm and rewarding, but he has little respect for the effort going into the establishment of these things, and so seldom accepts and responsibility for their maintenance. When he is viewed from any long or real perspective, he is very shallow, although he is immeasurably deep in every immediate relation. His chameleonlike capacity for change enables him to participate broadly, widely and effectively in the total of possible experience—normally to a greater extent than most of the other eleven types—but he ends up with little more than the persisting necessity for making new ties and finding new equilibriums in reality.

GEMINI

Life is a loom, weaving illusion.
VACHEL LINDSAY, *The Chinese Nightingale*

Gemini is the common sign in the air group, and this means that it reveals, in every horoscope, the characteristic way in which the native insinuates his way into the personal reality of every interesting situation. This is where he divides up his interest on any provocation, and carries the channelship or canalizing function which, with Libra, is a matter of linking the elements in everyday circumstances, on forward to a more enduring species of relationship among people and things. The keyword for this mode of action is VIVIFICATION. Man feels himself most successfully the social creature, or gains the greatest immediate satisfaction in the exercise of his own personality, as he is able to see himself emulated, imitated or otherwise reduplicated in a twinlike reflection of his own being. The emphasis at this point of the zodiac is upon his efforts to achieve the greatest intimacy of participation in events by (1) consistent attempts to enlist others in behalf of his own interests and projects, and (2) an instinctive and wholehearted throwing of himself into everything around him. There is as much enthusiasm in Gemini as in Libra, and as great a power of anticipation, but a complete absence of the deeper moods, together with a far greater capacity for sustained co-operation with various associates. The me-too spirit of the opposite and complementary Sagittarius is found in a more ulterior form, but with a more admirable desire to pay in full as well as share completely. These two opposing signs give the points of maximal personal interest in the zodiac, but Gemini is characteristically friendly in a vicarious and highly self-exalting satisfaction, not in the direct or simple self-indulgences symbolized by the centaur.

Thus Gemini indicates the fundamental usefulness or facility of the native in the social world around him, and reveals his ability to meet the conditions of everyday living without distress of mind. It shows whatever capacity may exist for political adjustment—that is, being on good or bad behavior as a matter of deliberate policy—and this can end up either as unselfish devotion or high superficiality. The self is charted here in its gift for (1) doing more than one thing at once, (2) revivifying its attack upon any ramification of loose ends in tasks to be accomplished, and (3) giving a highly personal attention to the daily activities which otherwise would be dull and difficult. This is simple practicality in the sense of an ease in doing whatever normal and usual things are to be brought to the service of other things more important than themselves.

The Gemini Type

The Gemini individual—in the case where this sign is rising or contains the sun, moon or an unusual concentration of planets—is the personal epitome of the air and common characteristics. He is the happy-go-lucky person who will do anything for which he finds an authoritative permission, and is essentially the outstanding man-of-affairs whose nose is out of joint only when he is ignored by the people around him. At his worst he is the busybody, the playboy and the dilettante, and at his best the friend-in-need, or the tireless soul who loves to engineer a rescue. He sets the pace for business in general, and in the most conventional dress is the merchant or trader, the executive or promoter. He works in first-hand contact with his fellows, and wins them by personal appeal and intimate advertising, especially in lines where he can achieve success by making their desires more real to them. He has a flair for practical techniques in every walk of life, and is almost a professional comforter. Socially, he will always sing for his supper. On higher levels of effort he is an artist or mechanical genius, able to catch some facet of reality and make it his own through a portrait, a gadget or some sort of clever adaptation.

He insists upon knowing everyone by name, and upon having their telephone numbers. He is inclined to be casual, however, and to see no more in an acquaintance than what he can call to life within himself, or for himself, through the given relationship. He is not so much faithless as ingratiating, since he has to find himself included very definitely in the activities of other people—in a sort of twin relation where the externally real is inwardly assuring—and so he seeks, continually, to strengthen whatever normal ties he is able to establish with those around him. He is a great dues-payer. He encourages clubs, fraternities and such organizations as an easy way to get a finger in current and popular activities. He is not particularly concerned with the transmission or movement of things, but rather with their significance as representing people and their problems. He strives to enlarge the potentials of general experience by persuading as many as possible of his intimates to do as many given things as they can, and he applauds every achievement to which he can lend any aid or encouragement. Like a Libra native, his main objectives in life often seem to center in a determination to keep everything active, and to avoid every threat of inertia or insignificance in any part of his own private world.

AQUARIUS

The ideal should never touch the real.
SCHILLER, *To Goethe*

Aquarius is the fixed sign in the air group, and this means that it reveals, in every horoscope, the characteristic way in which the native makes use of his vicarious experience to give himself an inner or psychological steadiness, and to sharpen his basic urge to live. The keyword for this mode of action is LOYALTY. Here is where any individual leans the most heavily upon the ideals he has found established in life about him, or upon the standards he has had the chance to test or refine for himself. It is at this point that man seeks to insinuate himself into some form of immortality, although he may never have any sense of the philosophical implications involved. What with Libra is a coupling function, and with Gemini a more personal channeling of the self in human relations, with Aquarius becomes the effort to live or actualize ideas and inner conceptions. The sign shows the native's determination to achieve a permanent self-establishment, thereby balancing his conventionality, on the one hand, against his capacity for utopian idealization and a complete flowing of self into new and novel enterprises, on the other. What here may often seem an idle quest for knowledge is really a persistent effort to stabilize the values in living by an adequate realization of life's meaning. This is where inner perspective anchors itself in the outer milieu, ultimately becoming an eager anticipation, or an enthusiasm which frequently takes the form of an exaggerated curiosity.

Thus Aquarius measures man's greatest possible adherence to his ideals and theories, together with his wildest roaming about in his effort to find new ones if ever the old come to fail him. The mansion always shows his practical obsession with immediate ends in personal fulfillment, or what statically is his everyday aplomb, and dynamically his unleashed desire. Here is his capacity for self-sacrifice at the call of an ideal, and so for a real austerity of character. Going too far, however, the individual may lose himself in some remote or purely theoretical consideration, and so betray his ultimate interests through an everyday vacillation. This is the part of the zodiac which charts the false concepts, the erroneous perspectives and the outwardly perverse notions by which the being is led astray. It also shows how anyone can master the inadequacy or disillusion of his own experience by a quickened ideal interest.

The Aquarius Type

The Aquarius individual—in the case where this sign is rising or contains the sun, moon, or an unusual concentration of planets—is the personal epitome of the air and fixed characteristics. In the extreme case this one of the twelve types may be a person of great vision, possessing the most exalted insight and calling humanity to a cosmic destiny. More often, and at the other extreme, he is a dreamer of dreams, a seeker of utopian satisfaction upon the lazy pastures of his own imagination. Normally he is a conventionalist, and rather gregarious. He likes to play the altruist, and does so when he can. Beneath whatever surface veneer he acquires in life, he is a seeker after guiding principles for himself. These he shares with others who will listen to him, thereby gaining a psychological encouragement. When his highest potentiality is achieved, he is carried along by the wonder of the exaltation he experiences. Then he is delightfully naïve, and at the disposal of all the less inspired souls around him. He is apt to be a person of high passions when compelled to function on any low level of self-fulfillment. Hence he is interested in ideals only to the degree that his own identity may have a safe refuge in them. When devoid of effective emotional anchorage, he is blindly jealous and unreasonable. He will give great loyalty to every sort of cause in which he can find any promise for his inner hopes, and so is very prone to indulge his wishful thinking, and to embrace some purely rationalizing philosophy.

He is of a disposition to make the best of whatever lies at hand, idealizing things as they are when potentialities become too elusive. Hence he is practical in fact, even when running wild in the realms of his thinking. He never gives up what he has until whatever he expects is delivered. He is a realist in the minor affairs of every day, simply because these do not interest him. As a result he is often lackadaisical, following along on the easiest lines in anything not definitely a matter of broader issue. At his best he makes a contribution to everyone around him, largely because his exceptionally active allegiance to whatever inspires him is genuinely infectious. He may accomplish much by his sensitiveness to the more remote implications of experience, as in research and real intellectual analysis. He is inclined to focus his interest on the significance of what happens, rather than in the passing event as such, and so he may prove very quiet and unobtrusive most of the time.

THE TRIBES OF DILIGENCE
CAPRICORN

The Athenians do not mind a man being clever, so long as he does not impart his cleverness to others.

PLATO, Euthyphro

Capricorn is the cardinal sign in the earth group, and this means that it reveals, in every horoscope, the characteristic way in which the native anticipates various crises, in his efforts to justify his being through the everyday world in which he finds himself. The keyword for this mode of action is DISCRIMINATION. The sign is the most practical of all the twelve, in the simple sense of that word, and it is the point in the chart where the greatest possible resourcefulness of an individual is to be found. Among those of little social background it may be no more than cunning, and in those with any refinement of character it will reflect a deeply rooted perseverance. Whenever the immediate situation gets out of hand, however, and an individual is made to feel inadequate, the mansion shows the unreasoning suspicion of which he is capable. Here is where man gives attention to all passing responsibilities, and develops his real facility in restoring order, repairing objects and mechanisms, straightening out the emotional or mental involvements of individuals or groups, and in general gaining a sense of the world's reality through mastering the sphere of his own experience. The general competence can become an extraordinary flair for concern over the business of other people, and for making public and group affairs almost a private problem, but never in a mere busybody sense. This is where the native shows his ability as the architect, the builder and the statesman.

Thus Capricorn reveals the ultimate critical genius of a given person, and especially indicates his power of analysis in questions of morality and ethics, i.e., his moral sensitiveness, or its lack. Under unfavorable development, this is a dog-in-the-manger attitude which may hold others back. Here an individual is shown as he is most clever in uncovering the trends of a situation, and in recognizing its component elements in their reaction upon each other. He may develop the almost intuitive keenness, together with exceptional alertness to immediate eventualities, which constitutes the highest possible form of practical judgment under the sign. This does not strengthen any truly mystical or genuinely religious experience or capacity, but rather leads to a demand for a complete conformity to normal expectation in life and conduct, both by the self and others.

The Capricorn Type

The Capricorn individual—in the case where this sign is rising or contains the sun, moon, or an unusual concentration of planets—is the personal epitome of the earth and cardinal characteristics. He is the most persevering and untiring of all the types, and is usually found to be either (1) a rather useful person at the given moment, when his special competence is needed, or else (2) a quite unpleasant creature, at the times when his proclivity for taking charge of a current situation is something to be resented. He is distinguished by his utter practicality, a realism that becomes almost inhuman whenever something to be done offers him a special chance to tinker with his own fascinating universe of reality. The most paradoxical or truly cardinal part of his nature is his unreasoning insistence that he be consulted if changes are to be made anywhere, but that he be left severely alone otherwise, free to choose for himself the problems to which he applies his talents. He is at once completely conventional, in liking things according to expectation, and yet even fanatical—violent to the point of paroxysm—in his insistence that everything be adjusted according to the lines he adopts and the arrangements he makes. He is a Libra inside out, enthusiastic after rather than before the fact, with equally little interest in remote considerations. He may struggle valiantly to maintain some commonplace ideal, and be devastatingly critical of the ends envisioned. He has no use at all for any notion which is no more than a hope for the future.

He asks of life, primarily, a continuing opportunity to exercise his skills, and he is apt to be quite dispassionate when it comes to any relations with particular people or groups. He becomes the glutton easily, and is the most insatiable of men when he finds any form of self-release a stimulus to his manipulative gifts. In dissipation he is more the lone wolf than ever. He wears out the average person in short order, but he does not interfere with others if they keep their place. He is ungrudgingly splendid when asked for advice or help in the normal course of life. His philosophy is usually one of expedience, feeling that anything necessary has full justification by that fact alone. When undisciplined, he enjoys gaining and exercising any advantage over his fellows, but even then he is generous if he is allowed to express himself. He has great assurance when he feels himself in direct touch with all pertinent factors in the given situation, although he is curiously servile when events are out of hand as far as he is concerned.

VIRGO

A place for everything and everything in its place.
SAMUEL SMILES, *Thrift*

Virgo is the common sign in the earth group, and this means that it reveals, in every horoscope, the characteristic way in which the native attempts to further his own ends by building upon the efforts of other people, and by maneuvering various individuals into relationships according to his own convenience. The keyword for this mode of action is ASSIMILATION. Everyone establishes the totality of himself through a process of psychological aggregation, or a division of labor by means of which he specializes his energies in some directions, helping his fellows and accepting their help in turn. Virgo is the point in the zodiac where the mutual usefulness of men and women to each other is disclosed, both as (1) organized to the extent where, normally, no supervision is required, and as (2) necessitating reorganization to a greater or lesser degree. The sign shows the capacity, in any person's case, for initiating and maintaining the sort of living relations which can be made reciprocally utilitarian in this fashion. Hence it also indicates any individual's potential success in mobilizing himself efficiently enough so that society at large will endorse the broader functions in which he finds his wholeness of experience, and in that way will permit those around him to participate in them to his own advantage.

Thus Virgo indicates the possibility of a genuine preciseness in personal activity, or of a simple and immediate efficiency in productive enterprise. This means any ability to build everyday experience into the very fiber of self, as well as any gift for projecting the self into new and different facets of reality as these are dramatized in the lives of other people, particularly the leaders of the race or the giants of human potentiality. Here is an individual's response to personal relations in general, or to the unalloyed interest of all men *per se*. This mansion shows an individual's willingness to accept anyone else in a common reality, quite apart from special obligation or particular preparation, and charts his tendency towards a superficial manipulation of people in his effort to further a maximum conformity to their joint expectation. The organism seeks at this point to stabilize its own rhythm, and to develop its practical capacity for putting all the elements of ordinary living into mutually contributory relationships. The individually critical functions of Capricorn are broadened here into a more essentially social statesmanship.

The Virgo Type

The Virgo individual—in the case where this sign is rising or contains the sun, moon, or an unsual concentration of planets—is the personal epitome of the earth and common characteristics. He is the most happily and fussily particular of all people, never as delighted as when about his self-appointed tasks. At his worst he is overfastidious, destructively critical and definitely officious, and his relations with others are apt to become an attempt to take complete charge of their personal affairs. Even when he acts in loving kindness, he will tell them what to do, how to place everything, and so on down to the most minute detail. At his best, however, he is the most considerate of all types, insisting that experience be as rewarding to the other fellow as himself. Pliable to an extraordinary extent when it comes to most details of living, he is never disturbed by any need to wait upon his friends, nor is he impatient when it comes to being served by them in turn. He is a born commoner, not interested in the hierarchic orders which men establish but seeing, instead, the role of the community in bringing everyone into one unified world. At heart he is the great leveler.

He is an excellent disciplinarian because, in common with the Piscean type across the zodiac, he makes so little distinction among persons. He is capable of a self-abnegation which would be extraordinary self-sacrifice in someone else, all because he lives so largely in other people. He does this vicariously always, and often literally. He is one with whom association may be exceedingly easy in consequence. When he develops his best potentialities, he is fascinatingly understanding. However, he assiduously avoids too definite a tie with anyone who might dominate their mutual relationship. He feels he must be free to manipulate the factors of reality in his own world, and to seek the unity of experience which he may never gain but which he can anticipate in a commonness of function with the people around him. When uncertain in his own mind, as far as some particular relationship is concerned, he becomes detached and cold. He can be very vindictive if crowded too hard. Even at his meanest, however, he has real capacity for every sort of human fellowship. He will often have high intuitive gifts, through his instinctive human sympathy, and at no moment is he ever apt to be at a loss for simple, direct and intimate relationships.

TAURUS

Let us make hay while the sun shines.
CERVANTES, *Don Quixote*

Taurus is the fixed sign in the earth group, and this means that it reveals, in every horoscope, the characteristic way in which the native makes use of his vicarious experience, to give himself a practical, everyday and external steadiness in living. The keyword for this mode of action is INTEGRATION. Here is the most definitely physical point of all in the chart, showing the pattern of energy-release in the individual case, and also measuring the particular indomitability or simple root constancy of which an individual is capable. The indication is of relations behind the scenes, or the undercurrents of the given life, with an occasional extraordinary sensitiveness to these, and a continual reaction to what they are supposed to be. The sign gives a clue to whatever feeling a person may have of exclusion from any immediate reality—or of being left behind by a growing and expanding world—and so it shows an eagerness to act, and to react, which may seem too primitive or immature to be pleasing to others. Sometimes Taurus may chart a hopeless constriction, which denies all real chance for self-expression and so demands an explosive unbottling of self, that is, a resort to crude and second-best efforts to achieve the coveted wholeness in self-realization. This is the point of unalloyed articulation in the zodiac, disclosing a conscious self-appreciation as this arises from the stresses and strains in every underlying impulse of appetite and need.

Thus Taurus shows the requirements of the self its own functional continuance, not only in a native's release of energy but in his determination to put the whole of reality to use. Here is his development of a conscious self-validity. What discloses a selfish or willful and undisciplined self-seeking on the lowest level can become a gift for sentiment and a talent for a continual and creative contribution to real human ideals. The native is charted at this point in his true breadth of consciousness. This is the place in any horoscope where he refines his fundamental metaphysics. It shows the nature and strength of his hidden allegiances, or as he is oriented to the ideals he glimpses behind the superficial press of events. Here is where he develops his willingness to do and die, or to integrate all experience for himself and his fellows at no matter what cost.

The Taurus Type

The Taurus individual—in the case where this sign is rising or contains the sun, moon or an unusual concentration of planets—is the personal epitome of the earth and fixed characteristics. He is the type which at its worst is least able to gain the co-operation of others. He will seek, in his moments of defeatism, to eliminate himself from every context. He may refuse to play, almost pugnaciously, or else may retreat with hurt feelings to some lesser reality he can recognize on his own account. The literal extremes of proud self-sacrifice and pure martyrdom in maladjustment are found here. The motivation in the Taurus person is so little obvious to his fellows, normally, that he may seem on superficial observation to be the most self-centered and touchy of all. He is somewhat prone to live an interior life, especially when thwarted, although this is usually against his interest. In such a case he contributes to his own elimination from the more objective forms of experience, and so brings about a very real loss of self in a psychological regression to infinity.

This native is usually stimulated to an exceptional extent by the interplay of ideas about him, attempting in consequence to make them his own. The result is that he appears to be overly energetic, with little apparent capacity for relaxation or rest. At times he is tempted to force himself, and to enjoy situations in which he is compelled to resort to artificial sustainment, driving himself to exhaustion at the end. When life has a proper channelship for his efforts, he is the most invaluable of people, but if he goes unappreciated or lacks real affection he may dissipate his resources in idle fretting, pouring his energy into highly trivial issues. When there is nothing at stake in his own external world of reality, or when he cannot feel himself necessary in a very real way, he is the least alive among these astrological tribes. Under such circumstances he will appear quite unapproachable in any ordinary sense. Then he has no special context of being in which he can at once lose and so find himself. Pre-eminently the person who must prove the cosmic wholeness within himself, his extreme sensitiveness, his desire to follow through in pursuit of worthwhile consummations, his faithfulness to ideals of ultimate and practical substantiation, all make him magnificent in his own roots, and give him the simple dignity he is never able to lose.

TABLE VI

The Twelve Signs of the Zodiac

Name	Quadrature	Triplicity	Mode of Action
♈ ARIES	Cardinal	Fire	Aspiration
♉ TAURUS	Fixed	Earth	Virility
♊ GEMINI	Common	Air	Vivification

♋ CANCER	Cardinal	Water	Expansion
♌ LEO	Fixed	Fire	Assurance
♍ VIRGO	Common	Earth	Assimilation
♎ LIBRA	Cardinal	Air	Equivalence
♏ SCORPIO	Fixed	Water	Creativity
♐ SAGITTARIUS	Common	Fire	Administration
♑ CAPRICORN	Cardinal	Earth	Discrimination
♒ AQUARIUS	Fixed	Air	Loyalty
♓ PISCES	Common	Water	Sympathy

CHAPTER TEN

The Portmanteau Symbols

Human character, as the astrologer encounters it, is infinite in its potentials. Astrology, seeking to avoid any loss of perspective in an illimitable reality, has long since reduced its major zodiacal lore to a series of concrete or portmanteau symbols. The initial and more important implications of these have now been presented in a way designed to reveal both their origin in general experience and their measure of the individual in his assimilation of his fellows to himself. As the symbolization is condensed into its traditional form, it emphasizes the various types of personality in (1) a very objective differentiation and (2) a highly organic characterization. These descriptive approaches to man provide the two amplified or functional alphabets of the zodiac.

THE MACROSCOSMIC ALPHABET

So likewise all this life of mortal man, what is it but a kind of stage play, where men come forth, disguised one in one array, and another in another, each playing his part?

ERASMUS, *Praise of Folly*

When the original attempt was made to aid a visual identification of the zodiacal signs by arranging the stars behind them in fanciful figures, there was also an obvious effort to assist any recognition of the astrological types among men by likening the twelve psychological tribes to certain real or mythological animals. The purpose of each symbol, presumably, was to provide the best possible portrait of whatever generalized individuality would have a correspondence with the given heavenly mansion. The living person, however, is far more the picture of his fellows than any ram or bull, crab or scorpion ever could be. Hence astrologers always build up a rather private conception of each sign in entirely human habiliments, equipping themselves with an instrument of analysis which they can adjust for any particular context of race and national distinctiveness. This is primarily a cataloguing of astrological appearance, or of the more superficial reflection of any person's nature in his physical form and habits.

Taken understandingly, the zodiacal descriptions are of great usefulness, and they have a high degree of reliability. However, it must be remembered that the outer mark of horoscopic factors on the physical body is infinitely more slight than elements of (1) genetic background, (2) environmental modification, and especially (3) accident. Attention has already been drawn to the fact that the sun sign may not be predominantly suggested, as far as typical characteristics are concerned, by a given native. People who live in closest accord with group or racial expectation will usually show the greatest fidelity to these solar indications, and in general all men will reveal the skeletal structure suggested by the sun's position. The ascendant or rising sign is normally most important in charting the individual's appearance. Tendencies shown at the eastern angle are strengthened in the case of anyone who lives in close conformity to the superficial conditions of his existence, or who is dependent on a continual stimulation from exterior events and relationships. In the exceptional instance where the zodiacal signature provided by the moon or other planets is most evident, the life is abnormally individualistic, exaggerating the particular indications. The ascendant describes the characteristic set of muscle and flesh in the case of all people, and the moon's position delineates the typical nervous tension as a final or over-all factor in human appearance.

ARIES is the sign of the ram, or the butting male animal which symbolizes the pioneer temperament. The general essence of this is expressed in the emotional keyword, giving the self-idealization of this type at its best as HOPE. Aries is generalized by a slender or exceptionally well-knit figure, the body inclined to be rangy or lean with a long or scrawny neck, a broad forehead and a narrow chin. The nose is apt to be prominent, or its length an outstanding feature. The eyes are often piercing, and sometimes are given a sharp appearance by bony sockets, or by overhanging and bushy brows. The hair may be wiry and curly with a tendency to sandy red or black. The complexion can be swarthy, and it inclines to be ruddy if the skin is light. The height ranges from medium to tall.

TARSUS is the sign of the bull, symbolizing a parade of male strength, or a desire to share vitality. A bovine placidity may characterize the native outwardly, and his genius may express itself in moral sensitiveness. The emotional keyword, giving the self-idealization of this type at its best, is PEACE. Taurus is generalized by a full neck, emphasized shoulders and a rather well filled-out body. The face is apt to be round, the mouth full, cheeks or chin dimpled, and the hair in a widow's peak at the forehead or neck. The stature ranges from short to medium. If racial background permits, the complexion runs to the olive, and in most cases there is a suggestion of the old-fashioned doll, with features all in one plane. Hands and feet may be large. The eyes and coloring may be light, but the normal type is rather dark, with a tendency to abundant and sometimes curly hair.

GEMINI is the sign of the twins, symbolizing the very persistent, annoying and practical duality of human restlessness. Because this native is always able to find a happy and fellow-element in experience, the emotional keyword, giving the self-idealization of this type at its best, is JOY. Gemini is generalized by a tall and well-proportioned body, with long limbs, slender hands and long lines in the features. Usually the eyes will be quite round, the nose lengthy, and the mouth wide.

The complexion may be sanguine, or somewhat lusterless and spotted, with the hair brown or dark and straight. The eyes tend to be gray or hazel, and to possess the sharpness of Aries, if not a characteristic alertness or wide gaze of their own. The hands and feet are sometimes exceptionally short and perhaps fleshy, even though the body ranges to length.

CANCER is the sign of the crab, or the grim-holding claw-replacing crustacean which symbolizes the marked self-containment here. The emotional keyword, giving the self-idealization of this type at its best, is PATIENCE. Cancer is generalized by short and stout individuals, often showing marked protuberances and angles in form or feature. The chest is usually broad, occasionally high. The body is often fleshy, with small hands and feet. Occasionally a very round moon face characterizes the native. His nose may be quite prominent at the tip. His coloring is usually fair, but his complexion pale. In extreme cases the upper part of the body is exceptionally large, in proportion to the rest of it, and with heavy breasts in even little women. The hair inclines to brown. The eyes are commonly gray, frequently small or unusually deep-set, and there is often a very characteristic infant's forehead.

LEO is the sign of the lion, king of the beasts, as a symbol of pride and self-respect. Because of the native's great capacity for holding exalted ideals, the emotional keyword, giving the self-idealization of this type at its best, is GLORY. Leo is generalized by relatively short and slender but round persons, and there is normally a characteristic sleekness in flat frontal surfaces of the hips and thighs. The head is more than often full and curved, even wholly dome-shaped. Sometimes the figure becomes larger and bony, giving an impression of height. The face may be quite oval, the complexion ruddy or sanguine. The hair ranges from yellow to dark, with a tendency to curls. The general coloring is brown. Sometimes large goggle eyes are found under this sign, and occasionally a Leo individual may be miniature in dimension, but always with ideal proportions in such a case.

VIRGO is the sign of the virgin, or the dramatization of human perfection as an extreme of self-reservation, so that the emotional keyword, giving the self-idealization of this type at its best, is PURITY. Virgo is generlized by lean individuals of quite variable stature, sometimes prone to stoutness, or to a raw-boned condition in later life. The body is usually better formed than average before filling out, with a roundish face and strongly marked but not large features. Coloring ranges from light brown to dark. The forehead is apt to be wide, the brows square and sometimes bushy, the upper lip often very long, the nose tending to length. The mouth is normally quite straight, sometimes extraordinarily thin-lipped. The back may be characteristically flat and beautifully modeled, but a bony protuberance at the base of the neck, front and back, is hardly less typical.

LIBRA is the sign of the scales. Because this native seeks to balance everything, or achieve symmetry, the emotional keyword, giving the self-idealization of the type at its best, is BEAUTY. Libra is generalized by the figure apt to be the most sheerly elegant of all, often of the statuesque order in small dimensions, generally with an oval face and well-proportioned features. The coloring is as light as heredity permits, and a characteristic of the sign is a well-defined spinal dip, aiding the distinctive carriage. The features are inclined to be regular even if out of pattern, the hair line is somewhat low and peaked, and the brows symmetrical. The native always tends to beauty in youth, commonly developing bad complexion or color in later years. The bone structure is always evident, as in high cheek bones. Teeth and nails are apt to be exceptionally fine.

SCORPIO is the sign of the scorpion, or the insect which stings its prey into a state of helplessness. The emotional keyword, giving the self-idealization of this type at its best, is JUSTICE. Scorpio is generalized, for the major part, by short and thick-set individuals of sturdy appearance. If blood permits, the complexion is swarthy. The hair is apt to be curly or waved, its line at the forehead very low, the brows bushy. The eyes may be almost glittering in their brightness, and there is nearly always the Egyptian eyelid, i.e., an exaggerated droop at the extreme outer corners. The nose may be aquiline to a pronounced extent, heavy or rounded at the nostrils. The face is inclined to squareness and breadth, and the lips to unusual fullness. The body is often hirsute. Occasionally the native becomes bowlegged, or warped in some definite skeletal distortion.

SAGITTARIUS is the sign of the archer, or the bowman centaur who as half-man and half-horse must share both human and animal nature. This symbolizes breadth of perspective in experience, and establishes the emotional keyword, giving the self-idealization of this type at its best, as SAGACITY. Sagittarius is generalized by tall, large and often stout individuals who are especially prone to long legs and arms, with a typically protuberant abdomen or very large thighs. The native is apt to be very handsome, with oval face and round, clear and calm eyes, and sometimes satanic eyebrows. He presents an exceptionally free and frank appearance, but he also has a marked tendency to baldness, his hair nearly always well off the temples. In all cases the forehead is high or back-sloping, the features somewhat elongated. The body may be undersized, but it remains proportionately rangy. The coloring usually runs from blond to browns.

CAPRICORN is the sign of the he-goat, most indefatigable of common male animals. Because of his normally cheerful acceptance of things as they exist, the emotional keyword, giving the self-idealization of this type at its best, is REVERENCE. Capricorn is generalized usually by well-knit and slender people, showing a narrow jaw which suggests the goat's head. When rounded out, the face is apt to become circular, due to the high cheekbones. Diminutive individuals, fairly common, are inclined to be wizened. Other members of this group are prone to be bandy-legged, with knotted knees and joints, and tending to thinness, particularly at the chest. The hair is often scanty. A false impression of frailty may be given. The eyes are usually small, sometimes piercing, frequently suspicious. Coloring ranges to dark, and turns gray early.

AQUARIUS is the sign of the water-carrier, or the individual who feels it his special privilege to serve others. The emotional keyword, giving the self-idealization of this type at its best, is TRUTH. Aquarius is generalized normally by well-set, filled-out and strong people. The face is long and square, frequently marked by a very delicate countenance. Most characterisitc is an unusually clear complexion, and an exceptional regularity of features which, occasionally, may seem too small. The hair of the face and head may be quite bushy, giving an appearance of distinction. The stature is generally above medium, with a tendency to flesh. The eyes are apt to be light, even in very dark types, and to look out on the world in a curious, candid fashion. Bad teeth were a most serviceable mark of this sign before widespread dentistry. The lips often present a distinct cupid's bow.

TABLE VII

The Self-idealizations of the Zodiac

ARIES	Hope	LEO	Glory	SAGITTARIUS	Sagacity
TAURUS	Peace	VIRGO	Purity	CAPRICORN	Reverence
GEMINI	Joy	LIBRA	Beauty	AQUARIUS	Truth
CANCER	Patience	SCORPIO	Justice	PISCES	Love

PISCES is the sign of the two opposite-facing fishes, suggesting a persistently outreaching but confused desire to experience everything in the ocean of life. The emotional keyword, giving the self-idealization of this type at its best, is LOVE. Pisces is generalized commonly by people of medium stature. Their shoulder line often has a pronounced slope, and their posture is nearly always bad. Because they handle their figure poorly, they give every impression either of slovenliness or else of a distinct other-worldliness. The eyes are apt to be very full or prominent, the mouth big and the features otherwise rather round, at times altogether too large for the head. The coloring tends to brown or dark, but the skin is usually bloodless no matter how dusky the color. The eyes are sometimes characteristically watery, or actually weak, and unless particularly animated the native may appear definitely lacklustrous.

THE MICROSCOSMIC ALPHABET

> *. . . A grain of sand includes the universe.*
> SAMUEL TAYLOR COLERIDGE, *Additional Table Talk*

The astrological rulership of bodily parts and organic functions has long been familiar, even to the general public, through such common diagrams as shown on page 16. The one modern innovation is the additional set of keywords. These are designed to aid a realization which might parallel, on the subjective side, that offered objectively through the more familiar symbols embodied in the ancient star-patterns. The application of the sign rulerships in the body is fundamentally psychological and here, in contrast with the macrocosmic alphabet, all twelve must be taken into consideration in every horoscope.

ARIES rules the head and brain, and therefore shows the manifestation of simple identity as the native himself is heady or impulsive in any given complex of being, or as he is inclined to be brainy and to act on his own intellectual judgment. The keyword is TORCH, which expresses his sense of complete resource and power in self-existence.

TARSUS rules the neck and throat, and therefore shows the manifestation of self-completion as the native attempts to swallow or consume the substance of experience, and to articulate or resound the organic satisfaction he seeks from every complex of being. The keyword is PILLAR, which expresses his practical stability and his sense of strength in all experience.

GEMINI rules the shoulders, arms and lungs, and therefore shows the manifestation of self-confirmation as the native seeks to grasp or clasp real personal relationships throughout life, and demands inspiration or the chance to inspire others in every complex of being. The keyword is PENCIL, which expresses his penchant for putting his mark on every phase of experience.

CANCER rules the chest, breasts and stomach, and therefore shows the manifestation of wholeness as the native establishes his central source of supply in a complete giving or gaining of nutriment through every complex of being. The keyword is VALVE, which expresses his desire to control and experience every phase of receiving and supplying things.

LEO rules the upper back, spine and heart, and therefore shows the manifestation of simple identity as the native lends himself to establishing or maintaining a structure for the vital stabilizing of himself in every given complex of being. The keyword is DYNAMO, which expresses his capacity for centralizing the actual distribution of experience.

VIRGO rules the abdomen and intestines, and therefore shows the manifestation of self-completion as the native is most personally or organically conscientious in his own functioning within any given complex of being. The keyword is HOPPER, or the chute or box which expresses his gift for sifting, teasing or compacting experience into its most useful niche.

LIBRA rules the lower back and kidneys, and therefore shows the manifestation of self-confirmation as the native continually seeks to distill some vital essence out of his relationships in every given complex of being. The keyword is LINK, or the coupling which expresses the utter directness of his attempt to put experience through his own alembic.

SCORPIO rules the pelvis and lower ducts, and therefore shows the manifestation of wholeness as the native continually projects himself, often privately and even secretly, through every given complex of being. The keyword is FURNACE, which expresses the highly individual way in which he reworks the materials of his own experience.

SAGITTARIUS rules the thighs and flesh, and therefore shows the manifestation of simple identity as the native most definitely orients or sensitizes himself in his own outer personality, seeking to embody himself quite literally in every given complex of being. The keyword is LAMP, which expresses his naïve illumination of all potentials in experience.

CAPRICORN rules the knees and skin, and therefore shows the manifestation of self-completion as the native strives for an ultimate power of containment, together with a real flexibility in self-realization, throughout every given complex of being. The keyword is BOOK, which expresses his critical gifts for embracing and sharpening experience.

AQUARIUS rules the calves, ankles and blood, and therefore shows the manifestation of self-confirmation as the native learns to personify every inner and outer value of his own social achievement in some given complex of being. The keyword is CAMERA, which expresses the fidelity of his continual reconstructions of reality in everyday experience.

PISCES rules the feet, liver and lymphatics, and therefore shows the manifestation of wholeness as the native seeks to reconstitute reality in general, and as he wanders about receptively in every given complex of being. The keyword is POOL, which expressses the pure self-restoring potentiality on which he draws in his capacity for limitless appreciation.

These are the various manifestations which constitute character in its subjective make-up, and provide the foundation for any understanding of potentialities as such.

TABLE VIII

The Subjective Implications of the Zodiac

Sign	Physiological rulerships		Keyword
ARIES	Head	Brain	Torch
TAURUS	Neck	Throat	Pillar
GEMINI	Shoulders, arms	Lungs	Pencil
CANCER	Chest	Breasts, stomach	Valve
LEO	Upper back	Spine, heart	Dynamo
VIRGO	Abdomen	Intestines	Hopper
LIBRA	Lower back	Kidneys	Link
SCORPIO	Pelvis	Lower ducts	Furnace
SAGITTARIUS	Thighs	Flesh	Lamp
CAPRICORN	Knees	Skin	Book
AQUARIUS	Calves, ankles	Blood	Camera
PISCES	Feet	Liver, lymphatics	Pool

Potentialities

CHAPTER ELEVEN

The Magic
of Patterns

A common insight of human thinking is that existence is action, not a mere static state of something. Thus man knows he is of consequence, or that he possesses potentialities, even when he is unable to form any clear idea of himself in his own mind. This is the proposition to which Sir Lewis Morris, the Welsh poet, gives apt statement in his remark that "life is act, and not to do is death."

Astrology is not concerned with the philosophical problems here, but with practical considerations arising in the process of act. The two preceding parts of this text have been devoted to a charting of man's everyday circumstances by the equatorial houses of the horoscope, and to a measurement of his personal characteristics by the signs of the zodiac. What remains is the astrological delineation of doing—and so, of existing—as it is found to be a continual interaction between various given situations and individual character. The two-way impact, which has been exhibited so far through each of the orientations provided by (1) the horizons and (2) the constants of experience, must now be identified in terms of (3) a pure ACTIVITY, or the final and most important of the three great horoscopic perspectives.

Activity of itself—that is, when made a primary factor in astrological analysis, and so divorced for the moment from the particular situations and characteristics involved—can only be the possibility of proceeding with reference to a definite kind of consummation, or of not doing so. Under way or accomplished, act is at once circumstantial and functional. Potentially, however, it can be a transcendence of circumstances as well as a response to them, and as much an expansion or refinement of the character as any exercise of its nature. It is, ultimately, the simple more or less of anything in question. The planets in horoscopy, added to the houses and signs, are the means of (1) determining the precise nature of the potentiality involved in every possible complex of a native's situation and character, or (2) finding how experience may be increased or decreased in particular phases of itself. The complete scheme of distribution in astrological correspondences can be given diagrammatically, as follows:

TABLE IX

The Basic Scheme of Astrological Analysis

(1) Man establishes horizons, charted by the houses.

He reveals circumstances as the co-operation of two factors:
   Identity, or the manifestation of freedom;
   Condition, or the manifestation of order.

(2) Man develops characteristics, charted by the signs.

He reveals function as the co-operation of two factors:
   Objectivity, or fidelity to social convenience;
   Subjectivity, or fidelity to organic convenience.

(3) Man manipulates potentialities, charted by the planets.

He reveals activity as the co-operation of two factors:
   Momentum, or the integration of circumstances;
   Capacity, or the refinement of function.

The problem at this point, in any over-all exposition of the horoscope, is to provide the mind with fundamental planetary meanings, such as will permit an actual charting of act apart from the conditioning of circumstances and the compulsion of characteristics. The astrologer, to make use of his equatorial houses, must be able to understand money, as an example, in its wholly general or fundamental implication. Otherwise he cannot analyze the pertinent differentiations by which he is able to offer guidance in a given individual's case. Aries shows a head—hence an initiative, a self-sufficiency and a flair for leadership—which is not limited to any race, climate, nationality, family, sex, age in years or other purely personal adaptation. For this reason the sign at the vernal equinox provides a real measurement of individual functioning in the astrological techniques. What is needed for the planets is a correspondingly broad generalization.

The physical sciences have been able to deduce and verify the so-called laws of nature—the generalized principles on which so many great achievements have been built—by directing first attention to those classes of phenomena where all individual differences can be averaged out, in a statistical sense, as in dealing with atoms, molecules and infinite masses. The screening in this way of infinite chemical activity, or scientifically fixed potentiality, made it possible to proceed on the basis of exact prediction, and so led to every important technological advance of the modern age. This text is based on research which began its examination of planetary meanings in January, 1923, by a special study of microscopic life, using the amoeba as a convenient type of living organism. Here were infinitesimal animals, simple to the point of a near loss of themselves in the medium which sustained them, yet exhibiting all the fundamental kinds of action which seem to be necessary in organic existence. They shared these with every higher form of animate being, but disclosed them on the level where all possible individual differences were cancelled out as completely as in the case of the physicist's atoms.

What the amoeba does, every laborer or capitalist, every commoner or aristocrat, every drunkard or saint, does likewise, not only for the same reason but in precisely identical fashion at root. This utterly generalized differentiation of activity, according to kind of act, is what the planetary bodies chart in horoscopy. Men start, and they stop. They labor, and they rest. They make themselves active or passive at will. They enjoy, or they reject. These are the possibilities which now must be derived from experience, rather than theory, and which must be shown to have the same logical measurement through the planets, astrologically, as circumstances and function through the equatorial and ecliptical mansions.

The amoeba remains a hopelessly generalized creature, as far as he appears in man's perspective. He eats at any point of himself by a simple ingestion of food particles into the substance that makes him up, and he excretes by collecting waste materials anywhere within this substance in the form of vacuoles which can be ejected through the wall-less boundary of himself. Respiration takes place in the same ingenuous fashion. Locomotion is a ponderously awkward but ridiculously easy flow of self in any desired direction, and so on. This is function at its extreme in a lack of pattern, and is circumstances in their most haphazard form. As life grows in complexity, however, a relatively fixed organization becomes necessary. A head develops as a means for taking supplies into the body. Other specializations without number help to put down the foundation for a higher existence by making it possible to dismiss most organic functioning to automaticity. In human character and situation a progressive achievement of generalization, above these merely physical functions, leads to man's high and characteristic individuality. This essentially social activity is charted by the planets. They are taken not in isolation from each other, but as they establish definitely recognizable patterns, akin to life itself in its evolution of organic forms.

Men do not materially interrupt their own rhythm of existence, or vary their pattern of activity, in making their adjustments to the stream of events in which they have part. The person who finds he must wait for a train is able to get his shoes shined, or make a telephone call—desires in which he may have been thwarted only very shortly before—and the transposition of emphasis from one thing to another in this fashion is the means by which he keeps his act and choice free in a very real sense. W. J. Colville (1860–1917), a theosophical writer of importance in another generation, was fond of saying that when he brushed his hair he was in psychic rapport with everyone who was brushing his hair at that moment. The concordance of life in its activity is not a compulsion of man, except incidentally. He may leave the guild of hairbrushers to place himself in the fellowship of breakfast-eaters, and so on indefinitely. The facility with which every individual can align himself where he wills—in circumstances, function and activity—is the basis of his capacity or true incentive, exactly as the alignments which he has made already, and which persist to varying degrees, constitute the momentums that are the very substance of his being. Here is probability at work, and what must be understood is how astrology can use the planets to chart it.

MOMENTUM AS A PATTERN OF SELF

Against a lucky man even a god has little power.
PUBLILIUS SYRUS, *Sententiæ*

All things tend to run their course. A fever or a common cold goes through a regular cycle, which has to be taken into account by the physician, and the crisis in certain diseases is an important manifestation of the same phenomenon. Infection is always followed by a necessary period of gestation, which can usually be predicted. Many remedial measures have stages which show the degree of efficacy in the individual case. Plants and animals appear or reappear at set times, and the reproduction of their kind runs to schedules which hold to norm with a greater reliability than the seasons themselves. This tendency for the basic functions of organic existence to be rhythmic, or to reveal a dependable regularity of cycle, is a necessity in a universe characterized by order. Birth and death, hunger and satiety, activity and sleep, desire and self-realization, all involve that continuous reconstruction of experience by which consciousness is made possible. The rhythms as such are the foundation of circumstances, and their parallel planetary cycles are the basis of astrological charting.

The irregularities of existence are even more importantly periodic, if in a different fashion, than the familiar cycles of common experience. Every dog has his day, according to the suggestion first made by Homer, and opportunity knocks on the door at least once in each man's case, as Lewis Bates points out in his *Good Luck*. The whole of an individual's life has a span which seems to be more consistent with his family or genetic pattern, statistically, than with the wider standard of longevity for the country at large. Indeed, nature often seems to enter upon a conspiracy to preserve each special little *status quo* as a cyclic momentum in its own right. No truism seems to have more universal confirmation that the one of Jesus, put down in *Mark,* 4:25, "For he that hath, to him shall be given: and he that hath not, from him shall be taken even that which he hath." This, of course, is what makes individuality possible. It is the integrity of activity *per se.*

These cycles overlap each other continually, often in a most incongruous blending of both desirable and quite unwelcome patterns. Thus a long siege of sickness may accompany a fine financial year. An individual in serious business straits may have the comfort of an ideal wife, and become the master of his lodge. Every single course of events in personal experience operates through its own convenience, perhaps revealed but in no wise initiated, terminated or controlled of necessity by any other chain of relations, either in the given case or in nature generally. Its length of duration seems to be inherent in its make-up, not in its superficial connections, and this is the phenomenon which the astrological planets dramatize most strikingly. Practically every problem arising in human experience becomes at base the need for creating favorable momentums in the act-of-self, if not for an extrication from unfavorable ones. The universe is not moving in anyone's favor, or against his interest, but he is merely making a proper or improper use of his potentialities.

Man understands this well enough, in everyday matters. When he finds his business unsatisfactory, he looks around and makes some change to effect the end he has in view. He consults a doctor, dentist, or other therapeutist in connection with bodily deficiencies, or a real estate broker when he finds the neighborhood of his home unsuitable for the needs of his growing children. He is only defeated, for the major part, when he is swept along in cycles for which his perspective is inadequate. Horoscopy fails him, therefore, when it seeks merely to give him a knowledge of the probabilities under which he is operating, without showing him at the same time how to engineer the shifts that will bring him under the course of an altogether different set of potentials. A patient would hardly be justified in consulting the physician if that gentleman would only report, "You are badly infected with a malignant fever, and I predict that in five days your agony will be most acute, and that in ten you will be dead."

In its portmanteau implication a POTENTIALITY is the possible duration of a definable action, or body of acts, reactions and attitudes. Seen circumstantially, any one potential in question is a momentum serving as an integrating factor in experience, and so providing the basis for any estimation of outcome. Examined functionally, the same potential is a capacity, and analysis moves on from predictive measurement of the situation—that is, a judgment upon its integration—to the shaping of events which are controlled rather than suffered. The possibility of this control, as against naïve eventuality, is shown by the identical heavenly body, of course, in the same astrological chart. The planets in the horoscope are used to determine the twofold potentiality of things (1) as encountered and (2) in the light of what may be desired. They show what tendencies in a particular life are of value, and so are either to be left undisturbed or helped and strengthened, and what ones, contrariwise, are fruitless and hence require redirection. The planetary relations of an astrological wheel thus reveal themselves as patterns of expediency, entirely as the native's momentums give a varying value to his capacities.

CAPACITY AS A PATTERN OF SELF

*Every man has his gift, and the tools go
to him that can use them.*
CHARLES KINGSLEY, *Saint's Tragedy*

The myth of talents as inborn, and marvelously mysterious, is helped by the exceptional appearance of the infant prodigy, or other precocious members of the human species. The average person assumes himself without hope in his own drab milieu, and decides to content himself with whatever conditions of lack have become the principal momentums in his own life. This does not mean that anyone can be a musical genius, as an example, but it is the very rare man indeed who does not have many potentialities which, with an adequate nurture, could not be advanced to a degree of unusual excellence. The extraordinary case involves over-all cycles of larger compass—some untoward emphasis of racial or group potentials—but it does not require any special factors to account for it, over and above those applicable to the less spectacular instance. Certainly it does not diminish the opportunity offered the little fellow. Times of unusual stress, such as war, show how far an abnormal culture of outstanding capacities can be brought about in the mass. The principle has long been recognized, as in the old Latin proverb that necessity is the mother of invention.

What astrology presents to every native is an outline of the chance which he may have to develop himself, or to improve the circumstances of his being, as this is scaled against the greatest rather than the merely average encouragement of his given age and set of relations. Genius which classifies as art has its special limitations, but so has a mechanical talent, a flair for politics, the psychic sense of the gambler, the muscular timing of an athlete, and so on through the endless list where even the least of men must surely find potentialities of himself in several categories. An individual always has the gift—that is, the ability to act—by which his capacities can so emphasize the more rather than the less, in the enhancement of some particular competence, as to make him superlative indeed within his own special self-chosen niche of reality.

Capacity exists because of the very important and basic fact that nature always does things in the same way, as far as possible, thereby establishing the integrity of pure doing in man and all other living creatures. An indestructibility of matter and a conservation of energy, the enduring principles which so fascinated classical physics and chemistry, are pieces of this same cloth. The preponderance of the expected event in a spread of possible instances, under the normal curve of statistics, is another manifestation of the same proposition. It is probably illustrated most dramatically, however, in the field of biology. Just as particular genius needs its special setting, so do all genera of life above a unicellular stage require the stability of the highly analogous organic pattern.

This is curiously evident in the embryological limb buds. Thus, among the Upper Jurassic fossils of geology, there is an early form of bird known as Archaeornis, distinguished by the fact that his wings had fingers as well as feathers. He was at the transition stage where he carried over reptilian character-istics into his new functioning, and the arrangement must have been altogether awkward, since hands can have little articulation when placed at the edge of arms already special-ized for flight. In the statistical sorting out of the various sports in nature—the process overliteralized by Herbert Spencer as a survival of the fittest—the prehensile functions of the fingers gravitated to the mouth, in the case of all birds, and the de-fense mechanism was centered in flight instead of prowess with the claws, showing how a particular form of evolutionary development became a special capacity.

The point is that the gravitational interrelations of circum-stances and function, as mediated by that complex of momen-tums and capacities which constitute the individual entity, operate together—under the recapitulatory activity of evolu-tionary progress—to produce more and more convenient complexes of reality on the circumstantial side, and more and more efficient organisms or living forms on the functional.

Thus the bird's wings are the arms of man, and the forelegs of lower mammals. The housefly's wings, contrariwise, have their evolutionary correspondence with man's hair, since they do not arise from limb buds at all. Nature holds to her established path except when, by following another, she can accomplish what for the moment is a greater result. This suggests the extent to which doing the same thing in the same way is not limitation, but opportunity, since it can be abandoned whenever convenient.

A sport in one direction is sustained by conventionality in a thousand others. Mediocrity can always become genius within the channel of available potentials, and this is the magic of patterns in their ultimate implication. Cinderella could blossom forth as a princess, something her sister were unable to do. The ugly duckling found himself as a swan. What is everywhere evident, through all organic and psychological adaptations, is the division of labor which fundamentally distinguishes potentiality from potentiality and so gives the most important clue to the nature of the planets, each as a sort of limb bud—withal a movable and restless one—in the universal or generalized man. In other words, the patterned wholeness of self is found embryonically as well as organically in the zodiac. Each of the heavenly bodies, in practical astrology, comes to represent a special sort of self-assertion. The essential realization for the astrologer is that the horoscope, by charting the particular potentials through which existence brings circumstances and function into co-operation with each other, can guide a development of each or any embryonic limb bud of capacity, as it were, into forelegs, arms or wings, exactly as may be most convenient or pleasing.

CHAPTER TWELVE

Self-Assertion
and Reality

Man most commonly preserves his integrity by his will to be unhurried in his major activities. This procrastination may have destructive results at times, but it also has been responsible for striking accomplishment. Ennius (as quoted by Cicero in *De Senectute*) says that the Fabian policy initiated by Quintus Fabius Maximus in the face of Hannibal's successes was such that "by delay he restored the state." Jesus, when advised that Lazarus was dead (*John,* 11:6), waited two days before proceeding to Bethany to perform the miracle. Here is no dignifying of an uncertainty of mind, or of a dilatoriness in facing the actualities of experience, but a realization that the self must be self-activated in every possible combination of circumstances and function. Any manifestation of the individual pattern of activity is impossible without a choice in the direction and nature of impact, an actual squaring off in time and space. Man's self-assertion is a manipulation of potentialities by using or rejecting them, to the end that duration serves rather than enslaves him, and that spatial relations sustain rather than deny his self-fulfillment.

The universe is not made up of indeterminate factors which blend together in becoming actualities, but of elements rigorously persistent in a process of continuing to be what they are. They co-operate with each other constantly in circumstantial and functional relationship, but no one of them can sacrifice its own nature and remain in existence. Everything encountered in experience is completely obsessed with its own business, and goes about its own affairs through every moment of time, no matter what its significance may be otherwise. When A becomes part of the reality in which B functions, A in that respect is a transient construct in B's complex of reality. It is true that this is made possible by the nature of A on his own account, but in no instance can B, acting in the periphery of A's self-assertion, maneuver any change in A, or depreciate A's integrity. Here is a further definition for a potentiality, i.e., a dependable changelessness in things as far as their own existence is concerned.

THE MEASURE OF REGULARITY

To do nothing is in every man's power.
SAMUEL JOHNSON, *The Rambler*

A cycle is a negative phenomenon. It is essentially a momentum, or something which of necessity expends itself and slows to a stop. Hence most individuals discover, sooner or later, that when they avoid self-assertion they often diminish rather than nurse their capacities. Sometimes they lose all point to this discovery by blaming on a lack of inspiration what after all is only the slow decay of ennui. Momentums are necessary, and highly desirable when they support the continuance of anything valued or enjoyed by man, but they are not self-sufficient. Moreover, in their mere continuance, they do not constitute any part of actual experience. No one knows, as personal fact, that the earth has two primary motions, or that the cells of his body engage in constant and highly vital enterprises of a cyclic nature. The procession of the seasons is hardly experienced, simply the individual impact of summer, or some other of them, in a special connection.

A momentum becomes critical, entering experience in a genuine sense, when it begins to lose dependability in the given situation, or when another one becomes necessary. Cycles, as a consequence, are only important in astrological analysis through their inception and cessation. The planets measure the terminal points when self-assertion is needed, not any mere continuance, that is, any interim devoid of significant act. The power of man to do nothing is his capacity to take advantage of whatever momentums sustain his own special contexts of reality, thus handling these negative factors in a positive fashion. He must face the falling away of much on which he counts, with the passage of time, and he must always be prepared to reinaugurate activities by which he integrates his existence, establishes his identity and gains his satisfactions. However, he can avoid purely side issues, together with all worry over trifles or concern with what is in no way a direct responsibility, by the simple orientation of his personal activity in its general content.

The sun, moon and other bodies become the PLANETS of horoscopy through their ultimately regular cycles of geocentric motion, and these cycles in their turn provide a statistical correspondence to the everyday momentums of normal existence. The original astrological correlation between the planetary movements and human events has an entirely empirical foundation, with the earliest roots of the horoscope lying in the simple relations observed in a time concordance between the heavenly positions and many regular fluctuations of human experience. The cyclic factors provided by the sun, in daily and seasonal distinctions, and by the moon, through periods in natural function which duplicate or multiply its phases, have been obvious to man from the dawn of his conscious existence. The phenomenon of morning and evening stars certainly caught his attention at the beginning of his myth-building, and unquestionably led to his various attempts to equate the planetary circling with the more subtle tides in his existence. The relatively free passage of Jupiter, Mars and Saturn through the night, lacking that limiting tie with the sun which makes Venus the particular lord of the dawn or twilight, merely helped expand a primitive astrolatry.

What the planets measure must of necessity be recognized in experience itself. There is a rhythm to inorganic reality, long before a perspective arises with the equally rhythmic self-assertion of conscious life. Thus the seasons and other natural phenomena of a cyclic sort exist before man employs them, although he creates the convenience which they instrument. Momentums always evolve out of other ones, giving origin in turn to more of their kind. Regularity as such is not significant, as has been pointed out; only the transition from one phase to another. Any integration of circumstances, indicated in horoscopy by the planets through their cycles, charts the relation of self to the potentialities which sustain it, and this is the basis for any astrological overview of the individual's further potentials in their everyday significance.

Experience is always a matter of conscious action or reaction, never the case of a completely passive receptivity. Self-assertion is the outreach of self in an inauguration or adoption of fresh momentums, therefore, never a mere coasting along upon the basis of repetitions dismissed to automaticity. No cycles are knowable of themselves, as already indicated. Any self-act is evident in a quickening of some potentiality, with a resulting regrasp of reality. Astrology charts a doing, even if this be no more than the willful maintenance of a change-lessness. The planets are acting, even in their extreme of regularity or non-deviation.

THE MEASURE OF DEVIATION

Dare to be wise: begin! He who postpones the hour
of living rightly is like the rustic who waits for the
river to run out before he crosses, yet on it glides
and will glide on forever.

HORACE, *Epistles*

Success gravitates to those individuals with the ability to press forward, or to make new starts and act creatively in all possible situations. This does not mean that the irresponsible souls are the ones on whom fortune will look with the greatest favor, but rather that those who know how to assert themselves properly will achieve ultimate mastery in the life that swirls about them. They preserve a dynamic foundation for their own reality by their continual employment of the patterns of activity established in their own special make-up. By their constructive procrastination they escape every limiting momentum. They demonstrate an irrepressibility, not an incompetency. They are resourceful rather than happy-go-lucky. They put limitation to use, rather than suffering it, simply because they have order under contract to their self-assertion.

Patience and law-abiding conformity to the rules of society have their place in life, obviously, yet the supineness of a populace serves the purposes of tyranny as nothing else. This is illustrated often enough. Thus a long line of automobiles waits at a railroad crossing. A collegiate chassis with a party of adolescents comes rattling and coughing down the wrong side of the narrow two-lane road, arrives at the gates just as they start to lift, and cuts over to the right out of the way of the counter traffic at just the exact moment to weave ahead of the whole properly regimented and more respectable chain of cars. No great spiritual injustice is revealed. There is always a place for the extremely individualistic factor in a statistically ordered universe, provided only that the self-assertion be creatively real. A person cannot become blindly anarchistic with any degree of social reward, but he may well learn that the cosmic orderliness exists, primarily and in every true sense, for those things which he dismisses to automaticity in natural course. These may, indeed, prove to be the vast bulk of acts and reactions through which he remains himself, but only in the background of the major processes through which he asserts his own continuance. Eccentricity or difference is a root necessity of personal existence or identity in any definable form. Anything that is without distinction is devoid of self-capacity, since it then melts into the indeterminate mass of an unknown and unknowable indefiniteness.

The principle here has had an apt and dramatic illustration in the field of astronomy, through the discovery of Neptune as the result of a purely theoretical analysis of deviations in the conduct of Uranus. The latter planet, found a half century earlier, showed the unmistakable gravitational influence of some more distant solar satellite. The momentum of the nearer body was not sufficiently non-deviate to be dismissed as the mere ground of its existence. The reality was critical or alive in the sense that the cycle was irregular, showing the co-operation of a potentiality as yet undiscovered, that is, not yet reduced to the status of a static fact.

The irregularities in planetary movements actually appear to increase in a progressive series with the addition of orbits to the sun's system—while at the same time diminishing in observable effect, on to infinity—and the same phenomenon is common in organic existence. Thus the appearance of some limitation, as a distractive factor producing an irregularity in the cycles of experience, identifies an unrealized or unutilized potentiality which must be turned to account. Thereupon the deviation becomes a moral dynamic, a new possible momentum of personal value, whether its urge is to an actual cyclic transition or to an adjustment in existing patterns.

The planets in horoscopy represent the basic potentials of activity because, as they move around the entire heavenly vault with differing positions and patterns in the zodiac and celestial equator, they can be used to dramatize the ramification of individual deviation in every possible pattern of self-assertiveness. The solar system must be viewed, not only as the physical instrumentation of cosmic order, but as an accurate reflection of the universal statistically coherent eccentricities of existence on the terrestrial globe. Thus these ten bodies are of the greatest value in their most marked deviation from ideal or mathematical norm. Their exceptionality provides the correlation to human events.

They are employed, astrologically, as seen by the eye or telescope, since the earth is central in the frame of reference. The increased distinctiveness of planetary conduct, arising largely from this geocentric rather than heliocentric point of view, is the most important source of their astrological meaning. Thus the sun moves with an approximate real regularity, as it takes on the orbital revolution of the earth. Next in orderly cycle is the moon, a true satellite which must revolve around the globe with only minor deviation. All the other bodies swing around the sun counterclockwise through the ecliptic, each of course moving in its own orbit. Those which are closest to the sun, still the center of the energy system, have the fastest zodiacal motion as a necessity of celestial dynamics. Since all are viewed from the earth, their movement becomes highly irregular, leading to recurrent periods of retrograde motion. The situation in such a case is not unlike that of trains operating at different speeds on adjacent tracks. A local may move forward, yet seem to be backing up when observed from an express which overhauls it. RETROGRADA-TION is highly important in skilled horoscopic judgment, not in changing the particular implication of the planet so moving, but in charting a subjective condition, due to the special excess of control, in a sense, by the earth itself.

The sun and moon are termed planets in astrology, a convenient if somewhat loose extension of meaning for that word, and they are treated precisely the same as the other bodies. The earth itself, in becoming the basis for the geocentric scheme, disappears from active consideration. The fixed stars provide the general background in charting the planetary positions, since any movements or changes among them are too slight for any but the most technical and hypotetical measurement. Meteors, and all irregular bodies, encountered at closer range in their approach to the terrestrial atmosphere, lack sufficient regularity or predictability to be of much practical use, although a few of them, as Halley's comet, have had suggestive possibilities. Planetary fragments, such as the asteroids, are for the major part too small to be employed effectively, and there are no adequate tabulations of their positions. The satellites of the other planets, as the prominent moons of many among them, have no measurable distinction in geocentric reference. The rule may be put down, however, that anything changing place in the sky against the relative motionlessness of the starry field can be given astrological validity. Hence planets are used as they are discovered, although horoscopy is not bound to its heavenly bodies in any specific sense. Each particular one of them is valuable, but not essential, so that no difficulty results from the lack of an integrated solar satellite between Mars and Jupiter.

Astrological practicality has been able to accomplish much in the other direction, by utilizing wholly intangible elements of celestial relationship. Phenomena which under other circumstances might be the result of a planet's presence in the operation of the closed system of energy can be accepted as the basis for a theoretical planet, and have horoscopic validity, as in the case of the suggested but probably non-existent intramercurial Vulcan. The fact that Neptune is an exception to the orderly arrangement of the other solar satellites including Pluto, according to Bode's law, does not militate against its value in the stellar art. Arabian astrology has made quite effective use of these oddities, including the functional stresses identified by the intersection of orbits and the like. The Moslem astrologers endowed the horoscope with multitudinous nodes and parts, taking subordinate relations between various points of the chart, whether symbolical or actual, and giving a ramification of significant focuses which, with proper skill, may have as high value in horoscopic indication as the actual physical bodies. Indeed, these mental constructs may be treated in exactly the same way as planets. The mid-points of relation are an extreme example of this procedure, and the employment of planetary positions in a projection or extension of time relations—the background of all work with progressions or directions—is another instance of it.

DRAMA IN THE SKIES

*There is one glory of the sun, and another glory
of the moon, and another glory of the stars; for
one star differeth from another star in glory.*

I Corinthians, 15:41

The planets are very real masses of matter, administering the kaleidoscopic stresses of the self-contained energy-system in which man has no less a part, at least in proportion to his gravitational bulk. Their practical relation to him is that of the general to the specific, so that they may be said to represent his potentialities as these are founded upon the common cycles of momentum in one or another direction of his experience. The planets are players in his drama of the skies, identifying symbolical limb buds in his zodiacal organism and charting processes by which it is conditioned and refined. Each has its own character, with a statistical correlation to some one of the basic ways of acting by which he continues to be what he is. All together, they reveal the pattern of his individuality. As focuses of cosmic activity in the larger scheme, they become the dynamic indicators of his momentums and capacities in the smaller. They are actors in the comedy or tragedy of himself as this is portrayed on the heavenly screen, and each has the implication it gains from its complete attention to its own business as an active body in the field of energy.

THE SUN is obviously the most important of astrology's planets, and it takes its position as a moving body in the geocentric scheme by replacing the earth. Its apparent motion is in its satellite's orbit, at the exact opposite point in the zodiac from the globe's actual position. This fact expresses, rather accurately in astrology's naïve symbolism, the most direct possible terrestrial outlook in terms of zodiacal perspective. Hence it represents, in horoscopy, the prime focus in the total situation which the earth, through the horizon established on its surface, makes manifest in man's existence. By the logic of suggestive parallels between planetary and human experience, the sun indicates the central or fundamental factor in any given reality because (1) it provides the most regular of all zodiacal movements, and also (2) determines the ordering

221

or designation of time *per se,* both diurnally and annually. In taking the earth's place, it occupies the fourth position among the ten planets in the sequence through which much of their nature is determined, and this means that it was actually central or focal in the original Chaldean system of seven. Although no one ever refers to this body by name, but rather designates it descriptively as the sun, it is properly known as Sol. There is far less relationship with Greco-Roman mythology than in the case of the true solar satellites, and no attempt has been made to associate the astrological sun with Apollo, into whom the earlier but minor worship of Sol or Helios was assimilated. Its symbol is the circle, suggesting infinite and undesignated potentiality, with the point or symbolization of manifestation placed at the center to indicate its fundamentally focalizing activity. Here is self-assertion at simple root.

THE MOON takes the place of the sun as the starting point in astrological sequence among the planets. Its name is Luna, but like the sun it is identified in common practice by the descriptive term. It has horoscopic primacy because of its exceptional swiftness of motion, and its intimate relation with the earth as a true satellite. Its greater speed enables it to distribute the implication of the other planets through the minutiae of everyday circumstances. As the general executor of the dynamic relations in the native's pattern of activity, it shows his degree of conscious self-participation in events, and becomes the indicator of emotion or of personal experience in its broadest possible potentiality. Moons in general are not regarded by occultists as the evolutionary offspring of a parent body—the common astronomical theory—but instead as the residual elements of original source material which the larger mass has failed to build into the substance of its being, hence aggregates of star-stuff from which it derives a sort of inverse, queer and psychic nutriment or support. This hypothesis, popularized by medieval thinkers, runs through the whole structure of lunar superstition. The light of the moon has been regarded as baneful throughout man's history, and the observable correspondence between its phases and meteorological phenomena, tidal cycles, parturition, and the like have led men to respect and fear it. Mythology early expanded man's instinctive sense of an organic link with this queen of the night, an idea taken over into astrological symbolism far more definitely than any relation with Artemis, Diana or the Roman goddess known as Luna. Its close functional association with the earth has made the moon the astrological indicator of life process *per se* in quite a literal fashion. Its symbol is the circle of infinite potentiality as this is bent in half and folded back upon itself to become the crescent, suggesting the reflexive self-awareness or fundamentally organic self-assertion which it dramatizes.

⊕

While the EARTH is not used as a planet in a geocentric astrology, its symbol is employed for the Part of Fortune in the Arabian system.[1] The ideogram consists of the cross of matter—or the double dichotomy of the equatorial house-axes, representing experience in general—set in the circle of infinite potentiality.

With the cross, the three essential components in the graphic symbolism of the original seven Chaldean indicators have been introduced, comprising a special notation for the drama in the skies. The CIRCLE, in its most simple significance, becomes the ideogram for spirit, or for infinity *per se*. It suggests a constancy of approximation to the ideal, which can

[1] The Part of Fortune is used widely, as a favorable indicator, together with the moon's north and south nodes, or dragon's head ☊ and tail ☋, as significators of special protection and self-undoing, respectively.

have no specific existence, and offers the most basic generalization possible in the form of any figure. It can be visualized as a regular polygon with an infinite number of sides, representing spirit as the constancy of experience through the illimitability of its own potentials. The CRESCENT, or the half-circle which is used in the composite ideograms rather than the original or conventionalized pictograph of the increasing moon, is a character for soul in its simple form, i.e., that which by nature is part spirit and part spiritually incomplete, hence under necessity to fulfill itself. The CROSS, apart from the particular theological meaning it has acquired, suggests the basic idea of a self-assertion operating vertically from spiritual resources and horizontally from a focalized self-consciousness or personality, and so establishing a self-identity in experience or everyday self-discovery. Hence it comes to represent MATTER as the allegorical crucifixion of spirit.

$$\male\kern-0.4em\female$$

MERCURY is first of the actual planets in the solar system, considering their orbits heliocentrically or outward from their common center. It becomes second in the astrological or symbolical order, following the moon. The name comes from Greco-Roman mythology, where Mercury is the Latin equivalent of Hermes, and the designation probably arose from the association of communication or messenger capacities with both the planet's activity and the wing-footed Olympian god. Its symbol expresses its directness of relation to the solar source, on the one hand, and to the necessary singleness of self-assertion as a ramification out from this center, on the other. This is because the ideogram of spirit, placed upon and dominating the one for matter, is surmounted by the pictograph for soul with its points upward, calling for a universal self-fulfillment out of a purely personal experience.

$$\female$$

VENUS is the planet next in order of solar orbit from Mercury, hence it holds third position in the ancient sequence. The name is that of the Latin goddess corresponding to Aphrodite, and the astrological implication links esthetic and other summations with the concept of love typified by the romantic lady of Olympus. These correlations between planets and mythological figures are quite superficial on the whole, remaining little more than a convenience of nomenclature. The immortal hierarchies of popular Greco-Roman religion originated through a rather casual stringing together of various dramatizations of natural law and superstition, during an age when graphic suggestion seemed much more important than logical consistency. The myths offer high symbolism for the planets, but they give no effective description of the planetary activities in actual human affairs. Aphrodite's cults were many in number, often divergent from each other in their main features, and with practices which certainly would give a wrong notion of the astrological implication in modern times. The symbol of Venus is the ideogram for spirit poised on that for matter. This indicates a self-assertion which subordinates physical realities to the conscious act-of-self, and which seeks to resolve all experience in some sort of personal satisfaction.

♂

MARS is the first planet beyond the earth in the solar system, and it holds fifth position in the ancient order, ranking next after the sun in fourth. Its name is from the Latin deity identified with the Greek god Ares, and the symbolism arises from the fact that the warrior, among human occupations, was once the figure of chivalry and creative initiative. Because the disgraceful antics of the immortals in the familiar Olympian stories have completely unseated the ideals originally deified, a notion of bestiality has attached itself to the planet, along with every possible destructiveness of war and pestilence. The symbolization of Mars exactly reverses that of Venus, but the pictograph has been conventionalized with the cross of matter becoming a scorpion's sting. Since the ideograms of these two planets are employed commonly in biological notation to represent male and female distinctions, special care is needed to keep the one from indicating a primarily feminine expression, and the other a specific masculine emphasis. The original form of the Martial symbol has been employed at different times, with or without modification, to identify the earth, Uranus and Pluto, which fact must be remembered in examining various astrological materials. The symbolism dramatizes a self-assertion of the sort which demands that spirit be subordinated to matter, or that a practical employment be given to spiritual potentials.

♃

JUPITER is the next planet out from the sun in the position of its orbit, occupying sixth place in the ancient order and representing the first of two ideas in the earlier astrology's effort to measure a transcendence of merely physical relationships. It is named after the Latin ruler of Olympus, in correspondence to Zeus, a selection which probably symbolized man's conscious and effective manipulation of circumstances according to his own desires and needs. The astrological designation took over none of the god's lecherous significance, but instead presented the unalloyed good fortune and the full favor of nature which Jupiter was supposed to command. The ideogram of soul is placed upon the cross of matter, but the arrangement is conventionalized with the former facing east from the horizontal or rising point of the house axis, thus emphasizing a type of self-assertion which is particularly eager to enter upon experience, or to give wholesouledly of itself in the act of being.

♄

SATURN is the seventh and final planet in the original group.

Its name comes from the Latin god corresponding to Cronus, one of the Titans and so a superior deity to Zeus in the hierarchical arrangement. Through what was apparently a confusion of his name with chronos, the Greek word for time, he became known as a god of cycles, and this notion has crept into astrology to give the planet a rulership over all time succession, an idea supported to some extent by the fact that its period in years is close to that of the moon in days. Saturn's symbol originally was the exact reverse of Jupiter's, but it has become much more highly conventionalized. It dramatizes self-assertion as a willingness to undergo experience in a subjective rather than objective fashion, suggesting a sensitiveness quickened by the compulsion of material necessity, i.e., the ideogram of soul placed at the nadir of the material cross.

♅

URANUS, also known as Herschel for a considerable period after its discovery by Sir William Herschel in 1781, is the first of three new planets located in modern times, and it occupies the eighth position in Chaldean order as extended by the necessity for including the newcomers in astrological techniques.[2] Its name is taken from the Greek personification of the heavens, head of a mythological dynasty superior to the Titans in the same way that they held priority over the Olympians. Here is a symbolization of a self-assertion directed towards the illimitable, or of human life as newly manifest in some enlarged dimension of self-act. The pictograph of Uranus, expressing powers beyond normal activity and capacity, is fundamentally phallic, although it came into being quite fortuitously or in much the same manner as the best of human symbolism. Superficially it is the initial letter of Herschel with a planet suspended from the crossbar, but it can be described

[2] Chaldean order was originally the sequence of Saturn, Jupiter, Mars, sun, Venus, Mercury and moon, which creates the planetary hour and day rulerships.

more fundamentally as the ideogram for male potency combined with a limiting or conditioning fence or ladder, thus representing the necessity for personal re-orientation in a greater reality.

$$\Psi$$

NEPTUNE, second of the new planets and ninth in position by the modernized Chaldean order, was discovered in 1846, and soon was named from the Latin diety who in his correspondence to Poseidon was lord of the seas, and who suggested the source of all experience in the eternal roots or springs of being. This dramatized the form of self-assertion by which an individual distributes his total obligation to society, or is compelled to do so, whether or no. The symbol superficially is the god's trident. More basically it is also phallic, suggesting the operation of a deeper reference in human capability, or illimitable personal capacity, through a modified pictograph of the female power in nature. As in the case of the Mars and Venus symbolization, the Uranus and Neptune ideograms do not involve masculine or feminine distinctions.

$$\cancel{\varphi}$$

PLUTO, third of the new planets and tenth in position by the modernized Chaldean order, was discovered in 1930, and named after the god of the nether regions more usually called Hades by the Greeks and Dis by the Romans. The lower world symbolizes the farthest or most ultimate possibility of extension in consciousness, and as such typifies the actual function of the planet in horoscopic procedure. The symbolization again is fortuitous, but the pictograph has not yet gained a universal acceptance in astrological practice, and so has a number of forms. The astronomers generally have settled upon a monogram made up of the first two letters, or ℗, and this is employed by many astrologers. As above, and in this and most recent American texts, the universalized upreach of soul embraces the circle of spirit, while resting on the cross of matter. This shows self-assertion through the creation of an illimitable potential for the orientation of self, rather than the mere communicating or messenger activity represented by Mercury, the other planet closest in nature to Pluto.

Additional Note on the Planetary Symbols

The symbol of Mercury is also identified as the caduceus of Hermes, or his head and a winged cap. The pictograph of Venus is variantly taken as the goddess' lookingglass, which euphemistically covers the phallic indication whenever it becomes a simple ideogram for female in biological literature. The representation of the earth is sometimes explained as showing the four quarters of the globe. The pictograph for Mars is occasionally described as the head, helmet and nodding plume of a warrior, or as his shield and spear, and this again is a cover for the indication of male functioning in the biologist's shorthand. The symbol of Jupiter is identified at times as the conventionalized delineation of an eagle, or as the letter Z of Zeus with a line through it to indicate an abbreviation. The ideogram of Saturn may be recognized as a primitive scythe or sickle, taken as an emblem of time.

TABLE X

The Ten Astrological Planets and Their Symbols

THE SUN (Sol)	☉	Infinite potentiality in manifestation
THE MOON (Luna)	☽	Infinite potentiality in awareness
MERCURY	☿	Soul lifting spirit out of matter
VENUS	♀	Spirit supreme over matter
MARS	♂	Matter supreme over spirit
JUPITER	♃	Soul on the ascendant of matter
SATURN	♄	Soul at the nadir of matter
URANUS (Herschel)	♅	Self-potency entirely uninhibited
NEPTUNE	♆	Self-potency entirely circumscribed
PLUTO	♇	Soul creating spirit out of matter

CHAPTER THIRTEEN

Patterns of Simple Expediency

Self-assertion must be identified and measured through its impact upon tangible elements in experience. Considered in any special sense apart from circumstances and function, activity is unknowable, remaining a generalization. Whenever the astrologer attempts to get the act-of-self disentangled from the totality of its involvements, he succeeds only in putting his own point of view in the vacuum he has hoped to create for his examination. He becomes at once a victim of what William James identified as the psychological fallacy, merely uncovering the reflection of his own ideas. Men of necessity see themselves in others, since the single vision has its own characteristic twist. In consequence the judgment of anyone must rest upon a common experience, never upon any supposed grasp of individual differences in isolation. The actual assertiveness of a given person is recognizable only as others are able to share in its implication. Hence astrology is compelled to chart all activity in terms of its significance within a social complex.

This means that an act-of-self is measurable not at source, but rather in its terminal relations, or through the ends to which it is directed. Action is knowable as it has an object, therefore, or as it can be described in some phase of purpose, move towards potentiality or response to possibility. The planets dramatize this, whether in terms of momentum or capacity, as simple EXPEDIENCY, i.e., activity objectified or reduced to measurement. There are four patterns of simple expediency by which man becomes sovereign within the periphery of his own consciousness, in both large or small compass and for both long or short periods. Thus he can (1) alter the emphasis in his own life processes, (2) re-examine and modify the personal values which motivate him, (3) change the superficial situation in which he finds himself, and (4) create new significance in the over-all social reality. These modes of self-assertion, to be explained at length in the following pages, constitute the four domains of activity in the astrological schematism. They correspond in fundamental fashion to the four worlds of experience in circumstances, and to the four alchemies in function.

The geometrical basis for the equatorial and ecliptical mansions gives a certain rigidity to the fourfold and similar distinctions among them, but these groupings of the planets are no less grounded in a fundamental unity—since they map the total activity of a closed system of energy—despite the fact that the domains can as easily be three, as they once were, or five, as is possible with Pluto's discovery. The utilization of four provides a closer parallel to the house and sign schemes, thereby aiding the mind's organization of these relations. The classification is obviously a logical construct which does not exist in nature but which does, nonetheless, give an understandable form to the actual unity charted by the planetary interrelations. This is an organic completeness which follows of necessity from the fact that the positions of the planets, as well as their significations, are established by the earth, very literally.

The criteria by which the planetary bodies are arranged in groups are (1) sequence in the heliocentric places of the orbits, (2) relative swiftness of mean geocentric movement, (3) adjacency of orbital situation to the earth or sun, (4) special affinity in physical characteristics, and (5) date of discovery or entrance into human experience. The first two of these standards have a positive correlation, and it is not necessary to distinguish between them in identifying the fundamental pairs, although both considerations have their part in creating the symbolism.

Of the ten planets now employed by astrologers, the sun and moon stand apart from the rest, and are known as the luminaries or LIGHTS. The first of these takes on the earth's own zodiacal motion, and becomes the positive member of the pair. The other, as the only true satellite of the earth, becomes the negative. Their mathematical relationship to the ecliptic is that of no deviation in a direct orbital circling, a species of self-sufficiency which couples them in the drama of the skies as the domain of VITALITY. They present, together, the greatest regularity of geocentric movement, and they also differ from the other eight bodies in the fact that neither is a solar satellite.

Mars and Venus occupy orbits adjacent to the ecliptic and can be said to represent the practical nextness of relationship to the earth, thus symbolizing everyday activity or a continual immediateness in experience. The superior planet, as astronomers designate the former, presents the positive factor as the simple outreach of self-assertion to superficial potentialities. The inferior body charts the negative implication, or the lean back upon the surface momentums in normal life. These two, therefore, establish the domain of EFFICIENCY. In their geocentric mean motion they are quite close to each other—identical with the sun in the case of Venus, and showing their near approach to the earth's norm—and in physical makeup they have the greatest degree of demonstrated affinity with the sphere on which man finds himself. They become a horoscopic pair on the pattern of the sun and moon, very naturally.

Jupiter and Saturn, outermost of the seven bodies known to the ancient and medieval astrologers, are linked as a third pair by the lack of (1) that adjacency in orbit to the ecliptic which brings Mars and Venus together, and (2) the special relation to the earth which couples the sun (as a geocentric body) and moon, as well also as by (3) the slowness of their mean motion and (4) the relatively slight condensation of matter which characterizes them as physical masses. This consistency of both remoteness and alien nature has constituted them the domain of MOTIVATION, or of man's subjective disjunction. The nearer body of the two becomes the positive member of the group because its positon suggests the mediative function by which the cosmos is drawn inward to man in a rather symbolical sense, the outer planet thereupon suggesting the corresponding negative distribution of man's conscious substance back and out into a universal totality. The greater intimacy of indication provided by this domain, in contrast with the superficial relations charted by Mars and Venus, gives it second place in the fourfold schematism.

Uranus and Neptune have a special kinship through (1) their relatively recent date of discovery, (2) the progressively outward positons of their respective orbits as solar satellites in relation to Saturn, with (3) their consequent increasing deliberateness of zodiacal movement, added to the fact that (4) they are invisible without a telescope.[1] They create the domain of social efficiency or SIGNIFICANCE. Uranus, as the nearer and first discovered of the two, becomes the positive member. The basic theory behind all meanings assigned to the three new planets is that they should parallel, in their indication, whatever factors in racial history have come into actuality more or less coincidentally with the years when they were identified in the heavens. Thus they have been given rulerships over specific activities and inventions unknown at the time the older books were compiled, such as the telegraph, telephone, motion pictures, radio broadcasting, airtravel and the like. Also they have been welcomed as a sort

---

[1] Uranus can be seen by the eye alone at times, but would be hardly distinguished as a planet, indeed, it was not recognized as such, even with the use of the telescope, for nearly two centuries.

of catchall for those things which astrologers with insufficient skills were unable to fine in a horoscope with the other bodies alone.

Modern astrology actually encounters a unique human society. It is one marked by a growing universal interdependence, and it reflects a machine age which has developed concurrently with the almost complete disappearance of the world's frontiers. The ravages of war and pestilence, the consistent deficiencies in food and other essentials of health and economic stability throughout the earlier periods, kept down populations and permitted each social group to remain essentially primitive, at least definitely discrete. A world-wide trade existed, but it concentrated on luxury articles. With the Renaissance, however, life achieved a larger potential. The mechanical inventions, following upon the socio-economic revolution, completely redistributed the people of the globe. Cities were built on a entirely new pattern, and society was recreated in such a way that few if any units could depend upon their own hinterland. As long as available frontier country provided for the general overflow from social pressures, the old modes of life could continue to function, and they did so. For them the more simple, three-domain or older Chaldean astrology was wholly adequate. But with the exhaustion of all possibility for more horizontal expansion, the economic strain became wholly internal, giving social growth a vertical dimension. A different basic way of life became necessary for the first time in the many long millennia of known history, and the three outermost planets have their major usefulness in charting the new problems to be solved.

Mercury, originally the odd planet when its six fellows were paired, and now Pluto, an equally extraneous body which is significant through its discovery in the present generation, are much alike through the exceptional irregularities in the position and shape of their orbits. Thus they stand apart from their eight companions in the stellar drama no less sharply, if more subtly, than the luminaries and other pairs, and it would be entirely possible to constitute them a fifth group. A more practical end is achieved, however, by viewing them as supernumerary bodies, each serving within the domain of activity where its position and motion naturally classify it otherwise, and thereby providing a means for mapping a specially mediative type of self-assertion. This technique is more effective than any establishment of the additional pair because it adds a dimension to the more simple or basic business of being, permitting the two planets to become indicators of heightened potentials, greater skills and abnormally stimulating or inspiring agencies in man's modern experience.

Here is the one-remove perspective, found as a vicarious or entirely theoretical and tentative act-of-self, i.e., a purely mental or intellectual activity. It is something which has always been identified through Mercury as mind, and through Pluto it is charted as the new vertical outlook or instinct in a mass intelligence. The first of the two mental indicators—in this assignment of their dramatic roles for the purposes of horoscopy—takes its place as a supporting player in the domain of efficiency, where it has the same type of mean motion as Mars and Venus, and Pluto is given the task of delineating the current generalized trends of thought, the broad lines of racial interest, in the domain of social significance.

The four domains of simple positive and negative potentialities are unified continually in the total act-of-self. Each of them charts a special degree of co-operation with some one of the others, depending on whether the emphasis is upon (1) circumstances, or a problem of time and place, (2) function, or a problem of character, and (3) activity, or a problem of more or less assertion. Thus VITALITY is personal with MOTIVATION in any emphasis upon circumstances, is objective with EFFICIENCY in any emphasis upon function, and is conjunctive with SIGNIFICANCE in any emphasis upon activity. EFFICIENCY is impersonal with SIGNIFICANCE in any emphasis upon circumstances, and is disjunctive with MOTIVATION in any emphasis upon activity. MOTIVATION is subjective with SIGNIFICANCE in any emphasis upon function. Here is the anatomy of planetary relationship, corresponding to the interweaving of axial and triadic distinctions in the houses, and of quadrature and triplicity in the signs.

TABLE XI

The Anatomy of Planetary Relationship

Planetary Domain	Circumstances	Function	Activity
VITALITY Sun, moon	Personal	Objective	Conjunctive
MOTIVATION Jupiter, Saturn	Personal	Subjective	Disjunctive
EFFICIENCY Mars, Venus, Mercury	Impersonal	Objective	Disjunctive
SIGNIFICANCE Uranus, Neptune, Pluto	Impersonal	Subjective	Conjunctive

Planets which together constitute one of these domains whenever significantly linked in a given horoscopic pattern, show the particular specialized act-of-self to be a conflict between positive, negative and supernumerative phases of an individual's more narrowed experience as perhaps constituting certain of his basic momentums. Contrariwise, planets more essentially different in their nature and symbolism are, when so linked, significant in their measurement of an outreaching towards a greater self-fulfillment, thereupon suggesting—according to the table—that an individual's interest or proper concern is a matter of broad issues in circumstances, function or activity, as the case may be. Significant linking, as far as this text is concerned, is the position of two or more of these bodies in the same house or sign. The relation through planetary ASPECTS, while adding a real dimension to horoscopic analysis, is beyond the scope of the present survey.[2] The classification of the sun as positive, personal,

---

[2] A simple but adequate outline of the aspects will be found in the author's *How to Learn Astrology*, to which reference has been made in the footnote on page 26. The full treatment of this vital factor in both the basic and the dynamic horoscopy is provided in the larger context of analytical postulation by a seventh volume in the major series, *Fundamentals of Number Significance*, still in preparation.

objective and conjunctive is exactly akin to the designation of Aries as positive, northern, fiery and cardinal, and of the first house as angular, horizontal, occidental, of the self's triad and below the earth.

VITALITY: SELF-ASSERTION IN PURE MOMENTUM

> *Life is a pure flame, and we live by an*
> *invisible sun within us.*
> SIR THOMAS BROWNE, *Hydriotaphia*

The sun and moon, in any horoscope, reveal the pattern of expediency by which the native gives attention to the necessities of life itself. They do this because their cycles afford the closest approximation to the rhythms of individual identity. The sun, the positive indicator, takes the keyword PURPOSE, and the moon, or negative or complementary focus of living as such, is FEELING.

The Sun

The sun as an indicator of purpose shows self-assertion through its most simple and essentially naïve impact on life in general. It reveals the character at its point of greatest consistency in circumstances, or where the native is most indomitably himself in welcoming or creating the sort of situation in which he feels the most comfortable. The heredity—all family and racial background—is manifest through the will in this necessary fidelity of itself to itself, hence the horoscopic typification of the individual, that is, the astrological dramatization of the being as a whole, has its basis in the sun's place. It has been pointed out that a person's appearance gets its broad outline here, the ascendant showing the environment modifications, and the moon (or some special aggregation of planetary bodies on rare occasion) adding elements of manner, and perhaps even physical deviation, as the manifestation of any overlying subtle, psychic and wholly intangible influences. Individuals tend to conform predominantly, in their

237

external appearance and characteristics, to (1) the sun sign, (2) the rising sign or (3) to the sign containing the moon (or exceptional grouping of planets). A TYPING indicated by the sun testifies to special directness in the life, the native largely fulfilling the converging lines of his blood and training throughout his act of being himself. This is in contrast to the case where an ascendant-typed person holds more consistently to circumstantial leading, or where a moon-typed person remains essentially deviate by all normal standards. Where the sun is prominent or focal in the planetary patterning, the life is inclined to function more simply, on the one hand, and with an excess of ego or unconditioned self-reliance, on the other. Contrariwise, the native's career is shaped rather opportunistically—by the actual events constituting his unfolding experience—whenever this planet has no particular horoscopic emphasis, and when he does not particularly favor its sign indications.

Will, the primary self-assertion of any person, differs from the identity in the fact that the latter, a circumstantial indication, is the composite of the self as known in surface and wholly exterior contact with others. The will remains the eternal core of personal being, totally unconditioned and necessarily devoid of dependence on anything other than itself. Here is the focus of all existence in its dynamic potentiality of continuing to be whatever it is. This is what can say "I," and what in consequence is identified as the ego or entity presupposed to stand behind or beyond qualification. Hence the sun provides the measure of inherent integrity or self-confidence, i.e., the act-of-self as viewed entirely in its own terms. All the other planets show a form of activity which depends on this inner or under and unswerving flow of the being. There is a foundation sequence of personal reality in the fact that a self is experiencing its own existence. The ramifications of personality are an addition to this, somewhat after the fashion of beads strung on a cord. The sun presents the practical more or less of the native's simple continuance as the phenomenon of identity *per se*, revealing how and under what conditions he may increase or decrease his personal reality by what adds up to an activity of will. The power to do nothing certifies his capacity to do anything or everything in any given particular. Here is a pattern of expediency shown in the horoscope by the sun's relations. The will is (1) positive because it acts in and of itself, (2) personal because it has no possible connection with anything which it refuses to accept as its concern, (3) objective because it instruments the utterly direct and unmediated relations of self to everything other than self, and (4) conjunctive because it centers reality within itself through its own self-assertion. Hence the sun is the planet of individuality *per se*, the continuingly original act-of-being underlying experience.

The Moon

The moon, in its indication of feeling, shows the self's act of being itself in its most simple and essentially naïve response to external stimulus. It reveals the character at its point of greatest pliability in circumstances, or where the native is most completely unconditioned in his ability and willingness to go along with any given phase or direction of human activity. Thus the planet measures the particular receptivity to experience in the pattern of a given life—which is the negative expression of vitality—and this has two important horoscopic implications. In the first place the moon charts any lack of self-restraint. This can have adverse consequences, contributing to a very primitive spread of the being, or what may be a complete absence both of privacy and of any desire for it. In the second place, it patterns an indivdual's personal touch with his total context of reality, the possibilities as well as actualities of all general relations with other people, thereby establishing the point of public emphasis and impact in any astrological wheel. This is where feeling is grounded on the lowest level, to become a more specialized emotion whenever these contacts with the outer and practical world, at any phase in their manifestation, begin either to encourage or threaten the act-of-self in its negative phase of vitality, that is, its wholly instinctive more or less of unconditioned response. The moon in consequence reveals experience as it has yet to acquire the modifications in self-assertion which the other planets measure. Hence this swiftest of the ten bodies becomes the natural distributor of personal relationships in events, a role often compared by astrologers to that of the minute hand on a clock, or the second hand on a watch. The lunar indications in everyday counseling are largely neutral in this sense, carrying the implications of the other bodies to every minutiæ of function and circumstances, and so ever demonstrating the nature of vitality in its receptive aspect. Here is the general activity of pure organic functioning.

The moon is negative because it maps the basic response of self to everything other than itself, but it is as personal as the sun in having no concern with that which does not enter dynamically into the substance of being. It charts personality, in contrast with the individuality shown by the sun. This is the warm and acquiescent focus of selfhood in living relationship. What the first house rules as the knowable aggregate of the being—that is, the point of ultimate mobilization by the self against a specific need or crisis—the moon measures in the self's fundamental experience of itself. Whatever the native constitutes the basic mood of self-assertion through his moon's sign and house is revealed by him to the world as a *fait accompli,* namely, a person, at the ascendant. Hence, if the eastern angle is the place of the moon in any native's case, he is apt to be overeager in human contacts, or prodigal in his vitality, simply because he lacks a spread through circumstances as a means for orientation in this process. Thus the lesser light is no less objective than the greater, and it is as conjunctive in respect to the minutiæ of other reality. Vitality is predominantly lunar when individual activity is peripheral rather than central. All aimless and experimental outreach of selfhood, becoming in due course a ramification of emotion, is charted by the moon. This can be sympathy as the sheer more of self in its willingness to grow, expand and increase in a dynamic fullness of itself, or antipathy in the corresponding less of self whereby, in its basic distribution of its energies, it feels itself flowing out of rather than into its own reality. The potentialities of personal feeling, in general, support the anticipatory experience of individuality in what it has yet to become in particular. Consequently the moon indicates imagination, on the constructive side, but also hallucination or psychological unbalance of every sort whenever the self-act is inadequate.

MOTIVATION: SELF-ASSERTION IN PURE CAPACITY

When a man does not know what harbor
he is making for, no wind is the right wind.
SENECA, *Epistulæ ad Lucilium*

Jupiter and Saturn, in any horoscope, reveal the pattern of expediency by which the native gives attention to the motivation of his personal activity. They do this because their cycles afford the closest approximation to the typical rhythms of a true social world. Jupiter, the positive indicator, takes the keyword ENTHUSIASM, and Saturn, the negative and complementary focus of inner life as such, is SENSITIVENESS.

Jupiter

Jupiter, in its indication of enthusiasm, is the great benefic of traditional astrology, long regarded as the most fortunate planet in the horoscope. Early astrologers visualized its activity as that of a policeman, in the sense of providing a tireless and continual protection over life, hence establishing order and bringing events in line with man's best personal interests. It measures the point of greatest factor of encouragement in a native's experience, since it reveals that natural expansiveness or indomitable spontaneity of self by which he is able, in varying degrees, to achieve the ends he desires. Because this is usually a pleasant sensation, the blessing of Jupiter has always been sought assiduously by devotees of the stellar art.

241

The planet rules the expediency in shaking off any particular shackles of limitation, and the thrill in any genuinely fresh experience. Perhaps most commonly indicating the simple joy of adventure, as in a first journey along and the like, it has a still more important role in charting the elements of self-discovery. These may be quite destructive, although very gratifying for the moment, as in prodigality and many forms of wantonness. The planet fundamentally shows the positive activity of motivation—or of life as made personal on the conscious level of responsible realization—and this is subjective, or creatively self-contemplative. Here is the deeper participation in experience, as compared with the more simple continuance in existence as an objective organism which the sun and moon reveal. It is the disjunctive self-assertion of basic selfhood, in contradistinction to the conjunctive vitality mapped by the lights, i.e., a conscious and discrete sense of self according to its own inner realization. Jupiter in the horoscope is the point of emphasis in the continuing process of birth and rebirth, as in contrast with the degeneration and death ruled by Saturn. It describes the early unfoldment of selfhood, exactly as the negative planet of motivation outlines the maturity of life, on through the declining years and up to the final withdrawal of consciousness from physical existence. Jupiter, as the positive disjunction in the personal and subjective act-of-self, shows the actual maturing—i.e., growth *per se,* especially as this remains wholly under the direction of self—but Saturn charts the surrender to exterior domination by other people, not only with the lessening of interest in living or senility but also through the formative period of discipline in childhood.

Jupiter always measures whatever serves to expand or fulfill the actual, conscious or immortal selfhood. Among other things, it gives a horoscopic clue to any tendency towards social accumulation of wealth and position as well as physical fleshiness, together with any proclivity to indulge ambitions and appetites which produce or accentuate swollen possessions, overweight and any psychological sense of importance. The quickening of the soul or conscious selfhood to the potentialities of experience becomes a native's capacity for discrimination, or good sense, the sagacity which this planet rules as in distinction from the dispassionate intelligence of Mercury. This becomes religion or spirituality as an awareness of moral or ethical standards. These values exist because they are commonly accepted, so that their pursuit facilitates a normal self-expansion. It is obvious that the individual who is inclined to destructive expression, who is appreciably anarchistic or freakish in tastes and conduct, can have but a minimal assistance from the life in which he participates. Things are not good because Jupiter identifies them, but because human society prefers them, and it is this moral preference which makes them expedient when it comes to entering into experience. Unsocially disjunctive acts are the result of weakness in character relative to some particular norm or potentiality, indicated by an inadequate emphasis of Jupiter, and any positive activity on the level of motivation is therefore, in general, a breadth of inclination towards encouraging everything at its finest, or responding on the basis of whatever best potentiality can be visualized. This is consciousness *per se,* or the type of act by which the ego becomes an actual discrete entity, capable of an immortal existence. When such a self-appreciation is exalted, as in the sense of a touch with some higher or supernal reality, the native may achieve a genuine spiritual inspiration. He may take on a priestly function among his fellows demonstrating a public spirit or a real altruism, but he may also fall short in a smugness or bigotry.

Saturn

Saturn, in its indication of sensitiveness, has a much greater concern than Jupiter with the deeper, interior and eternal phase of motivation, charting the personal self-realization as more consciously disjunctive because it is negative and essentially reflexive. Here sagacity becomes wisdom, or a completeness of inner resolution. In the astrological tradition the planet has been the dreaded great malefic, always measuring the certainty of ill in an age where men expected the worst.

What is actually shown is the uncompromising fidelity of the self's act to motivating decision, or of consequences to their contributory origins, whenever the self takes or accepts a definite set of its own. Because medieval man depreciated himself, he put himself under bondage to a certain pattern of idea, and was compelled to live in the world he established. Any uncertain individual today may prefer a definite ill, relatively easy to precipitate, than some uncertain good calling on him to expand his own powers and to develop his own constructive potentialities. This is the negative phase of motivation, or consciousness on its lowest level. More happily, however, Saturn has also been symbolized as the judge, giving assurance of a final just verdict on human intention, effort, and achievement. This is disjunction as truly subjective or creative in the sense that nothing is lost ultimately. Death is not cancellation, but rather reassignment. The negative indication of motivation, seen outwardly or from a foreview, may be the literal termination of the given life—more commonly the end of some particular cycle of experience—but this is an assurance of continuity, giving a time measure in existence by making consequences significant. The planet fundamentally charts whatever remains in consciousness as real beyond or through the focus of any particular form of interruption or superficial alteration in the self or its affairs. Thus it rules the support gained from land or exceptionally fixed possessions. Unfortunately the older astrologers saw this subjective and disjunctive persistence of personal sequence on the destructive side only—when they encountered it in the Saturnine or negative phase—and so they identified it with the self-sustaining karma of the East, or the pervading ill-fate of the Dark Ages. Because consciousness here rests so largely in the depths of its own potential, it may seem as unpleasant as the spontaneous out-spilling of Jupiter is the reverse. Hence Saturn is the point of fear or suffering in the horoscope, not as an immutably bad fortune, but rather the possibility of self-activated change. Superficially it is illness and maladjustment, but the indication may be taken much more constructively as a definite key in any problem of health. Personal subjectivity may be seen to determine the physical condition of the native, and organic well-being may be taken as conscious self-adjustment.

Saturn shows the psychological sensitiveness of a native as his self-delimitation in a personal well-being. It reveals his disjunctive withdrawal from various outworn phases of experience, sometimes smoothly and so evident as little more than a loss of interest, and equally often in quite dramatic fashion, the retreat then becoming a distinct defeat at the hands of circumstances. When such an event represents a definite embarrassment, there is real suffering or distortion in consciousness. If the situation is serious, there may be tragic concomitants. All these details are mapped by this planet in the general pattern of expediency. Sometimes the attempt at self-extrication from a situation will lead to an unwitting or deliberate and calculating deception, to an unsocial and perhaps unfair manipulation of others, or to an acceptance of a personally distorted world of treachery and criminality. Disappointment, discouragement and dissatisfaction are all forms of inadequacy in the self's disjunction in experience. The constructive mobilizations of consciousness may be no less high-strung, but in their touch with the depth of the native's potentials, in their refinement of sensitivity and their capacity for real suffering, they offer a sure foundation for further experience. Saturn thus indicates how completely the self may be stabilized within itself, individually, in a co-operation point by point with Jupiter's spontaneity.

EFFICIENCY: SELF-ASSERTION IN PURE CONVENIENCE

*The end of good is an evil, and the
end of evil is a good.*
LA ROCHEFOUCAULD, *Maximes Posthumes*

Mars, Venus and Mercury, in any horoscope, reveal the pattern of expediency by which the native gives attention to the everyday and relatively impermanent eventualities which he must manipulate in his own interest. They do this because their cycles afford the closest approximation to the rhythms of transient superficiality in ordinary experience. Mars, the positive indicator, takes the keyword INITIATIVE; Venus, the negative and complementary focus in this surface activity, is ACQUISITIVENESS; and Mercury, the supernumerary and mind factor, is MENTALITY.

Mars

Mars, in its indication of initiative, provides the basic approach for any understanding, through the horoscope, of man's day-by-day efficiency. The passing and shifting thresholds of choice or decision are his objective means for an impersonal disjunction of life's relations as he encounters them. This process of an opportunistic self-act when seen as pure convenience, is little more than efficiency in affirmation or negation, in commencement or refusal to begin. Neither vitality nor motivation are involved, since existence is now to be measured on the impersonal side, or where simple trial and error become the rule. The objective disjunction of activity is accomplished by bringing every potentiality of self and its situation to the immediate moment and location of experience, over and over again in the kaleidoscope of events. The familiar ruddy planet charts the way in which a native starts things, or the pattern of expediency under which he releases, directs and applies force or energy of a tangible sort in the world about him. It identifies the point at which each successive and experimental phase in his external affairs is inaugurated. Venus, by the same token, shows how he stops his action, completes his endeavor, or reaches the corresponding point of consummation in some given context of passing events. Mars, therefore, is pre-eminently the planet of superficial or practical impulse. This at its most aggressive extreme becomes undisciplined or brute force, and it may be manifest either in violent action against others or else in temper and a psychological and reflexive whipping of the self to a state of heat and excitement. The astrological literature has been filled with various interpretations of the dogged or unquench- able martial energy, not always making it clear that there is no potential of self-continuance in the expenditure. Here, rather than the persistence of the personal planets, is a reiter- ative or recurrent effort which not only requires stimulus but a continued restimulus also. An overcoming of resistance to self, through some inertia exterior to self, is always involved. This may or may not imply a species of actual conflict, but it necessarily includes an act of precipitating or inaugurating, whether conventional or original in nature, and whether lead- ing to approval or disapproval.

Life, in its general or impersonal efforts towards the recog- nition or disjunction of reality, is highly competitive, and Mars represents a native's simple effort to capitalize upon whatever element of conflict seems to concern him. This is the aggres- siveness at the root of all objective experience of self in its relations to its everyday world. Manifest constructively, it is generosity and courage, but in its inadequacy it becomes ill- temper and the high destructivenesss of fear. Mars in the horoscope reveals the fashion in which anyone finds the things at hand most useful, thereupon seeking to control them without assimilating himself to them in any personal degree. Here is the foundational self-assertion underlying all skill, or trained and habitual distinctions of an impersonal and objec- tive nature. It is activity which is potentially creative as it leads to the development and refinement of methods for ac- complishing specific tasks. In consequence the planet rules mechanization and technical as well as manual dexterity, both in their perfection and their employment. This does not mean outstanding inventiveness, or any true genius with its neces- sarily subjective foundations, but the direct and impersonal employment of tools and instrumentalities in all cases where they remain convenient agencies for the simple and immedi- ate inauguration or administration of act in response to stimu- lus.

Venus

Venus, as an indicator of acquisitiveness, complements Mars—as has already been indicated—by showing how man stops or completes action, or consummates his relations with all factors immediately at hand in experience. The negative phase of the impersonal and disjunctive self-assertion represented by this planet is found in two entirely distinct forms of expediency, however, both of which constitute the termination of activity on the level of everyday efficiency, but each of which may seem very much the contrary of the other. First is the careful preservation of things in general, whether animate or inanimate, and whether a matter of tangible objects or of the transient ties and relations among them. This is terminal to the act-of-self in the sense of a dismissal to automaticity. It is a direct and conscientious cherishing of something at the stage when it is not felt necessary to do anything about it. Other types of activity may come into play, as the organic functioning of life in terms of vitality, the conscious realization or affirmation of values, and so on, but physical action for the moment is no longer stimulated. Cessation, if experienced, is merely an enjoyment of satiety. Second of these expedient phases of action shown by Venus is a stoppage through direct destruction, and this must be distinguished carefully from the positive antagonism of Mars. It is fundamentally the careless or self-indulgent dissipation or abuse of whatever lies conveniently at hand, commonly including all types of degeneration and drifting in ordinary relations. The planet thus gives a valuable clue to any carelessness, slovenliness, or stubborness in normal act and attitude, as well as their psychological counterparts in vanity, conceit and gullibility. Where Saturn charts a reduction of reality to conscious values, Venus indicates the more simple cancelling out of this same reality in a deficient or entirely false appreciation, or a totally unwarranted taking of things for granted.

The cherishing of all human possessions, measured in principal part by this negative indicator of pure convenience, is the act-of-self as simple enjoyment. There is no more continuance *per se* in consummation than initiative, so that such consummatory realities as money and resources have to be put to use, all genuine love has to be quickened, every possible variation of esthetic fulfillment must have its exercise through an expediency of everyday relations. Static accumulation is shown by Jupiter, as has been pointed out. The self-challenging vitality of human interest is no less a personal matter, hence acquiring its rulership by the lights. Venus is of great importance in horoscope interpretation through its identification of money and property as the one wholly impersonal means for the objective disjunction or efficient placement of various higher facilities. Financial resources make it possible for any individual to dismiss multitudinous acts-of-self to the care of others. Romance is a climactic phase of everyday relationship—as is all esthetic efficiency in general—permitting a very similar resting of the being in a possession or accomplishment which differs only as a matter of language, or the deeper ideas involved, from other consummations. Great emotion, as an organic experience in co-operation with an object, is personal and conjunctive, and so measured by the moon. Efforts to create beauty or adorn life, however, are a move to bring the act-of-self to efficiency, and thus to experience a reward for the effort in the entirely disjunctive enjoyment to which it leads. Perfumes and luxuries, as well as food, clothing and all possible possessions of a transient sort, are facilities of self-fulfillment of the impersonal sort which Venus shows in astrological analysis.

Mercury

Mercury, in its indication of mind, provides the horoscope with a reliable guide to whatever general potentials of self-orientation may be brought to focus in any immediate or practical experience. It is supernumerary in nature because the expediency it charts transcends the necessarily direct stimulus to which activity under Mars and Venus must respond. It shows an act-of-self which is no less impersonal, objective and disjunctive, but one which is basically responsive to the persisting center of individuality on the one hand, and to the constancies of all experience on the other. The planet derives its meaning in part from its particular astronomical eccentricities, and in larger part from the closeness of its orbit to the sun. Venus is linked to the center of the physical system in a similar fashion—so that the consummations and enjoyment charted by that planet are always a folding in of superficial reality upon the self—but Mercury can get only a little more than half as far away from the parent body and in consequence represents a greater dependence upon center, in a type of activity akin to the will expressed on the personal level by the sun itself. Mercury is particularly impersonal in its move now to one and now to the other side of the great luminary, while yet partaking of a definite centrality in experience as the most inward of the true solar satellites. Normally retrograding three times a year, in an accentuation of this looking now forward and now backward, the planet becomes a point of mediative activity in practical being, enabling the individual to make choices in an almost complete freedom from time and space. This is essentially the intellectual act *per se,* because it depends upon neither beginning nor end and has no necessary relations to anything other than itself. Intelligence centers reality in full and continual conformity to individual convenience, and mind in consequence can be seen as the completely disjunctive focus of awareness.

Mercury, in its rulership of man's focalizing power in everyday affairs, primarily charts methods and modes of communication and thought, together with immediate action which has indirect but practical effect, such as oratory, dramatization and educative effort. It measures the general operation of memory, reason and any individual capacity for utilizing values, symbols, tokens and the like for self-orientation in any particular situation at hand. This includes the employment of language in every phase of articulation, ramifying to comprise all means for the exchange of ideas or reactions, and ending up as any ability for seeing how man's generalized or codified knowledge and science can be put to work. It identifies tools when they are automatic, mechanical or otherwise developed so that anyone can use them without the expression of particular initiative, and shows all active development of community, national and racial skills or facilities. In every case this means act or choice by proxy and delegation, together with the pre-emption for self by adoption or orientation of another's action and choice. It rules nothing possessed of actuality in separation from other considerations, that is, its disjunctive activity is objective or efficient in function. Man's mind does not operate by itself, but must use borrowed notions, images and symbols. It is impossible to think, except in or against the thoughts of other people as these in some way express a common reality. Therefore the planet ultimately outlines the various forms of rationalization, explanation, justification and self-realization by means of which human intelligence remains competent in its self-delimitation. Hence the planet has its greatest horoscopic significance in disclosing whatever genius the native may have for controlling his own practical focus of awareness, and for recognizing his own efficient center in everyday experience.

SIGNIFICANCE: SELF-ASSERTION IN PURE ADAPTABILITY

All power is a trust; that we are accountable for its exercise; that from the people and for the people all springs, and all must exist.

BENJAMIN DISRAELI, *Vivian Grey*

Uranus, Neptune and Pluto, in any horoscope, reveal the pattern of expediency by which the native maintains his basic position in the society of which he is a member. They do this because their cycles afford the closest approximation to the broad social changes in the given age. Uranus, the positive indicator, takes the keyword INDEPENDENCE; Neptune, the negative and complementary focus of group concern, is OBLIGATION; and Pluto, the supernumerary and mental factor, is OBSESSION.

Uranus

Uranus, in its indication of independence, brings social reality down to the point of individual opportunity, showing the instinct to act for the group—and so impersonally—as in contrast with simple self-assertion in a more primitive and personal reality. The planet reveals that area in the horoscope where the native is most free to express himself according to his own subjective but conjunctive notions, that is, where he will have the maximum co-operation and appreciation from his fellows in his especially deviate or unique efforts. It therefore provides the measure of originality and genius, over and above the power of initiative shown in the horoscope by Mars—and is the act-of-self in the larger social dimension which transcends both the primitive will charted by the sun and the naïve spontaneity indicated by Jupiter. It describes any person's gifts for social as against purely superficial self-expression, and gives important light upon the directions and conditions under which the native may participate in the larger potentials of civilization. Here is more than personal distinction, which was known to the world long before 1781. Uranus is essentially a planet of deviation in a highly creative sense, actually inoperative in any area of conscious experience unless there are elements in the individual life which are somehow challenging to the entire context of a modern world. There must be something to endow each new-age man with a justification for himself through some species of definite contribution to higher existence in the lives of those around him. This is where impersonality is as subjective as conscious motivation. The masses are carried along in the events measured by these new bodies in astrology, however, and the impersonality is thereby as conjunctive as organic vitality. Uranus is positive in blazing the new way for the race, but what it reveals may never have any direct psychological significance for the individual.

Racial progress, of course, must continue in its own terms. Uranus indicates these new and original facets of group activity, such as are consequent upon the evolution of a machine-age culture, but only at the stage where they remain a novelty to men in general, and especially to the average narrow and self-blinded native. The first necessity of interdependence in social institutions is a continual emphasis upon the interweaving co-operations as such, and in consequence the planet indicates the large-scale ideals and schemes which are being carried to a point of achievement, not those which the race as a whole has been able to dismiss to the common place. What is shown is the outreach to uncharted and broader potentials of human activity, but entirely as these are anchored in known and ordered realities already possessed, i.e., as they are conjunctive despite their uniqueness. A wild utopianism is as foreign to racial and personal independence as the conventional and constricted individualism of tribal life at the other extreme. Uranus is a normal planet in every respect, and the beginning of any effective pioneering into broad and more theoretical or artificial dimensions of existence must be founded upon that regularity of touch with ordinary life which is dramatized in the very arrangement of the three new bodies. Thus Neptune begins to be strikingly exceptional in its heavenly situation, and Pluto carries the irregularity further. These points, already explained, reveal how the sequential development of implication through the bodies of recent discovery presents a move from lesser to greater deviation, and seems to indicate that a progressively larger dimension in man's experience is correlated with a mounting distortion in cosmic orderliness. This suggests that the independence of Uranus calls for an increasingly common sharing of greater potentials in all possible new experience. The planet charts the expansion, never the loss, of the creative normality involved.

Neptune

Neptune, in its indication of obligation, charts the negative facet of cultural self-realization or the fundamentally impersonal, subjective and conjunctive activity of modern social compulsions. It identifies that point in the horoscope where the individual is under the greatest necessity to do what the group as a whole wishes him to do, or where any extreme of co-operation or allegiance is demanded of him by other people in general. These are the native's required relations to the new and interdependent culture, revealing his continuing bondage in varying detail to necessities larger than his comprehension as the price he must pay, whether or no, for any enhancement of his social liberties. Thus Neptune, in every chart, describes the situation under which anyone is brought up short most definitely, whenever he fails to respond to the opportunities for this larger mode of being. It indicates the way in which he finds his strength dissipated by the psychological drag of a complicated community organization. His social sensibilities may be reassured or confused below the level of consciousness, since Neptune is both negative and subjective, but the whole complex of his personal experience may yet be hampered here by the continual demands of overwhelming realities about him, if he does not make some voluntary contribution to the current community vision. The planet descIplines him constantly, to make him creatively aware of group values, and it maps the conditions under which his act-of-self may be given exemption from a necessity to support things which, to him as an individual, may seem inconsequential and unreal simply because of their remoteness.

Here in consequence is the area of the horoscope where the personality finds itself under its actual obligation to alien ways of action. The self-enslavement, when an individual's general social interest is deficient, may take the form of a substitution which, more often than not, may be a resort to unsocial perversions instead of an enlargement of self-function. Often there will be an employment of artificial compensations in the form of drugs, or other facilities of modern life, as these may be twisted into a false service and final betrayal of self. Psychological escapism, or fantasy as a direct surrender of conscious control over ordinary experience, is shown by the moon on the lower level, since a mere emotional overflow is involved. As an adverse effect of the maladjustment indicated here, under Neptune, the conjunctive activity may become a social despair, however, and the person who cannot rise to the full significance of things in a larger society is apt to become anarchist if not mentally unbalanced, with the ultimately destructive tendency to resist rather than utilize the compulsions upon him. Then he tilts against windmills, and becomes a voice of malcontent in every situation. An adequate or creative interest in the intricacies of community organization, contrariwise, may awaken an individual to the unfolding potentials of his own equally intricate constitution, especially in the instance of someone who possesses or develops the skills to make an enduring contribution to his day and age. Thereupon Neptune charts the higher type of group intuition, the social insight or possibly even prophetic capacity which enables the more competent native to express the race destiny in some measure, and hence to capitalize spectacularly upon his place in the scheme of things.

Pluto

Pluto, in its indication of obsession—taken as potentially no less constructive than unfortunate, or as the compelling vision by which men are caught up out of themselves in a transcendence of lesser living—is the planet of mediative activity in cultural self-realization, or is the mass mind which directs the basic formulation and communication of social concepts in modern life. It is, as a matter of subjective conjunction, what Mercury continues to be as the objective disjunction of ideas and notions in experience. Neither are personal, or concerned with organic well-being, on the one hand, and with motivating norms or values on the other. Pluto shows the native's impersonal response to his group's needs and dangers. Where the capacity for social vision is inadequate in a given case, it reveals the resultant unawareness of the more significant trend of events, and so shows any inclination to become involved in some wrong, unprofitable or purely visionary line of effort. Most simply, it identifies the point in any astrological wheel where the personality is affected primarily by group or race ideas, thus becoming stimulated or repressed, as the case may be, by the impact of generalizations arising outside individual experience. Pluto is best seen at all times as a cosmic Mercury, indicating in every respect, on the larger scale and in the universal dimension, what the longer-known planet shows normally. It thus identifies, quite conveniently, the great isms by which men are either welded into group actuality or else divided among themselves. It also shows the underlying and often entirely unsuspected general orientation in the presuppositions of every modern individual. It discloses the nature and influence of propaganda, whether put forth consciously or unconsciously, and whether with essentially good or bad fruits.

When the native co-operates with the best of world-wide developments in a given generation, he is inspired to a continuing and genuine social service, one which is both actual and intellectual. This is the only way in which he achieves a maximum conjunction of the potentials inherent in any larger pattern of his own self-assertion. Pluto's most important role is thus to outline the effectiveness or discordance of any individual's obsessing vision in the light of the dominating potentials in group progress, and to give him guidance in grasping his opportunity as a cosmic citizen. This outermost planet reveals the universal mind of mankind in its witting or unwitting attempt to achieve and share the social insights which make living significant in any real sense, co-operating here with the indications of Uranus and Neptune. These three planets move so slowly that they can give but the slightest indications of any true personal difference. However, even when their individual testimony in the horoscope fails to be very illuminating, they aid in classifying the native according to his fundamental orientation to the current over-all scheme of things. They provide a frame of reference in which the other planetary indications may be seen with exceptional effectiveness, since they provide each generation with its own particularly modern character. In this the new planet of obsessing vision or visionariness discloses the real social intelligence of each separate personality, irrespective of any inadequate response on his part to the immediate challenges of today's interdependent society.

TABLE XII

The Planets and Their Keywords

THE SUN	Purpose	JUPITER	Enthusiasm
THE MOON	Feeling	SATURN	Sensitiveness
MARS	Initiative	URANUS	Independence
VENUS	Acquisitiveness	NEPTUNE	Obligation
MERCURY	Mentality	PLUTO	Obsession

CHAPTER FOURTEEN

The Mastery
of Circumstances

An individual's manipulation of his potentialities in circumstances is a practical proposition of increased or decreased self-assertion, entirely as this is convenient or profitable, at the points of momentary emphasis in his situation. Horoscopy guides him effectively by (1) showing him where, in the relations set up through his fundamental pattern of identity, he may gain the maximum degree of co-operation with his various purposes, and (2) describing the necessary nature of the interaction between himself and his general milieu in every case.

The ten planets identify the particular ways in which he asserts himself, the place of each in the houses of his chart giving the specific direction of expediency. Exactly as a businessman, knowing that a train departs for the city he wishes to visit, can arrange to take it, so the native, as he becomes aware that some one capacity of his has a special momentary value in the world of reality in which he finds himself, can act with a more rather than a less of himself. Thus he moves, in the given area of potentiality, towards a fulfillment rather than frustration. He masters circumstances by proceeding according to the genius of his personal pattern, in accordance with a conscious use of the universal timetable. There is no departure or arrival on the tracks of potentiality which astrology cannot give him, if he approaches the stellar art with an adequate skill and a proper discrimination.

THE SUN IN THE EQUATOR

Wake! for the Sun, who scatter'd into flight
The Stars before him from the Field of Night,
Drives Night along with them from Heav'n, and strikes
The Sultan's Turret with a Shaft of Light.
OMAR KHAYYÁM, *Rubáiyát* (Fitzgerald)

THE SUN IN THE FIRST HOUSE places the practical focus of life in a determination to exalt the ego, whether in a subtle or blunt fashion. This position always encourages a conscious effort to dominate the immediate situation, and to keep the center of any stage. At his best the native is able to master his circumstances through direct and simple sincerity, and at his worst he is apt to meet every issue with bombast or some inept self-assertion.

THE SUN IN THE SECOND HOUSE places the practical focus of life in a determination to possess and use the best of everything at hand. This position always encourages a conscious realization of personal advantages, and of the value of individual resources. At his best the native is able to capitalize upon the potentials of any given situation, and at his worst he is apt to lose out through his greedy and unreasonable demands upon others.

THE SUN IN THE THIRD HOUSE places the practical focus of life in a determination to have a finger in every immediate concern. This position always encourages a conscious passion for contributing to the convenience of himself and others. At his best the native is able to find or create the proper niche of the moment for everyone around him, and at his worst he is apt to bring confusion everywhere through his own vacillation or disorganization.

THE SUN IN THE FOURTH HOUSE places the practical focus of life in a determination to win and enjoy security for the self and its own. This position always encourages a conscious conservatism, either as isolationist in temperament or as concerned over getting down the roots of self. At his best the native is able to bring an enduring stability to the things in which he interests himself, and at his worst he is apt to let the world go by unnoticed.

THE SUN IN THE FIFTH HOUSE places the practical focus of life in a determination to flow out into every possible expression of selfhood. This position always encourages a conscious interest in the passing parade of events, and a tendency to make life an ever-varying carnival. At his best the native is able to bring a heightened enjoyment to himself and everyone around him, and at his worst he is apt to exploit others for his own pleasure.

THE SUN IN THE SIXTH HOUSE places the practical focus of life in a determination to test the mettle of reality in every possible sort of hard effort. This position always encourages a conscious desire to bring everything down to a utilitarian basis. At his best the native is able to organize or redirect the energies of himself and others to an increased advantage, and at his worst he is apt to become wholly malcontent and unsocial.

THE SUN IN THE SEVENTH HOUSE places the practical focus of life in a determination to enjoy human relationships at every point of contact. This position always encourages a conscious flair for seeing an advantage or recognizing an opportunity. At his best the native is able to persuade all people to cooperate with whatever catches his interest, and at his worst he is apt to precipitate conflict or ultimate difficulty by his dominating opportunism.

THE SUN IN THE EIGHTH HOUSE places the practical focus of life in a determination to refine the self in every crucible of experience. This position always encourages a conscious concern over the adequacy of the self's skills and effort. At his best the native is able to find the place where his energies will have the greatest support from others, and at his worst he apt to play the busybody and count upon a competency he does not possess.

THE SUN IN THE NINTH HOUSE places the practical focus of life in a determination to exalt the ego through high standards and broadened interests. This position always encourages a conscious lean towards an intellectual understanding or a religious orientation. At his best the native is able to bring effective insights or genuine wisdom to every situation, and at his worst he is apt to meet all reality with a complacent intolerance or bigotry.

THE SUN IN THE TENTH HOUSE places the practical focus of life in a determination to elevate the self by catering primarily to the welfare of the group. This position always encourages a conscious passion for enduring distinction and the external or immediate seal of public dignity. At his best the native is able to administer any responsibility with very real skill, and at his worst he is apt to be rather pompous and to develop dictatorial whims.

THE SUN IN THE ELEVENTH HOUSE places the practical focus of life in a determination to expand the self by some difinite program of achievement. This position always encourages a conscious alertness to general potentials and objectives. At his best the native is able to bring the divergent desires of himself and others to a common reconciliation, and at his worst he is apt to concentrate on side issues, or lose out through sheer partiality.

THE SUN IN THE TWELFTH HOUSE places the practical focus of life in a determination to get on the inside of things and to control the machinery of life. This position always encourages a conscious response to the undercurrents of the moment. At his best the native is able to recognize the basic unity in experience, or to bring unsuspected and helpful relations into play, and at his worst he is apt to cultivate suspicion or encourage half-baked effort.

THE MOON IN THE EQUATOR

What is there in thee, Moon! that thou should'st move
My heart so potently?

KEATS, *Endymion*

THE MOON IN THE FIRST HOUSE centers all personal experience in the passing situations of an everyday here and now. This position exaggerates a delight in all direct contact with life, and gives a sharpened emphasis to immediate relationships. The native at his best is able to bring a creative intimacy to everything he does, and at his worst he is apt to dissipate his energies in activity which is unworthy of him.

THE MOON IN THE SECOND HOUSE centers all personal experience in a general sharing or utilization of human resources. This position exaggerates the sense of immediate possessiveness in every phase of life. The native at his best is able to bring a living significance to any event in which he participates, and at his worst he is apt to waste his own substance as well as that of everyone around him.

THE MOON IN THE THIRD HOUSE centers all personal experience in the transient activities which occupy people in general. This position exaggerates a dependence upon the reliability demonstrated or dramatized by others. The native at his best is able to adjust himself to any set of circumstances, and to be himself in all eventualities, and at his worst he is apt to be a busybody, never getting down to his own affairs.

THE MOON IN THE FOURTH HOUSE centers all personal experience in matters of great general moment or unusually private concern. This position exaggerates a desire for settled conditions, and a tendency to develop selfish me-and-mine instincts. The native at his best is able to bring peace and security to himself and everyone close to him, and at his worst he is apt to insulate himself against all surrounding reality.

THE MOON IN THE FIFTH HOUSE centers all personal experience in a continual exhibition of individual skills. This position exaggerates a joy in abandoning all restraint, whether for adventure or sense indulgence. The native at his best is able to be the life of the group wherever he goes among his fellows, and at his worst he is apt to yield to every vagrant impulse in order to gain or hold attention.

THE MOON IN THE SIXTH HOUSE centers all personal experience in the problems and issues of human obligation, or the practical divisions of labor in a normal society. This position exaggerates any concern over the subordination of some people to others. The native at his best is able to further every social adjustment for himself or his fellows, and at his worst he is apt to meddle in affairs quite beyond his province.

THE MOON IN THE SEVENTH HOUSE centers all personal experience in particularly partisan relationships, whether on a large or small scale. This position exaggerates an interest in the passing opportunities of life, and develops a realization that the self must press for its own advantage at all points. The native at his best is able to find common elements in his associations with any other individual, and at his worst he is apt to make things unnecessarily hard for himself.

THE MOON IN THE EIGHTH HOUSE centers all personal experience in situations controlled for the major part by others. This position exaggerates a sense of touch with deep-seated considerations, and makes the life quite subjective. The native at his best is able to conform to expectation, shaping the cycles of events as he wishes, and at his worst he is apt to discourage all accomplishment by those around him, and to fail them at all points.

THE MOON IN THE NINTH HOUSE centers all personal experience in issues of morality, elevating ends and reasons above practical needs. This position exaggerates every concern over ideas and motives. The native at his best is able to approach reality with an understanding support for every human capacity, and at his worst he is apt to worry over abstractions and dissipate every impulse to action.

THE MOON IN THE TENTH HOUSE centers all personal experience in public affairs, great or small. This position exaggerates the assimilation of the individual to the group, and enhances his pleasure in large-scale or responsible act. The native at his best is able to further the interests of everyone with real success, and at his worst he is apt to betray those who trust him by an unhealthy love of the spotlight.

THE MOON IN THE ELEVENTH HOUSE centers all personal experience in affairs with an established momentum. This position exaggerates a joy in anticipation, planning, consultation and the general framing of individual effort in some greater pattern. The native at his best is able to create stimulating vistas everywhere in life, and at his worst he is apt to concern himself with wild and fruitless enterprises.

THE MOON IN THE TWELFTH HOUSE centers all personal experience in the psychical and wholly institutionalized phases of life. This position exaggerates the tides of mood in the personality. The native at his best is able to order events by his sympathetic response to the deeper sweep of impulse in others, and at his worst he is apt to antagonize everyone through a sheer incapacity for consistent action.

MARS IN THE EQUATOR

Push on, pursue, in no wise faint of foot!
ÆSCHYLUS, *Fragments*

MARS IN THE FIRST HOUSE cultivates a type of initiative which, primarily, meets the needs of simple self-realization. This position demands an everyday experience where the issues of life are encountered in concrete fashion. The native at his best is able to face everything directly, cutting across any lines of unnecessary subtlety, and at his worst he is apt to defeat his own ends by hesitant or undependable conduct.

MARS IN THE SECOND HOUSE cultivates a type of initiative which, primarily, meets the needs of simple acquisition and expenditure. This position demands an everyday experience marked by a great deal of manipulation or negotiation. The native at his best is able to take a very efficient part in any human enterprise, and at his worst he is apt to neglect his responsibilities and dissipate everybody's resources.

MARS IN THE THIRD HOUSE cultivates a type of initiative which, primarily, meets the needs of simple movement and change in the community. This position demands an everyday experience with a great ramification of superficial relationships. The native at his best is able to locate the source of any trouble, helping life to run smoothly, and at his worst he is apt to disrupt every course of events.

MARS IN THE FOURTH HOUSE cultivates a type of initiative

which, primarily, meets the needs of simple self-assurance and social security. This position demands an everyday experience where home ties and ultimate values are dominant. The native at his best is able to profit continually from the consistency of his actions, and at his worst he is apt to miss out in life by stirring up trouble in his own foundations.

MARS IN THE FIFTH HOUSE cultivates a type of initiative which, primarily, meets the needs of simple self-discovery and self-refinement. This position demands an everyday experience of a particularly fluid sort. The native at his best is able to develop an unquenchable enthusiasm in both himself and others, and at his worst he is apt to precipitate inharmony by his presumptuousness and instability.

MARS IN THE SIXTH HOUSE cultivates a type of initiative which, primarily, meets the needs of simple adjustment in the social milieu. This position demands an everyday experience where human inequalities and cross purposes are a problem. The native at his best is able to play the role of conciliator, thriving on the chance to reach high and low, and at his worst he is apt to breed dissatisfaction everywhere.

MARS IN THE SEVENTH HOUSE cultivates a type of initiative which, primarily, meets the needs of simple co-operation with others. This position demands an everyday experience where all men are encountered as equals. The native at his best is able to bring a new impetus or an enlarged horizon to every phase of life, and at his worst he is apt to antagonize people or stimulate their energies fruitlessly.

MARS IN THE EIGHTH HOUSE cultivates a type of initiative which, primarily, meets the needs of simple orientation to the interests and rights of others. This position demands an every-day experience where definite social necessities challenge the ingenuity of self. The native at his best is able to rise to any occasion, and at his worst he is apt to disparage his fellows and their capacities in abrupt fashion.

MARS IN THE NINTH HOUSE cultivates a type of initiative which, primarily, meets the needs of simple adjustment to ideas and values. This position demands an everyday experience where the lessons learned in life have a chance to prove themselves. The native at his best is able to act with consistent good judgment, and at his worst he is apt to outrage everyone by his naïve self-justification and big ideas.

MARS IN THE TENTH HOUSE cultivates a type of initiative which, primarily, meets the needs of simple self-achievement or social recognition. This position demands an everyday experience where group activity has an exceptional emphasis. The native at his best is able to demonstrate leadership or responsibility in every special field of effort, and at his worst he is apt to be a petty dictator or troublemaker.

MARS IN THE ELEVENTH HOUSE cultivates a type of initiative which, primarily, meets the needs of simple orientation to life's possibilities. This position demands an everyday experience where there is a marked and friendly drift, or an intelligently directed ordering, in all activity. The native at his best is able to contribute a dramatic power to any given objective, and at his worst he is apt to be the dilettante.

MARS IN THE TWELFTH HOUSE cultivates a type of initiative which, primarily, meets the needs of simple adjustment to the undercurrents or totally ordered phases of life. This position demands an everyday experience where all minor things are dismissed to the care of others. The native at his best is able to uncover unsuspected advantages in every situation, and at his worst he is apt to disorganize everything.

VENUS IN THE EQUATOR

Venus smiles not in a house of tears.
SHAKESPEARE, *Romeo and Juliet*

VENUS IN THE FIRST HOUSE shows that any self-satisfaction is gained, primarily, through an essentially naïve self-exploitation. This position requires a practical reward for effort which, ultimately, can be exhibited and enjoyed here and now. The native at his best is able to follow through with any responsibility he accepts, and at his worst he is apt to sacrifice everything through an excessive vanity.

VENUS IN THE SECOND HOUSE shows that any self-satisfaction is gained, primarily, through the manipulation of various resources. This position requires a practical reward for effort which, ultimately, increases the self's everyday gift for meeting the exigencies of its experience. The native at his best is able to put everything to use advantageously, and at his worst he is apt to defeat himself by inertia or greed.

VENUS IN THE THIRD HOUSE shows that any self-satisfaction is gained, primarily, through an uninhibited capitalization upon ordinary human relations. This position requires a practical reward for effort which, ultimately, keeps life interesting. The native at his best is able to maneuver any immediate combination of circumstances into a desired pattern, and at his worst he is apt to lose himself in trivialities.

VENUS IN THE FOURTH HOUSE shows that any self-satisfaction is gained, primarily, through an essentially naïve regard for the self and its own. This position requires a practical reward for effort which, ultimately, can be preserved and enjoyed in seclusion. The native at his best is able to bring security to everyone he likes, and at his worst he is apt to be unsocial and very jealous of his own privileges.

VENUS IN THE FIFTH HOUSE shows that any self-satisfaction is gained, primarily, through a direct refinement and exhibition of individual skills. This position requires a practical reward for effort which, ultimately, augments the channels for self-expression. The native at his best is able to dramatize himself most inspiringly, and at his worst he is apt to cheapen himself in his desire for superficial applause.

VENUS IN THE SIXTH HOUSE shows that any self-satisfaction is gained, primarily, through an uninhibited capitalization upon simple hard work. This position requires a practical reward for effort which, ultimately, reconciles any differences among men through a mutual service. The native at his best is able to balance life's account as he goes, and at his worst he is apt to make unfair demands everywhere.

VENUS IN THE SEVENTH HOUSE shows that any self-satisfaction is gained, primarily, through an essentially naïve concentration on momentary contacts. This position requires a practical reward for effort which, ultimately, develops appreciation for everyday opportunity. The native at his best is able to win everyone through the fullness of his attention, and at his worst he is apt to develop very bizarre relationships.

VENUS IN THE EIGHTH HOUSE shows that any self-satisfaction is gained, primarily, through the recognition and use of purely social resources. This position requires a practical reward for effort which, ultimately, provides fresh cycles of experience. The native at his best is able to call out new and constructive effort in every situation, and at his worst he is apt to encourage every human disintegration.

VENUS IN THE NINTH HOUSE shows that any self-satisfaction is gained, primarily, through an uninhibited capitalization upon the religious, scientific or philosophical concepts of the moment. This position requires a practical reward for effort which, ultimately, opens some door to understanding. The native at his best is able to create real values, and at his worst he is apt to defeat all sound judgment.

VENUS IN THE TENTH HOUSE shows that any self-satisfaction is gained, primarily, through an essentially naïve elevation of the self among its fellows. This position requires a practical reward for effort which, ultimately, can be enjoyed in public or in ceremonial fashion. The native at his best is able to gain the good will of all people, and at his worst he is apt to truckle to every selfish influence.

VENUS IN THE ELEVENTH HOUSE shows that any self-satisfaction is gained, primarily, through an unswerving fidelity to major vision. This position requires a practical reward for effort which, ultimately, strengthens every objective ambition. The native at his best is able to bring everything within effective sight of its goal, and at his worst he is apt, by bad counsel, to destroy all hope for achievement.

VENUS IN THE TWELFTH HOUSE shows that any self-satisfaction is gained, primarily, through an uninhibited capitalization upon objective or subjective limitations. This position requires a practical reward for effort which, ultimately, gives a deeper meaning to life. The native at his best is able to create an immediate reality of any desired sort, and at his worst he is apt to make everything quite unreal.

MERCURY IN THE EQUATOR

Neither snow, nor rain, nor heat, nor gloom of night stays these couriers from the swift completion of their appointed rounds.
HERODOTUS, *History*

MERCURY IN THE FIRST HOUSE identifies a focus of awareness which depends primarily, for self-orientation, upon simple trial and error. This position develops a rational tendency to visualize everything in the immediate context without either foresight or hindsight. The native at his best is able to meet people on their own terms, and at his worst he is apt to jump to conclusions in everything he does.

MERCURY IN THE SECOND HOUSE identifes a focus of awareness which depends primarily, for self-orientation, upon a consistently conventional approach to all experience. This position develops a rational tendency to think of things in terms of immediate value. The native at his best is able to handle all people and property advantageously, and at his worst he is apt to dissipate everything through his bad judgment.

MERCURY IN THE THIRD HOUSE identifies a focus of awareness which depends primarily, for self-orientation, upon familiar settings or established conveniences. This position develops a rational tendency to visualize life as organic or mechanical. The native at his best is able to help people get along together in every sort of human relationship, and at his worst he is apt to treat them as mere pawns in his game.

MERCURY IN THE FOURTH HOUSE identifies a focus of awareness which depends primarily, for self-orientation, upon whatever actually has proved to be a basis of security. This position develops a rational tendency to think of things in terms of their dependability or intrinsic worth. The native at his best is able to strengthen the more stable elements in experience, and at his worst he is apt to lean on very frail reeds and contribute to every instability.

MERCURY IN THE FIFTH HOUSE identifies a focus of awareness which depends primarily, for self-orientation, upon breaking away from the conditioning background. This position develops a rational tendency to visualize life as a stage, a playground or a schoolroom. The native at his best is able to find fascinating potentials in everyone, and at his worst he is apt to concentrate on justifying his own self-indulgence.

MERCURY IN THE SIXTH HOUSE identifies a focus of awareness which depends primarily, for self-orientation, upon a continual readjustment in human relations. This position develops a rational tendency to think of everything as material for manipulation. The native at his best is able to solve any social dilemma, and at his worst he is apt to blind himself to inequalities and so encourage every injustice.

MERCURY IN THE SEVENTH HOUSE identifies a focus of awareness which depends primarily, for self-orientation, upon a consistent rising to the occasion. This position develops a rational tendency to approach life as an opportunity for self-fulfillment in others. The native at his best is able to bring all people to a point of co-operation and at his worst he is apt to precipitate constant conflict.

MERCURY IN THE EIGHTH HOUSE identifies a focus on awareness which depends primarily, for self-orientation, upon a conformity to the general social trend. This position develops a rational tendency to think of things as representing a greater reality than themselves. The native at his best is able to stimulate all people to real accomplishment, and at his worst he is apt to surrender everything to his own fantasy.

MERCURY IN THE NINTH HOUSE identifies a focus of awareness which depends primarily, for self-orientation, upon a definite anchorage in experience, tradition or knowledge. This position develops a rational tendency to visualize life in highly abstract terms. The native at his best is able to put everything in its proper frame of reference, and at his worst he is apt to lose all reality in an intellectual chaos.

270

MERCURY IN THE TENTH HOUSE identifies a focus of awareness which depends primarily, for self-orientation, upon a dramatization of human standards. This position develops a rational tendency to look upon life opportunistically. The native at his best is able to recognize and clarify every social need, and at his worst he is apt to develop a distorted and destructive view of his own place among his fellows.

MERCURY IN THE ELEVENTH HOUSE identifies a focus of awareness which depends primarily, for self-orientation, upon the prevailing social vision. This position develops a rational tendency to visualize life as determined by purpose, or shaped by desire. The native at his best is able to aid everyone in capitalizing upon current developments, and at his worst he is apt to accept and give fundamentally bad advice.

MERCURY IN THE TWELFTH HOUSE identifies a focus of awareness which depends primarily, for self-orientation, upon a sense of supporting foundation in life's hidden trends. This position develops a rational tendency to think of things in terms of deeper values. The native at his best is able to see the basic reality beneath all phenomena, and at his worst he is apt to create a completely imaginative world of his own.

JUPITER IN THE EQUATOR

What makes life dreary is the want of motive.
GEORGE ELIOT, *Daniel Deronda*

JUPITER IN THE FIRST HOUSE reveals a psychological orientation which primarily seeks to exalt the personality, and so enhances every intimate relationship. This position encourages personal incentive through direct and immediate self-fulfillment. The native at his best is able to demonstrate real diplomacy in every passing situation, and at his worst he is apt to be gullible or faithless.

JUPITER IN THE SECOND HOUSE reveals a psychological orientation which primarily seeks to multiply possessions and resources in every walk of life. This position encourages personal incentive through an increasing success in business and social detail. The native at his best is able to strengthen and often underwrite the efforts of all his fellows, and at his worst he is apt to exploit anyone conveniently at hand.

JUPITER IN THE THIRD HOUSE reveals a psychological orientation which primarily seeks to keep the whole world running smoothly and happily. This position encourages personal incentive through a simple efficiency in living. The native at his best is able to keep everyone around him in good humor, and at his worst he is apt to raise petty issues, or sidetrack every consideration but his own aplomb.

JUPITER IN THE FOURTH HOUSE reveals a psychological orientation which primarily seeks some inner assurance for the self in every phase and turn of existence. This position encourages personal incentive through success in stabilizing the immediate milieu of interest. The native at his best is able to help others achieve enduring fruits of experience, and at his worst he is apt to pre-empt everything for himself.

JUPITER IN THE FIFTH HOUSE reveals a psychological orientation which primarily seeks to expand self-expression on every level of reality. This position encourages personal incentive through the untrammeled refinement or broadening of personality. The native at his best is able to call forth an unlimited creative capacity in everyone, and at his worst he is apt to cheapen all human relationships.

JUPITER IN THE SIXTH HOUSE reveals a psychological orientation which primarily seeks to capitalize upon human differences, or to put all life in pigeonholes. This position encourages personal incentive through success in handling others according to their own special gifts. The native at his best is able to glorify hard work and struggle, and at his worst he is apt to override the feelings of everyone around him.

JUPITER IN THE SEVENTH HOUSE reveals a psychological orientation which primarily seeks to make others do battle for self, or to achieve things by negotiation and co-operation. This position encourages personal incentive through the fruits of a sheer opportunism. The native at his best is the perfect partner in a real reciprocity of interest, and at his worst he is insatiable in bending everyone he can to his whims.

JUPITER IN THE EIGHTH HOUSE reveals a psychological orientation which primarily seeks to obtain support for the self's desires by guarding the interests of others. This position encourages personal incentive through success in meeting current eventualities. The native at his best is able to lead men to accomplishment through new experience, and at his worst he is apt to lean on second-hand ideas or sheer imagination.

JUPITER IN THE NINTH HOUSE reveals a psychological orientation which primarily seeks to keep life aligned to its own genius or heritage. This position encourages personal incentive through an expanding intellectual discovery and insight. The native at his best is able to bring everyone to real wisdom, and at his worst he is apt to remain pedantic or to sacrifice actual knowing to mere opinion.

JUPITER IN THE TENTH HOUSE reveals a psychological orientation which primarily seeks to dominate every situation. This position encourages personal incentive through success in directing the lives of others. The native at his best is able to serve his fellows through a superior executive ability, and at his worst he is apt to stoop to every form of politics and to demonstrate a very short memory.

JUPITER IN THE ELEVENTH HOUSE reveals a psychological orientation which primarily seeks to further the objectives of significant people. This position encourages personal incentive through an ever widening popularity. The native at his best is able to contribute a real vision to everything in which he takes an interest, and at his worst he is apt to become the social climber and advocate of every passing fad or empty hope.

JUPITER IN THE TWELFTH HOUSE reveals a psychological orientation which primarily seeks to reduce everything to some fixed pattern. This position encourages personal incentive through success in adjusting to life's undercurrents. The native at his best is able to develop an effective emotional sustainment for himself and all his fellows, and at his worst he is apt to give voice to every human apprehension.

SATURN IN THE EQUATOR

These flashes on the surface are not he.
He has a solid base of temperament.
TENNYSON, *The Princess*

SATURN IN THE FIRST HOUSE centers all personal motivation in the immediate potentials and consequences of the experience at hand. This position creates a special sensitiveness to any and all restraint upon the personality. The native at his best is able to bring depth to even the most trivial contacts with others, and at his worst he is apt to rebel against the slightest subordination of his own appetites and feelings.

SATURN IN THE SECOND HOUSE centers all personal motivation in the practical give and take of everyday life. This position creates a special sensitiveness to the possessions, rights and general privileges of normal human affairs. The native at his best is able to bring depth to every phase of self-expenditure, and at his worst he is apt to rebel against every responsibility for his own well-being.

SATURN IN THE THIRD HOUSE centers all personal motivation in immediate factors of efficiency and superficial functioning. This position creates a special sensitiveness to social and business contacts as convenient or necessary in self-fulfillment. The native at his best is able to bring depth to all human fellowship, and at his worst he is apt to rebel against every transient courtesy of ordinary living.

SATURN IN THE FOURTH HOUSE centers all personal motivation in considerations of security or ease for the self and its own. This position creates a special sensitiveness to entrenched prerogatives and cloistered luxury as ends to be demanded or defended. The native at his best is able to bring depth to any place of retreat, and at his worst he is apt to rebel against the slightest private responsibility.

SATURN IN THE FIFTH HOUSE centers all personal motivation in the efforts of self to express itself without restraint and despite consequences. This position creates a special sensitiveness to the personality's right to order its own destiny. The native at his best is able to bring depth to all human experimentation, and at his worst he is apt to rebel against every creative or inner instinct.

SATURN IN THE SIXTH HOUSE centers all personal motivation in matters of priority or relative advantage in the necessary functioning of human society. This position creates a special sensitiveness to any inadequacy in the common rewards for effort. The native at his best is able to bring death to both labor and suffering, and at his worst he is apt to rebel against the least social or economic duty.

SATURN IN THE SEVENTH HOUSE centers all personal motivation in the competitive relationships or opportunities of life. This position creates a special sensitiveness to the personal significance, for better or worse, of everyone with whom experience is shared. The native at his best is able to bring depth to every contact with others, and at his worst he is apt to rebel against every necessity to co-operate with them.

SATURN IN THE EIGHTH HOUSE centers all personal motivation in any necessary conformity to social pressure. This position creates a special sensitiveness to the psychological adjustment of personality to its lot in life. The native at his best is able to bring depth to every self-ordering, thereby contributing real poise to others, and at his worst he is apt to rebel against every challenge to his own potentials.

SATURN IN THE NINTH HOUSE centers all personal motivation in intellectual considerations or vicarious experience. This position creates a special sensitiveness to the particular competency of individual judgments. The native at his best is able to bring depth to every effort of men to understand themselves, and at his worst he is apt to rebel against even the least appeal to wisdom or normal reasoning.

SATURN IN THE TENTH HOUSE centers all personal motivation in group experience and matters of authority or individual prominence. This position creates a special sensitiveness to political and business advantage. The native at his best is able to bring depth to every function of society as a whole, and at his worst he is apt to rebel against the slightest dignification of anyone other than himself.

SATURN IN THE ELEVENTH HOUSE centers all personal motivation in the group momentums of the moment, or in the individual ambitions which they further. This position creates a special sensitiveness to man's vision of his own progress. The native at his best is able to bring depth to the least of hopes and objectives, and at his worst he is apt to rebel against every demand that he commit himself to any goal.

SATURN IN THE TWELFTH HOUSE centers all personal motivation in the psychological stress of society. This position creates a special sensitiveness to passing undercurrents, and the institutional limitations which support them. The native at his best is able to bring depth to every inner mobilization of personality, and at his worst he is apt to rebel against any demand upon his own deeper sense of things.

URANUS IN THE EQUATOR

*Longing not so much to change things
as overturn them.*

CICERO, *De Officiis*

URANUS IN THE FIRST HOUSE indicates that any individuality is encouraged, most definitely, by direct and intimate relationships. This position requires an expression of independence through some effective achievement by the self. The native at his best is able to bring new life to any situation in which he can develop an interest, and at his worst he is apt to become contrary, whimsical or even queer.

URANUS IN THE SECOND HOUSE indicates that any individuality is encouraged, most definitely, by the chance to manipulate possessions. This position requires an expression of independence through some adequacy of personal resources. The native at his best is able to discover or develop whatever is needed to meet any emergency, and at his worst he is apt to precipitate real loss by his cocksure attitude.

URANUS IN THE THIRD HOUSE indicates that any individuality is encouraged, most definitely, by the casualness, smoothness and convenience of the general situation. This position requires an expression of independence through a definite and practical cleverness. The native at his best is able to develop a lively fellowship everywhere, and at his worst he is apt to create a bedlam through his shifting whims.

URANUS IN THE FOURTH HOUSE indicates that any individuality is encouraged, most definitely, by a background of unimpeachable security. This position requires an expression of independence through well-established or commonly venerated channels. The native at his best is able to bring a genuine zest to the enjoyment of simple foundations, and at his worst he is apt to destroy all peace or assurance for everyone.

URANUS IN THE FIFTH HOUSE indicates that any individuality is encouraged, most definitely, by situations or relations without inhibition. This position requires an expression of independence through a dramatic exaggeration of life. The native at his best is able to stimulate everyone to fascinating self-discovery, and at his worst he is apt to pursue the unconventional or outrage human feelings.

URANUS IN THE SIXTH HOUSE indicates that any individuality is encouraged, most definitely, by a continual adjustment to definite social needs. This position requires an expression of independence through some intensified division of labor or exaltation of effort. The native at his best is able to bring real adventure to duty and at his worst he is apt to make it impossible for men to work with each other.

URANUS IN THE SEVENTH HOUSE indicates that any individuality is encouraged, most definitely, by some concrete challenge in a competitive situation. This position requires an expression of independence through a facility in assimilating self to others. The native at his best is able to bring men together in a dramatic co-operativeness, and at his worst he is apt to create inharmony by his consistent intractability.

URANUS IN THE EIGHTH HOUSE indicates that any individuality is encouraged, most definitely, by the chance to administer the practical affairs of others. This position requires an expression of independence through the continual reconstruction of the self. The native at his best is able to resolve every social impasse, and at his worst he is apt to disorganize the resources of everyone around him.

URANUS IN THE NINTH HOUSE indicates that any individuality is encouraged, most definitely, by the need to bring life to constant analysis. This position requires an expression of independence through a complete freedom of thought. The native at his best is able to help everyone to think things through, and at his worst he is apt to distort all perspective and to encourage every sort of utopian intemperance.

URANUS IN THE TENTH HOUSE indicates that any individuality is encouraged, most definitely, by participation in affairs of importance, or by unrestricted authority. This position requires an expression of independence through an acceptance of broad responsibilities. The native at his best is able to build an enthusiastic public spirit, and at his worst he is apt to divide all men among themselves.

URANUS IN THE ELEVENTH HOUSE indicates that any individuality is encouraged, most definitely, by situations or relations of great sweep or high future potentiality. This position requires an expression of independence through pouring the self into projects of significance. The native at his best is able to create new and exciting vistas of life, and at his worst he is apt to confuse everyone around him.

URANUS IN THE TWELFTH HOUSE indicates that any individuality is encouraged, most definitely, by the impact of the unexpected, or the chance to manipulate undercurrents. This position requires an expression of independence through a psychological self-sufficiency. The native at his best is able to give subconscious sustainment to every wavering effort, and at his worst he is apt to contribute to complete chaos.

NEPTUNE IN THE EQUATOR

The only certainty is that nothing is certain.
PLINY THE ELDER, *Historia Naturalis*

NEPTUNE IN THE FIRST HOUSE demands that experience remain naïve, and eliminates all direct psychological support for the self. This position invites self-limitation through a general indefiniteness of reaction to normal reality. The native at his best is able to rise for the moment to the most divergent of necessities, and at his worst he is apt to drift along or stir up trouble by his nebulousness.

NEPTUNE IN THE SECOND HOUSE demands that experience remain practical, and discourages all accumulation of resources except for transient needs. This position invites self-limitation through a general indefiniteness in utilizing the self's assets. The native at his best is able to mobilize whatever may be required for an emergency, and at his worst he is apt to invalidate everything he possesses.

NEPTUNE IN THE THIRD HOUSE demands that experience remain highly grooved, and tends to keep it very pointless. This position invites self-limitation through a general indefiniteness of participation in the everyday world. The native at his best is able to offer a subtle, intangible but helpful fellowship to everyone around him, and at his worst he is apt to develop an annoying ineptness.

NEPTUNE IN THE FOURTH HOUSE demands that experience remain relatively private, and challenges all assumptions of established security. This position invites self-limitation through an unhealthy cloistering of the self and its deeper interests. The native at his best is able to inspire everyone with a simple and universal goodness, and at his worst he is apt to repel everyone through a naïve self-absorption.

NEPTUNE IN THE FIFTH HOUSE demands that experience remain dynamically personal, and eliminates all self-satisfaction through mere sensation. This position invites self-limitation through an unhealthy dependence upon some exterior stimulus to the creative energies. The native at his best is able to call out unsuspected capacities for real self-expression, and at his worst he is apt to toady to human weakness.

NEPTUNE IN THE SIXTH HOUSE demands that experience remain intense, and denies every effort to adjust the distinctions among men. This position invites self-limitation through a basic inability to achieve any fair division of labor in life. The native at his best is able to serve everyone through his keen social instinct, and at his worst he is apt to make life difficult by an inability to rise to special needs.

NEPTUNE IN THE SEVENTH HOUSE demands that experience remain critical, and denies all real permanence in human relations. This position invites self-limitation through uncertainty or ulterior motives in dealing with people. The native at his best is able to bring men together for any specific opportunity, and at his worst he is apt to assume too much of others and so prevent real co-operation.

NEPTUNE IN THE EIGHTH HOUSE demands that experience remain self-challenging, and denies all release from censorship by life at large. This position invites self-limitation through a general nebulousness in the use of group resources. The native at his best is able to sacrifice himself superlatively for his fellows, and at his worst he is apt to pander to the prejudices of every person he meets.

NEPTUNE IN THE NINTH HOUSE demands that experience remain intellectual or vicarious, and eliminates all immediate attention to ideal realizations. This position invites self-limitation through a vacillation or inconclusiveness of judgment. The native at his best is able to bring an illimitable scope to human thinking, and at his worst he is apt to be either hopelessly opinionated or wholly visionary.

NEPTUNE IN THE TENTH HOUSE demands that experience remain public, and requires a continual re-establishment of the individual. This position invites self-limitation through a general resentment of criticism and a flouting of social standards. The native at his best is able to dramatize the unsuspected dignity of man, and at his worst he is apt to destroy his usefulness by making himself ridiculous.

NEPTUNE IN THE ELEVENTH HOUSE demands that experience remain exciting, and eliminates all value in fixed objectives. This position invites self-limitation through an unrealized dependence upon the encouragement of others, or upon the basic drifts in life. The native at his best is able to exalt all human expectation, and at his worst he is apt to encourage a dangerous wishful thinking in everyone.

NEPTUNE IN THE TWELFTH HOUSE demands that experience remain harrowing or disconcerting, and denies all efforts toward psychological self-assurance. This position invites self-limitation through an unreasoning dependence upon custom and inertia. The native at his best is able to reveal or shape the basic undercurrents of life, and at his worst he is apt to distort all experience through an unbridled imagination.

PLUTO IN THE EQUATOR

The eternal fitness of things
SAMUEL CLARKE, *Being and Attributes of God*

PLUTO IN THE FIRST HOUSE gives a social perspective which orients the individual to life as a whole by entirely direct or first-hand experience. This position enhances any analytical interest in the significance of personal action. The native at his best is able to understand and develop the fullest potentials of human nature in everyone, and at his worst he is apt to encourage a destructive self-sufficiency.

PLUTO IN THE SECOND HOUSE gives a social perspective which orients the individual to life as a whole through the ebb and flow of resources in ordinary living. This position enhances any analytical interest in the economic potentials of human relationship. The native at his best is able to uncover broader uses for everything at hand, and at his worst he is apt to discount every fruitage of experience.

PLUTO IN THE THIRD HOUSE gives a social perspective which orients the individual to life as a whole by his involvement in minor responsibility. This enhances any analytical interest in commonplace or neighborly relations. The native at his best is able to ferret out and capitalize upon the social capacities of everyone around him, and at his worst he is apt to belittle or sabotage any activity he cannot dominate.

PLUTO IN THE FOURTH HOUSE gives a social perspective which orients the individual to life as a whole through whatever private world he may establish. This position enhances any analytical interest in human comforts and personal security. The native at his best is able to bring memorable or immortal qualities to all personal relationship, and at his worst he is apt to undercut every basis for self-respect.

PLUTO IN THE FIFTH HOUSE gives a social perspective which orients the individual to life as a whole by the natural experimentation of everyday living. This position enhances any analytical interest in creative self-release through the talents. The native at his best is able to add dimension to any individual's psychological outreach, and at his worst he is apt to encourage a subtle self-wastage.

PLUTO IN THE SIXTH HOUSE gives a social perspective which orients the individual to life as a whole through recurring problems of socio-economic adjustment. This position enhances any analytical interest in the service functions of society. The native at his best is able to stimulate everyone to significant effort, and at his worst he is apt to contribute covertly to the maladjustments around him.

PLUTO IN THE SEVENTH HOUSE gives a social perspective which orients the individual to life as a whole by the direct issues of everyday affairs. This position enhances any analytical interest in human conflicts and co-operations as such. The native at his best is able to develop harmonious relations in any matter of common concern, and at his worst he is apt to intensify every lurking passion.

PLUTO IN THE EIGHTH HOUSE gives a social perspective which orients the individual to life as a whole through his sensitiveness to the social necessities placed upon him. This position enhances any analytical interest in the immediate significance of group resources. The native at his best is able to bring out the unsuspected capacities of everyone, and at his worst he is apt to reduce life to near-anarchy.

PLUTO IN THE NINTH HOUSE gives a social perspective which orients the individual to life as a whole by the impact of science, religion and philosophy. This position enhances any analytical interest in the competency of human knowledge. The native at his best is able to elevate the standards of any milieu in which he finds himself, and at his worst he is apt to develop a vicious muddlemindedness.

PLUTO IN THE TENTH HOUSE gives a social perspective which orients the individual to life as a whole through whatever authority he wins for himself. This position enhances any analytical interest in government, business and group projects. The native at his best is able to win a broad support for any enterprise, and at his worst he is apt to encourage an insidious callousness or tyranny.

PLUTO IN THE ELEVENTH HOUSE gives a social perspective which orients the individual to life as a whole by his completeness of self-assimilation into momentums and objectives. This position enhances any analytical interest in the dynamic vision which leads men to action. The native at his best is able to become exceedingly long-headed, and at his worst he is apt to reduce all ambition to a cut-throat level.

PLUTO IN THE TWELFTH HOUSE gives a social perspective which orients the individual to life as a whole through various psychological relationships. This position enhances any analytical interest in the unexpected and subtle developments which engulf the unwary. The native at his best in able to create a sustaining inner rapport of real power, and at his worst he is apt to become a subversive influence everywhere.

CHAPTER FIFTEEN

The Refinement of Character

The effective mobilization by man of his personal characteristics, or what becomes the functional manipulation of his potentialities, is a matter of utilizing the various resources in charcter and capacity, or of holding them in check. He can sing, or he can drop off into philosophical reflection. He can stir himself in a high physical sensitiveness to danger, or relax in a complete melting of the self through some esthetic enjoyment. He cultivates or strengthens the potentials of function whenever he has recourse to them, just as he contributes to their disintegration and ineffectiveness by his failure to put them to work. His choices in the one way or the other, taken all together, determine the refinement of his characteristics, whether for the better or the worse.

Astology reveals the pattern by which this refining process may have its most gratifying results. Exactly as any individual must know what clothes to wear for this or that occasion, what words or attitudes to use in social intercourse of a given sort, so must he have a better basis than mere chance, or primitive instinct, in calling upon one as against another characteristic facet of selfhood. The ten planets, by their place in the signs of his horoscope, show the particular ways in which his personality can operate in its exercise of its own nature, thus offering effective guidance for the very best cultivation of character, and for a genuine capitalization upon its worth.

THE SUN IN THE ECLIPTIC

Let not the sun look down and say,
Inglorious here he lies.
BENJAMIN FRANKLIN, *Poor Richard*

THE SUN IN ARIES identifies an individual in whom the cardinal and fire characteristics have their sharpest convergence. Life for him must be exciting, and he must be self-reliant. This means he is essentially fearless, and that he likes to move quickly and positively, taking the full consequences of whatever he does. He does not care much for abstract considerations, and gives little thought to other people.[1]

THE SUN IN TAURUS identifies an individual in whom the fixed and earth characteristics have their sharpest convergence. Life for him must be purposeful, and he must be easily influenced. This means he is eager for experience, but highly sensitive, and often made inarticulate rather than moved to the energy of which he is capable. He can be patient, steadfast and proud, or else touchy, possessive and a martyr.

THE SUN IN GEMINI identifies an individual in whom the common and air characteristics had their sharpest convergence. Life for him must be personal, and he must be readily stimulated. This means he is alive and keen, practical and impatient, the best of friends in an emergency and a rather shallow acquaintance in any long pull of accomplishment. He is intimate, inquisitive, enthusiastic and restless.

THE SUN IN CANCER identifies an individual in whom the cardinal and water characteristics have their sharpest convergence. Life for him must be exciting, and he must be self-consummating. This means he is willful, possessive, unhurried, and gifted with insight into the possibility of things. He

---

[1] The full description of the Aries type *per se*—that is, as determined by various combinations of sun, moon, ascendant or especially significant groupings of planets, but not by some one or other of these factors when the personality is largely or predominantly typed by a different sign—has been given on page 160, with the other characteristic signatures of the zodiac following according to the order by quadrature within each triplicity.

is unpredictable, stubborn in whatever course he adopts, ever opportunistic or calculating, and self-centered.

THE SUN IN LEO identifies an individual in whom the fixed and fire characteristics have their sharpest convergence. Life for him must be purposeful, and he must be self-reliant. This means that he is the magistrate at heart, inclined to dramatize values for all the world, and able to give special importance to everything he does. He is complacent, competent and highly imaginative. He thrives on adulation.

THE SUN IN VIRGO identifies an individual in whom the common and earth characteristics have their sharpest convergence. Life for him must be personal, and he must be easily influenced. This means he enjoys intimate relationships, and always finds a special niche for everything. He is capable of great self-sacrifice, and is a born commoner, but he may be very unreasonable and so lose all perspective.

THE SUN IN LIBRA identifies an individual in whom the cardinal and air characteristics have their sharpest convergence. Life for him must be exciting, and he must be readily stimulated. This means he is an unconditioned enthusiast, an extremist in all he does, and the moodiest of people. He rejoices in change and the chance to try things. He can be charming and exhilarating, or inconstant and ruthless.

THE SUN IN SCORPIO identifies an individual in whom the fixed and water characteristics have their sharpest convergence. Life for him must be purposeful, and he must be self-consummating. This means he is determined, clever and scheming, able to fathom the motives of others and so politically gifted. His ingrained impersonality makes him the most self-intent, creatively curious and single-minded of men.

THE SUN IN SAGITTARIUS identifies an individual in whom the common and fire characteristics have their sharpest convergence. Life for him must be personal, and he must be self-reliant. This means he is the promoter and administrator, delighting in companionship and incined to be the good sport always. He has no great discrimination, and is no intellectual, but he is hearty and able to inspire others.

THE SUN IN CAPRICORN identifies an individual in whom the

cardinal and earth characteristics have their sharpest convergence. Life for him must be exciting, and he must be easily influenced. This means he worries constantly, yet meets any emergency with a genuine ingenuity. He is a conformist, but often officious and prone to take an ell for an inch, characteristically insatiable in his interests and activities.

THE SUN IN AQUARIUS identifies an individual in whom the fixed and air characteristics have their sharpest convergence. Life for him must be purposeful, and he must be readily stimulated. This means he is high-visioned, optimistic, gregarious to a fault, and often gullible. He must be challenged to his best, or he becomes dogmatic and jealous. He is a realist in minor things, a do-or-die idealist otherwise.

THE SUN IN PISCES identifies an individual in whom the common and water characteristics have their sharpest convergence. Life for him must be personal, and he must be self-consummating. This means he is interested in himself and his own, but capable of broad emotional entanglements. He is mystically inclined, ever seeking poetic and hidden implications. He is universal in taste but intimate in manner.

THE MOON IN THE ECLIPTIC

Does the moon care for the barking of a dog?
ROBERT BURTON, *Anatomy of Melancholy*

THE MOON IN ARIES describes a temperament which is characteristically responsive to life as adventure, and which reacts to experience as an essentially thrilling means of self-realization. The native is emotionally independent of the people around him, his feelings sharp and often a conscious and very convenient instrument of his purpose. He is warm when interested, otherwise detached and inwardly unstirred.[2]

THE MOON IN TAURUS describes a temperament which is characteristically responsive to the revaluation it gains at the hands of others, and which reacts always to the actuality of life. The native is emotionally keyed to the ideals which are

[2] Compare footnote on page 285.

most familiar or useful, and he is incapable of any real feeling except in their terms. He is blindly faithful, sentimental and affectionate, often unoriginal and timid.

THE MOON IN GEMINI describes a temperament which is characteristically responsive to the interesting and intimate contacts of the moment, and which reacts to the challenge of accustomed experience. The native is emotionally sympathetic with every effort of his fellows, hurrying to encourage them on the slightest provocation, but he is generally incapable of sustained feeling or undivided loyalty.

THE MOON IN CANCER describes a temperament which is characteristically responsive to self-existence as an adventure, and which reacts to experience with a possessive and confident expectation. The native is emotionally maternal, hence often patronizing, and always sympathetic in his own individual fashion. He is naïvely trusting in his affections, but devastatingly exacting of anything he cannot encompass.

THE MOON IN LEO describes a temperament which is characteristically responsive to life as an individual responsibility, and which reacts to every eventuality as a necessity for decision, dictation or firm stand along some predefined line. The native is emotionally self-sufficient, inclined to let things alone unless they concern him, but bitterly resentful of criticism or interference when he decides to act.

THE MOON IN VIRGO describes a temperament which is characteristically responsive to direct encouragement or appreciation, and which reacts to others with a deep hunger for common experience or shared self-realizations. The native is emotionally overeager, and inclined to anticipate or dictate the course of development in all relationships. He is insistent, often petulant, but ever generous in service.

THE MOON IN LIBRA describes a temperament which is characteristically responsive to the trial or discovery of self as a continuing adventure, and which reacts with high opportunism to every opening for shared experience. The native is emotionally supercharged with an easy, gracious and impersonal fellow-feeling for mankind. He lives hard, although for the moment, and is up and down with every shift about him.

THE MOON IN SCORPIO describes a temperament which is characteristically responsive to life in its organic wholeness, and which reacts directly to inner motives, and to political rather than practical exigencies. The native is emotionally insatiable when it comes to enjoying and completing whatever activity or interest he initiates or adopts as his own, and he is almost devoid of ordinary sympathy or surface feeling.

THE MOON IN SAGITTARIUS describes a temperament which is characteristically responsive to experience in its greatest social naïveté, and which reacts to other people as so much a part of self that the personalities almost melt into each other. The native yearns to do things with everybody. He has the open friendliness of a young animal, and is blissfully unaware of real human differences.

THE MOON IN CAPRICORN describes a temperament which is characteristically responsive to life as a constant adventure in the justification of self, and which reacts with high opportunism to every chance for becoming necessary in some given situation. The native is emotionally supersensitive, often hypercritical of his fellows, but untiring and most considerate when interested.

THE MOON IN AQUARIUS describes a temperament which is characteristically responsive to experience as the proving-ground of self, and which reacts to everything on an idealistic or utilitarian pattern. The native is emotionally overloaded with potentials of self-release which may be spilled out as sheer desire, used to buttress some pet cause, or stored up in high frustration. He is prodigal, but careful.

THE MOON IN PISCES describes a temperament which is characteristically responsive to the depths of human experience, and which reacts in an underlying affection for all people everywhere. The native is emotionally naïve, continually excusing or overlooking personal deficiencies, and struggling against any subjection of living values to cold reason. Unselfishness is his god, and he often pauperizes others.

MARS IN THE ECLIPTIC

We sack, we ransack to the utmost sands
Of native kingdoms, and of foreign lands:
We travel sea and soil; we pry, and prowl,
We progress, and we prog from pole to pole.
                    FRANCIS QUARLES, *Divine Emblems*

MARS IN ARIES reveals a characteristic inclination to act with simple assurance, meeting the need of the moment and disregarding any consequences other than the immediate results in the practical situation at hand. The native asserts himself in the petty details of life by brushing aside unnecessary preparations, or any consideration of remote contingencies, and either does what he wants to do or else forgets it.

MARS IN TAURUS reveals a characteristic inclination to act with a calculated self-realization, able to put up an impenetrable screen to protect an extreme sensitivity, or else to mold and refine the ideals and hopes of others by an intensity of participation in events. The native asserts himself in the petty details of life by a practical and quiet attention, but he can rise to a white passion in emergencies.

MARS IN GEMINI reveals a characteristic inclination to act with an enthusiastic acquiescence in anything projected by others, or with a momentary throwing of the self into every phase of familiar routine. The native asserts himself in the petty details of life by taking more than his expected part in immediate affairs, destructively if he cannot do so otherwise, and by trying to be everywhere at once.

MARS IN CANCER reveals a charactistic inclination to act with naïve self-interest, paying as little attention as possible to the exigencies of the moment, and moving at whatever tangent promises to center any major developments upon the self. The native asserts himself in the petty details of life by a dynamic inertia, or by a consistent overruling, diverting or reshaping of every activity around him.

MARS IN LEO reveals a characteristic inclination to act with simple fidelity to the ideals or principles which the self has built into its own particular personality, ignoring exterior compulsions on the one hand and avoiding mere opportunism on the other. The native asserts himself in the petty details of life by dramatizing his own conceptions in everything he does, or by making a game of everyday living.

MARS IN VIRGO reveals a characteristic inclination to act with a calculated and selfish desire for comfort, willing to pay any reasonable or fair price for the co-operation of others, but draining everyone psychologically, if not actually manipulating their personal affairs. The native asserts himself in the petty details of life by making many demands while also proffering unlimited services or favors.

MARS IN LIBRA reveals a characteristic inclination to act with an enthusiastic letting-go of every available energy, and a constant if unwitting extension of the scope in experience through an insatiable experimentation in all possible relationships. The native asserts himself in the petty details of life by his willingness to face any situation, and to quarrel with all those who do not welcome his co-operation.

MARS IN SCORPIO reveals a characteristic inclination to act with a naïve confidence in every personal idea or notion, thus creating an exceptional efficiency in self-mobilization and leading to a long-headed preparation for contingencies. The native asserts himself in the petty details of life by consistently disregarding the immediate situation as it stands, and doing what he wants to do at his own convenience.

MARS IN SAGITTARIUS reveals a characteristic inclination to act wth simple faith in the good fellowship and fairness of all men, playing no favorites but making no specific connections and so accepting no particular obligation to definite people or occasions. The native asserts himself in the petty details of life by conforming rather easily to current procedures, and by following some convenient example.

MARS IN CAPRICORN reveals a characteristic inclination to act with a calculated self-interest, moving to make any issue a personal opportunity, and possessing a very competent instinct for meeting sudden emergencies in a way that turns out to be an advantage. The native asserts himself in the petty details of life by a simple practicality, ignoring what does not interest him and riding over all who get in his way.

MARS IN AQUARIUS reveals a characteristic inclination to act with an enthusiasm of vision, self-mobilization and unleashed passion which will usually carry through to the goal, irrespective of its wisdom or even its desirability. The native asserts himself in the petty details of life by the intensity of his interest in everything around him, and his willingness to expend himself whole-heartedly at any hour of the day or night.

MARS IN PISCES reveals a characteristic inclination to act with a naïve presumption of the sympathy and support of everyone concerned in any given situation, together with a confidence in the ability of the self to win others to whatever is undertaken. The native asserts himself in the petty details of life by an emotional resort to the imaginative, poetic and spiritual implications in every phase of experience.

VENUS IN THE ECLIPTIC

He who has put a good finish to his undertaking
is said to have placed a golden crown to the whole.
EUSTATHIUS, *Commentary on the Iliad*

VENUS IN ARIES discloses a characteristic fondness for life in its direct or immediate and fundamentally thrilling phases, and a tendency to bring things to completion by a ruthless elimination of all side interests. The native makes himself comfortable, under the everyday demands upon him, by letting most events take their course, and by mobilizing his charms or abilities where they will mean the most.

VENUS IN TAURUS discloses a characteristic fondness for life in its practical idealism or individual courageousness, and a tendency to round out experience in terms of tangible realizations. The native makes himself comfortable, under the everyday demands upon him, by his complete release of self in every situation he understands, and by his unerring sensitiveness to any inadequate or incomplete consummation.

VENUS IN GEMINI discloses a characteristic fondness for life in its essentially personal enthusiasms, and a tendency to bring things to completion speedily in order to make way for some new interest. The native makes himself comfortable, under the everyday demands upon him, by his cheerfulness in superficial favors as occasion offers, and by his skill in directing the vivifying impulses of everyone around him.

VENUS IN CANCER discloses a characteristic fondness for life in its simple or unconditioned universality, and a tendency to round out experience rather unpredictably in a ruthless self-interest. The native makes himself comfortable, under the everyday demands upon him, by insulating himself from any disturbing elements in his experience, and by maintaining an unswerving fidelity to his own desires.

VENUS IN LEO discloses a characteristic fondness for life in its common or spontaneous dramatizations of human values, and a tendency to bring things to completion arbitrarily or in response to an inner and private consideration. The native makes himself comfortable, under the everyday demands upon him, by ignoring his fellows except as they show an effective respect for his accomplishments and his notions.

VENUS IN VIRGO discloses a characteristic fondness for life in its transient human relations, and a tendency to round out experience in its own more personal terms. The native makes himself comfortable, under the everyday demands upon him, by his conscientious attention to routine or avoidance of all procrastination, and by his persistent focusing of all immediate interest in the most vital end results.

VENUS IN LIBRA discloses a characteristic fondness for life in its simple excitement, and a tendency to bring things to completion the moment fresh interests are ready to replace the old ones. The native makes himself comfortable, under the everyday demands upon him, by the grace with which he meets any new development, and by his gift for engineering consummations as pleasing to his fellows as to himself.

VENUS IN SCORPIO discloses a characteristic fondness for life in its ideal illimitability, and a tendency to round out experience through an entirely self-centered rationalization. The native makes himself comfortable, under the everyday demands upon him, by putting his own private meaning in everything that happens, and by extricating himself continually from any uninteresting participation in passing events.

VENUS IN SAGITTARIUS discloses a characteristic fondness for life in its kaleidoscopic surface phases, and a tendency to bring things to completion rather abruptly, either because of thinning interest or exhausted potentials. The native makes himself comfortable, under the everyday demands upon him, by moving from one relationship to another, and by feeling free to make demands upon anyone.

VENUS IN CAPRICORN discloses a characteristic fondness for life in its commonplace functioning, and a tendency to round out experience quite selfishly, the moment it serves its purpose. The native makes himself comfortable, under the everyday demands upon him, by working to eliminate whatever proves to be annoying in one fashion or another, and by his continual exercise and improvement of his own skills for his own advantage.

VENUS IN AQUARIUS discloses a characteristic fondness for life in its intellectual or ideal enthusiasms, and a tendency to bring things to completion in response to a very deliberate notion. The native makes himself comfortable, under the everyday demands upon him, by refusing to be involved in trivial matters, and by making everything around him significant in the light of his own personal ideas.

VENUS IN PISCES discloses a characteristic fondness for life in its personal illimitability or endless ramifications of human expression, and a tendency to round out experience by putting it into some frame of larger reality. The native makes himself comfortable, under the everyday demands upon him, by sharing his feelings with his intimates, and by exalting everything in a deep mystical fashion.

MERCURY IN THE ECLIPTIC

To flee from folly is the beginning of wisdom.
HORACE, *Epistles*

MERCURY IN ARIES delineates a type of mind which characteristically anchors itself in the immediate reality of life, and which relies more upon its initial than its final insights. This means a mentality which is alert rather than reflective, accepting events with a naïve impartiality. The frame of reference in all its thinking is the direct experience of the self in an actual context of everyday living.

MERCURY IN TAURUS delineates a type of mind which characteristically anchors itself in the idealized struggle of life, and which relies more upon its final than its initial insights. This means a mentality which is tentative, cautious and highly expectant rather than experimentative, unrestricted and indiscriminate. The frame of reference in all its thinking is the pattern of reality established in general experience.

MERCURY IN GEMINI delineates a type of mind which characteristically anchors itself in the socialized promise of life, and which relies more upon its initial than its final insights. This means a mentality which is impressionable, changeable and exhilarating rather than self-sufficient or inspired in any way. The frame of reference in all its thinking is the conventional expectation in human conduct.

MERCURY IN CANCER delineates a type of mind which characteristically anchors itself in the immediate satisfactions of life, and which relies more upon its final than its initial insights. This means a mentality which is culminative, dogmatic and circumscribed rather than original, adjustable and inquiring. The frame of reference in all its thinking is the self-completeness to which it necessarily challenges itself.

MERCURY IN LEO delineates a type of mind which characteristically anchors itself in the idealized reality of life, and which relies more upon its initial than its final insights. This means a mentality which is fundamentally stirred within itself, rather than influenced by exterior relationships. The frame of reference in all its thinking is the significance of the self in the experience of the moment.

MERCURY IN VIRGO delineates a type of mind which characteristically anchors itself in the socialized struggle of life, and which relies more upon its final than its initial insights. This means a mentality which is exacting rather than sure of itself, and which in consequence requires continual reaffirmation and repetition. The frame of reference in all its thinking is the practical problems of everyday living.

MERCURY IN LIBRA delineates a type of mind which characteristically anchors itself in the immediate promise of life, and which relies more upon its initial than its final insights. This means a mentality which is responsive to things rather than self-activated, and so definitely partial to each passing interest. The frame of reference in all its thinking is the world of special relations in which it functions.

MERCURY IN SCORPIO delineates a type of mind which characteristically anchors itself in the idealized satisfactions of life, and which relies more upon its final than its initial insights. This means a mentality which is given breadth and certainty rather than shaped or even remotely influenced by various climates of opinion. The frame of reference in all its thinking is the native's private pattern of reality.

MERCURY IN SAGITTARIUS delineates a type of mind which characteristically anchors itself in the socialized reality of life, and which relies more upon its initial than its final insights. This means a mentality which is opportunistic rather than thorough, and so inclined to seek quantity and surface value in knowledge. The frame of reference in all its thinking is the arena of human relationships in action.

MERCURY IN CAPRICORN delineates a type of mind which characteristically anchors itself in the immediate struggle of life, and which relies more upon its final than its initial insights. This means a mentality which is critical and realistic rather than comprehensive or consistent in any generalized fashion. The frame of reference in all its thinking is the momentary situation and its challenge to individual competency.

MERCURY IN AQUARIUS delineates a type of mind which characteristically anchors itself in the idealized promise of life, and which relies more upon its initial than its final insights. This means a mentality which is inspired rather than refined by experience, and so apt to overreach itself. The frame of reference in all its thinking is the pattern of values in which human vision is nurtured.

MERCURY IN PISCES delineates a type of mind which characteristically anchors itself in the socialized satisfactions of life, and which relies more upon its final than its initial insights. This means a mentality which is assured or encouraged rather than captivated or stimulated by experience. The frame of reference in all its thinking is the symbolical and wholly emotional background of the personality.

JUPITER IN THE ECLIPTIC

Two things fill the mind with ever new and increasing wonder and awe—the starry heavens above me and the moral law within me.
IMMANUEL KANT, *Critique of Pure Reason*

JUPITER IN ARIES indicates the development of a consciousness which is characteristically self-sufficient, and quick in its response to new situations. Its fundamental motivation arises from its own unimpeachable sincerity in every issue of life. The native as a real personage is interested in adequate fields for his talents, and his welfare demands a continual and insistent personal challenge.

JUPITER IN TAURUS indicates the development of a consciousness which is characteristically self-exploiting, and sure in its response to ideas. Its fundamental motivation arises from its own inexhaustible capacity for experience with an inner implication. The native as a real personage is interested in making an effective contribution to the values of life, and his welfare requires a genuine role in human progress.

JUPITER IN GEMINI indicates the development of a consciousness which is characteristically self-projective, and generous in its response to human relations. Its fundamental motivation arises from the full appreciation for its efforts which it is able to gain from others. The native as a real personage is interested in every chance to stimulate people, and his welfare demands a multiplicity of personal contacts.

JUPITER IN CANCER indicates the development of a consciousness which is characteristically self-satisfied, and quick in its response to new situations. Its fundamental motivation arises from its own complete tolerance for experience in any given phase. The native as a real personage is interested in the perfection of living, and his welfare demands a continual reinforcement of his own cloistered reality.

JUPITER IN LEO indicates the development of a consciousness which is characteristically self-sufficient, and sure in its response to ideas. Its fundamental motivation arises from its own unimpeachable sincerity in holding to values. The native as a real personage is interested in the meaning of life, and his welfare demands a chance to build up and dramatize some ideal in his own character.

JUPITER IN VIRGO indicates the development of a consciousness which is characteristically self-exploiting, and generous in its response to human relations. Its fundamental motivation arises from its own inexhaustible capacity for everyday associations. The native as a real personage is interested in making his world a more comfortable place, and his welfare demands the fullest chance for working with others.

JUPITER IN LIBRA indicates the development of a consciousness which is characteristically self-projecting, and quick in its response to new situations. Its fundamental motivation arises from the full appreciation for its efforts which it is able to gain in every issue of life. The native as a real personage is interested in an effective self-discovery, and his welfare demands a continually unfolding opportunity for himself and others.

JUPITER IN SCORPIO indicates the development of a consciousness which is characteristically self-satisfied, and sure in its response to ideas. Its fundamental motivation arises from its own complete tolerance for experience with any given implication. The native as a real personage is interested in the perfection of human ideals, and his welfare demands a definite chance to test all the values of life for himself.

JUPITER IN SAGITTARIUS indicates the development of a consciousness which is characteristically self-sufficient, and generous in its response to human relations. Its fundamental motivation arises from its own unimpeachable sincerity in dealing with other people. The native as a real personage is interested in the simple activities of every day, and his welfare demands a consistently free living.

JUPITER IN CAPRICORN indicates the development of a consciousness which is characteristically self-exploiting, and quick in its response to new situations. Its fundamental motivation arises from its own inexhaustible capacity in meeting any issue of life. The native as a real personage is interested in dominating the milieu in which he finds himself, and his welfare requires a continual proving of his talents.

JUPITER IN AQUARIUS indicates the development of a consciousness which is characteristically self-projecting, and sure in its response to ideas. Its fundamental motivation arises from the full approval for its efforts which it is able to gain from the established standards of life. The native as a real personage is interested in a genuine self-quickening, and his welfare demands a constantly broadening experience.

JUPITER IN PISCES indicates the development of a consciousness which is characteristically self-satisfied, and generous in its response to human relations. Its fundamental motivation arises from its own complete tolerance for experience with any given person. The native as a real personage is interested in the perfection of the ties among men, and his welfare demands a continual chance for sympathy with the people around him.

SATURN IN THE ECLIPTIC

And the Lord said unto Satan, Whence comest thou? Then Satan answered the Lord, and said From going to and fro in the earth, and from walking up and down in it.

Job, 1:7

SATURN IN ARIES shows a characteristic sensitiveness which may lead the native to attempt too hurried a perfecting of his special potentialities. An inner dignity of self requires him to

299

demand a more than normal recognition or encouragement from life at large. His basic personality is refined by the necessity that he reconstitute and re-establish himself with every new development in his general situation.

SATURN IN TAURUS shows a characteristic sensitiveness which may lead the native to an unnecessary agonizing over his deeper ideals. An inner dignity of self requires him to sustain a realization of some worthy destiny for himself. His basic personality is refined by the necessity that he translate his ideals into definite action, or in some way strengthen the *esprit de corps* of his own milieu.

SATURN IN GEMINI shows a characteristic sensitiveness which may lead the native to irritate the people who might contribute most to his experience. An inner dignity of self requires him to accept every normal channel of social intercourse. His basic personality is refined by the necessity that he clarify or deepen his everyday contacts with others by stimulating an inner potentiality in each case.

SATURN IN CANCER shows a characteristic sensitiveness which may lead the native to overreach himself in his effort to control the factors of a given situation. An inner dignity of self requires him to deal with every critical issue in an honest and complete self-interest. His basic personality is refined by the necessity that he perfect his hold on lesser things as a way for reaching out to the greater ones.

SATURN IN LEO shows a characteristic sensitiveness which may lead the native to jump to conclusions, or to act before he has thought things through. An inner dignity of self requires him to cultivate permanent insights from every passing detail of experience. His basic personality is refined by the necessity that he demonstrate or exemplify every virtue or capacity he chooses to applaud or make his own.

SATURN IN VIRGO shows a characteristic sensitiveness which may lead the native to reduce all personal experience to cheapness and inadequacy. An inner dignity of self requires him to approach life with a true humbleness, rather than self-depreciation. His basic personality is refined by the necessity that he exalt personal relations, bringing a special adventure in self-fulfillment to every human fellowship.

SATURN IN LIBRA shows a characteristic sensitiveness which may lead the native to antagonize others through his own impatience or willingness to compromise. An inner dignity of self requires him to make an unceasing impact of his best efforts upon all experience. His basic personality is refined by the necessity that he work with people generally in a mutual respect for capacities and motives.

SATURN IN SCORPIO shows a characteristic sensitiveness which may lead the native to lean altogether too readily upon his own unsupported notions. An inner dignity of self requires him to re-establish his personal perspective with every new turn in experience. His basic personality is refined by the necessity that he actually earn, in an everyday world, whatever moral support he needs.

SATURN IN SAGITTARIUS shows a characteristic sensitiveness which may lead the native to depend entirely too much on other people. An inner dignity of self requires him to plumb every possibility of relationship with those to whom he is linked by circumstances. His basic personality is refined by the necessity that he put his best foot forward in everything he does, even when not disposed to do so.

SATURN IN CAPRICORN shows a characteristic sensitiveness which may lead the native to hurry through all his experience, and so miss its real significance. An inner dignity of self requires him to give an intelligent ordering to everything in which he is concerned. His basic personality is refined by the necessity that he achieve any recognition for himself through the fundamental excellence of whatever he does.

SATURN IN AQUARIUS shows a characteristic sensitiveness which may lead the native to destroy his effective vision by compromising with lesser and transient considerations. An inner dignity of self requires him to develop a quickened understanding of all human idealizations. His basic personality is refined by the necessity that he take some interest in every significant movement or enterprise of his own day.

SATURN IN PISCES shows a characteristic sensitiveness which may lead the native to dissipate his underlying and vital rapport with others. An inner dignity of self requires him to make his principal ties with those who can hold him to his own highest promise. His basic personality is refined by the necessity that he cultivate an experience which challenges his poetic appreciation and puts his sympathies to work.

URANUS IN THE ECLIPTIC

*That so few now dare to be eccentric
marks the chief danger of the time.*
JOHN STUART MILL, *On Liberty*

URANUS IN ARIES encourages a characteristic emphasis of individuality through the native's gift for persistent self-assertion, or for seeking experience in which he can respond with the direct and simple naturalness of his own being. He is able to regrasp or master his destiny at any time by reverting to eccentricity, or permitting some unconditioned impulse to establish a new focus in reality.[3]

URANUS IN TAURUS encourages a characteristic emphasis of individuality through the native's gift for integrating all possible social acts and judgments, growing in personality through

[3] The three planets of social significance move so slowly that their indications apply of necessity to very large blocks of people, i.e., those who are born, raised and carried through experience together in more or less common patterns of general orientation. To have cases of Uranus in all twelve signs, the spread of nearly a century in births is necessary. The years needed for Neptune are double. It is practically impossible, in the instance of Pluto, to find living examples for more than four of the ecliptical mansions. This means that the characteristics now to be listed, particularly for Neptune and Pluto, will apply to whole generations of people. This fact must be kept in mind with all three newer planets, and it has a special importance in Neptune's case because that body seems to give a particular distribution of subdivisions in the theoretical great ages of man, that is, the sign-intervals in the precession of the equinoxes.

this depth of his interest in organized progress. He is able to regrasp or master his destiny at any time by re-ordering the pertinent considerations of his own affairs, and adopting a more promising frame of reference for them.

URANUS IN GEMINI encourages a characteristic emphasis of individuality through the native's gift for encouraging others to assert themselves in experience, and for developing new ways to do things. He is able to regrasp or master hs destiny at any time by dropping threadbare interests and turning his attention afresh to the life about him, cultivating new contacts where he can help and be helped.

URANUS IN CANCER encourages a characteristic emphasis of individuality through the native's gift for sustaining a definite personal uniqueness, either uninfluenced by events around him or else bringing everything to pivot upon himself. He is able to regrasp or master his destiny at any time by giving his exceptional self-interest a social significance, as in becoming a prophet of some sort.

URANUS IN LEO encourages a characteristic emphasis of individuality through the native's gift for dramatizing his own potentialities, thus giving his special assets an added social value. He is able to regrasp or master his destiny at any time by building upon some unusual development or situation in everyday experience, or by reshaping his own inner realization and developing a new personal intensity.

URANUS IN VIRGO encourages a characteristic emphasis of individuality through the native's gift for enhancing his own original usefulness in the commonplace functions he performs, and for bringing people into exceptionally practical relationship with each other. He is able to regrasp or master his destiny at any time by encouraging, organizing and utilizing various untried potentialities of the given milieu.

URANUS IN LIBRA encourages a characteristic emphasis of individuality through the native's gift for personal distinctiveness, or for a deliberate eccentricity which he employs to bring out the immediate potentials of a situation. He is able to regrasp or master his destiny at any time by his originality of approach to the given issue, or by demanding a completely new and different response from life as a whole.

URANUS IN SCORPIO encourages a characteristic emphasis of individuality through the native's gift for giving some unique twist or special pertinency to the ideas of his fellows, thereupon shaping their thinking or their prejudices to his own advantage. He is able to regrasp or master his destiny at any time by the basic originality of his own judgments, and the unconditioned self-sufficiency of his philosophy.

URANUS IN SAGITTARIUS encourages a characteristic emphasis of individuality through the native's gift for spontaneous and transient but fully rewarding relations with other people in the normal course of everyday living. He is able to regrasp or master his destiny at any time by making new and convenient social connections, profiting from his capacity for avoiding every hindering tie or trailing obligation.

URANUS IN CAPRICORN encourages a characteristic emphasis of individuality through the native's gift for capitalizing upon the unexpected eventualities of experience, and so opening new avenues of self-expression to himself. He is able to regrasp or master his destiny at any time by gathering the scattered threads of any special milieu, weaving them together with a unique and fascinating effectiveness.

URANUS IN AQUARIUS encourages a characteristic emphasis of individuality through the native's gift for quickening the vision of others and thereby putting human efforts into an intelligible pattern. He is able to regrasp or master his own destiny at any time by a simple intensification of his own personality, or by offering some unique and challenging way for a self-expending which makes life more worth living.

URANUS IN PISCES encourages a characteristic emphasis of individuality through the native's gift for an enduring sympathy or fellowship with men of all types and potentiality. He is able to regrasp or master his destiny at any time by developing these uniquely subjective ties with others, or by opening up some special capacity for sharing himself with his fellows in this emotional or spiritual fashion.

NEPTUNE IN THE ECLIPTIC

*I think there is a fatality in it—I seldom
go to the place I set out for.*
                STERNE, *A Sentimental Journey*

NEPTUNE IN ARIES requires a characteristic conformity by
the native to his astrological generation with its over-all culture of personality *per se*. He is able to achieve his own desires
fully when he demonstrates the genius of this individualistic
type. A contribution of this group in America was the establishment of Spiritualism, Christian Science and Theosophy as
a recrudescence of creative personality.[4]

NEPTUNE IN TAURUS requires a characteristic conformity by
the native to his astrological generation with its over-all culture of a new secular philosophy. He is able to achieve his own
desires fully when he shapes his actions to general standards
or idealized values. A contribution of this group in America
was the new conception of a democratic imperialism, i.e., the
rule of the world by self-made men.

NEPTUNE IN GEMINI requires a characteristic conformity by
the native to his astrological generation with its over-all culture of intellectualism as the hope of man. He is able to
achieve his own desires fully when he makes use of his social
resourcefulness or inventive faculties. A contribution of this

---

[4] It is impossible to specify—in terms of a definite number of years
with sharply defined boundaries—the domination of social events by
individuals whose horoscopes place Neptune in the given sign. A very
broad approximation is gained, in the delineations here given, by
taking these periods as beginning, in each case, some twenty-five
years after the planet's ingress. This does not mean that the pioneers
or leaders of the astrological generation were born with Neptune in
the particular zodiacal mansion, but rather that the great impetus
which they articulated has stemmed from the mass of those who were
so defined. Developments in the United States are used for illustration, but the phenomenon is world-wide, and can be traced out in
similar fashion everywhere. The thirteen or fourteen-year transitions
are subtle, although important and not difficult to recognize. They
are suggested here with only the briefest of pen strokes.

group in America was the recent wave of business efficiency, practical science and industrial development.

NEPTUNE IN CANCER requires a characteristic conformity by the native to his astrological generation with its over-all culture of an organic society. He is able to achieve his own desires fully when he co-operates in the struggle for a reconciliation of social conflicts. A contribution of this group in America was the socio-economic awakening, or individual perfectionism, interrupted by World War II.

NEPTUNE IN LEO requires a characteristic conformity by the native to his astrological generation with its over-all culture of an exalted personal leadership. He is able to achieve his own desires fully when he capitalizes upon his personal merits. A contribution of this group in America should in some way parallel the achievement of American independence by the previous Neptune-in-Leo generation.

NEPTUNE IN VIRGO requires a characteristic conformity by the native to his astrological generation with its over-all culture of a utilitarian society. He is able to achieve his own desires fully when he works his personal activities into the functional whole. A contribution of this group in the prior American cycle was the constitutional formulation of a middle-class democracy in its New World setting.

NEPTUNE IN LIBRA requires a characteristic conformity by the native to his astrological generation with its over-all culture of a rampant individualism. He is able to achieve his own desires fully when he centers his personal interests in enterprises which are challenging to his fellows. A contribution of this group in the prior American cycle was the great initial attack upon the open frontiers.

NEPTUNE IN SCORPIO requires a characteristic conformity by the native to his astrological generation with its over-all culture of an organized exploitation. He is able to achieve his own desires fully when he shapes his life to logical or scientific standards. A contribution of this group in America was the era of personal politics with the spoils system and a development of the periodic financial crisis.

NEPTUNE IN SAGITTARIUS requires a characteristic conformity by the native to his astrological generation with its over-all culture of national coalescences and compromises. He is able to achieve his own desires fully when he makes the fruits of his accomplishment available to others. A contribution of this group in America was in the exaggeration of free enterprise, and the intellectual awakening.

NEPTUNE IN CAPRICORN requires a characteristic conformity by the native to his astrological generation with its over-all culture of political opportunism, sectional rivalry and personal ingenuity. He is able to achieve his own desires fully when he capitalizes upon the community interest. A contribution of this group in America was the expansion of boundaries and a rising impetus to invention.

NEPTUNE IN AQUARIUS requires a characteristic conformity by the native to his astrological generation with its over-all culture of a new national idealism. He is able to achieve his own desires fully when he works to further the objectives of everyone. A contribution of this group in America was the scientific and industrial accomplishment of the Civil War period, and the abolition of slavery.

NEPTUNE IN PISCES requires a characteristic conformity by the native to his astrological generation with its over-all culture of creature comforts. He is able to achieve his own desires fully when he gives them an esthetic cast or humanistic implication. A contribution of this group in America was a new dimension of business functioning, and an effective intellectual revolt against traditionalism.

PLUTO IN THE ECLIPTIC

At night astronomers agree.
MATTHEW PRIOR, *Phillis's Age*

PLUTO IN ARIES creates a characteristic intellectual epoch marked by faith in the individual, or by an acceptance of his inviolability. The native is inclined to hail resourcefulness, welcome danger and employ violence as the most direct way to personal power. Here is *laissez faire* at its peak, represented by people born in the 1825–1853 period, and by the open-frontier spirit they intensified in America on through the Civil War and the 1873 panic.[5]

PLUTO IN TAURUS creates a characteristic intellectual epoch marked by an active interest in the practical integration of society. The native is inclined to look upon life in utilitarian fashion. Here is the extreme of psychological support for exploitation, represented by people born in the 1853–1884 period, and by the sensitiveness to world-wide potentialities they brought to experience upon their maturity.

PLUTO IN GEMINI creates a characteristic intellectual epoch marked by a high appreciation for human fellowship. The native is inclined to throw himself into any enterprise at hand, always seeking to speed life's course of action. Here is the psychological rejection of all traditionalism, represented by people born in the 1884–1914 period, and by the practical secularism developed with their rise to dominance.

PLUTO IN CANCER creates a characteristic intellectual epoch marked by an instinct for universal or absolute realization. The native is inclined to make the affairs of the world a very personal concern. Here is the psychological demand for authoritarian foundations, represented by people born in the 1914–1939 period, and by the struggle over global ideologies which they have begun to instrument in effective fashion.

PLUTO IN LEO creates a characteristic intellectual epoch marked by the individual's faith in his own ideas. The native is inclined to be very intense in his reaction to socio-economic and political problems. Here is the probable incentive, psychologically, for the coming conflicts over the spheres of

[5] This is description in historical perspective, yielding a significance which becomes pertinent only since 1930. These epochs of Pluto's influence, more a matter of intellectual orientation than social transition, are approximated on the same basis as the Neptune cycles in the preceding section. The positions of the third new planet are somewhat approximate, since astronomy as yet has no exact determination of its orbit, and cannot have for considerable time to come.

influence which support any balance of power, to be represented by people born in the 1939–1958 period.

PLUTO IN VIRGO creates a characteristic intellectual epoch marked by an active interest in human refinement and the perfection of social ties. The native is inclined to approach all life in somewhat clinical fashion. Here is the psychological drift towards a respect for personality, represented under the previous cycle and in England by people born in the 1711–1724 period, or the era of Methodism.

PLUTO IN LIBRA creates a characteristic intellectual epoch marked by a high sense of personal adventure. The native is inclined to an exaggerated opportunism in his reaction to the major issues of life. Here is the psychological enthusiasm over new experience, represented in Europe by people born in the 1724–1737 period, and by the particular humanistic ferment of Frederick the Great and Voltaire.

PLUTO IN SCORPIO creates a characteristic intellectual epoch marked by an instinct to psychological imperialism. The native is inclined to come to his own conclusions, and to advocate his ideas forcibly. Here is the will to self-determination, represented in America by people born in the 1737–1750 period, and by the rising political sensitiveness of the colonies, well dramatized at the Boston Tea Party.

PLUTO IN SAGITTARIUS creates a characteristic intellectual epoch marked by a full faith in human nature. The native is inclined to drive himself in a prodigal self-expenditure, whenever his own pattern of life proves of definite value to the group at large. Here is the psychological encouragement to mass political action, represented by people born in the 1750–1763 period, and by the American Revolution.

PLUTO IN CAPRICORN creates a characteristic intellectual epoch marked by an active interest in the over-all ordering of society. The native is inclined to be very critical in everything he does, impersonal and altogether unsparing of others. Here is the psychological support for any subordination of the individual to the group, represented by people born in the 1763–1778 period, and by the American Constitution.

PLUTO IN AQUARIUS creates a characteristic intellectual epoch marked by a high sense of group potentialities. The native is inclined to see possibilities in everything around him, and to give them high publicity. Here is the psychological support for social sharing, represented by people born in the 1778–1800 period, and by a first great surge of immigration, and of urban and industrial development.

PLUTO IN PISCES creates a characteristic intellectual epoch marked by universal aspirations. The native is inclined to live easily, but always exercising himself over world-wide issues. Here is the psychological encouragement for man's conquest of nature, represented by people born in the 1880–1825 period, and by exploration or discovery such as reached a climax in the California gold rush.

Appendixes

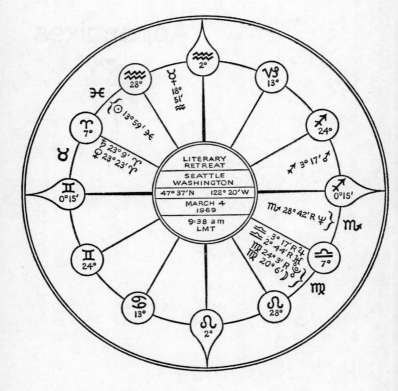

APPENDIX A

How to Cast
a Horoscope

The two great celestial circles, the equator and ecliptic that establish the astrological map of the heavens for any particular birth or event, have been shown in their fundamental relationship to each other on page 123 as follows:

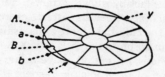

In erecting or setting up or casting a chart, as astrologers commonly describe the detailed calculations, the first task in terms of the diagram repeated here is to find the location of the notch A in the zodiac together with B and the other ten cusps of the houses.

A is Leo 6°36′ at Quito, Ecuador. At New York City, with x the autumnal equinox or Libra 0° lying at the same relative position, A would be Leo 20°35′ as explained on page 125. This involves much distortion of a mathematical sort that need never concern the newcomer to astrology, thanks to the fact that everything is worked out for him in the Tables of Houses. However, he must have a clear idea of the simple operations left to him in the ordinary course. Thus A may be anywhere in the zodiac, depending on how the two celestial circles lie together in respect to a particular horizon.[1] Hence y, the vernal equinox or Aries 0°, could replace x in the second house. Thereupon A, for New York City, would be Capricorn 16°30' as follows:

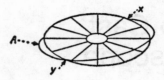

The equatorial divisions that actually are shown in the normal diagram have a fixed relation to the location on the earth for which the horoscope is calculated, since they represent the quarter segments in the heavens created by the horizon and meridian of that place. Astrological practice and convenience reflects this fact by showing the horizon as a horizontal line in the horoscopic wheel. Its eastern interception with the great circles, or the celestial sphere at its rising point from the perspective of an absolute north, is put at the left hand.[2] The equatorial mansions, presented above in perspective to indicate the situation of the zodiac in respect to them, are normally shown without distortion. The zodiacal lean is left to the imagination and the ecliptic itself omitted as on pages 126 and 310. The obliquity between these two planes established by the earth's motions has only a minor significance in the interpretation of an astrological chart despite its great importance in determining what zodiacal sign and degree correspond to a particular equatorial cusp when it comes to the given location on the globe's surface.

The horizon is the starting point in all astrological implica-

[1] Their relationship to each other is constant except for the almost negligible precessional crawl of about 50" annually.

[2] A few astrologers have reversed the procedure, giving the zodiac rather than houses a fixed position in their diagrammatic conventions, but this practice is seldom encountered.

tion but it is much more simple mathematically to begin the erection of a chart by calculating the position of the mid-heaven first, and this has become a universal practice. While the ascendant and descendant vary with geographical latitude, and the eight minor houses also in consequence, the tenth and fourth angles are the same at any particular longitude on the earth's surface from one pole to the other for any one individual position of the two great circles in the heavens. The midheaven cusp for all possible horoscopes is tabulated once for each day in the various ephemerides of the planets' places, and the initial step in casting a horoscope is to take this from the tables and to make any adjustment necessary when the birth or event is not at the precise time and place on which the ephemeris is based.

This meridian position is usually designated as sidereal time or given in hours, minutes and seconds rather than degrees of equatorial arc.[3] As an example if it is desired to know the cusps in an astrological map for 2:00 P.M., Greenwich mean time, July 4th, at London for a number of recent consecutive years and if both midnight and noon ephemerides for Greenwich (that is, London) are consulted, the sidereal times for midnight or noon may be listed for comparison.

		Midnight[4]			Noon		
1964	......	18h	48m	7s	6h	50m	6s
1965	......	18	47	10	6	49	8
1966	......	18	46	13	6	48	11
1967	......	18	45	16	6	47	14
1968	......	18	48	16	6	50	14

What the novice should notice here is that the change from

[3] In full, sidereal time of the midheaven and often in greater abbreviation merely S.T. when it is not to be confused with standard time. The term sidereal time is here a practical equivalent of right ascension since the emphasis is on the situation of the revolving heavens and not on the hour angle.

[4] This is the common but highly ambiguous term. What is meant is the 0h beginning the calendar day, as on a twenty-four-hour clock.

year to year is very minor, and that it is due mainly to the intercalary February 29th. Thus 1964 and 1968 agree within some nine seconds. What should be observed next is that when the twelve hours of the clock from midnight to noon are added to the sidereal times for each of the midnights and compared with the ones for noon there is a discrepancy of almost two full minutes.[5] This two minutes of course is essentially half the difference in sidereal time from one day to the next, and it represents the movement of the mean sun through the zodiac.[6] Hence the hours shown by the clock are not quite as long in everyday experience as those comprising a complete circle. The sun moving counterclockwise annually and clockwise daily meets itself so to speak by a little in each twenty-four hours, and every clock hour or fraction must be lengthened proportionately whenever used to adjust any position indicated in sidereal time. The two minutes of discrepancy make 120 seconds in the twelve hours, and so each hour of clock time elapsed after the midnight or noon for which an ephemeris is calculated must be corrected by the addition of ten seconds approximately or 9.856s exactly.[7] These hours and their correction are added to the sidereal time of the midheaven at Greenwich to find the sidereal time of the horoscope's midheaven. For 2:00 P.M. at London for July 4th, 1967, the computation from midnight is as follows:

S.T., July 4, 1967:	18h	45m	16s	
Time Interval:	14	0	0	
Interval correction:		2	18	
	32	47	34	= 8h 47m 34s

[5] 18 plus 12 is 30 which, minus 24, is 6. The twenty-four hours of the circle must always be added or subtracted as necessary.

[6] The mean sun is a fictitious body supposed to move uniformly in the heavens and varying from the actual movement by as much as a quarter hour twice a year. Apparent time shown by a normal sundial and created by the real sun is seldom used. All ordinary clocks and practically all astrological calculations and tables employ the mean time based on the fictitious movement, and in consequence there is

The computation from noon is similar, with the precise correction of 19.71s rounding to the 20s of simple approximation.

S.T., July 4, 1967:	6h	47m	14s
Time interval:	2	0	0
Interval correction:			20
	8	47	34

The most adequate Tables of Houses are the compilations by Joseph G. Dalton published in 1893 as *The Spherical Basis of Astrology* and those by Hugh S. Rice issued in 1944 as the *American Astrology Tables of Houses*. In the Dalton tables the 2:00 P.M. London midheaven sidereal time of 8h 47m 34s is close to halfway between the 8h 45m 44s of a Leo 9° midheaven and the 8h 49m 48s of a Leo 10° one, and can be taken precisely enough as Leo 9°30′. At 51° north latitude the difference of 43′ at the ascendant between Libra 29°18′ and Scorpio 0°1′ corresponding to the 60′ of difference between Leo 9° and Leo 10° at the midheaven would give Libra 29°39′ for the zodiacal rising point at 51° north, but half the difference of a diminishing 22′ of ascending point from 51° to 52° north means that 11′ must be subtracted from 29°29′ to locate the Libra ascendant at 29°18′.

In the Rice tables the midheaven sidereal time of 8h 47m 34s is between the 8h 44m 0s of Leo 8°34′24″ and the 8h 48m 0s of Leo 9°33′33″, and approximately within an eighth of the latter midheaven position. The movement in Leo corresponding here to the 4m interval in sidereal time is an almost precise 59′ of which an eighth is 7′ plus. Subtracting that from Leo 9°33′33″ gives a horoscopic midheaven somewhat more

---

nothing here for which the astrologer ever is likely to have to make adjustment.

[7] Most Tables of Houses list the exact corrections of mean to sidereal time for the entire twenty-four hours.

accurately at Leo 9°26'. At 51° north latitude the difference at the ascendant corresponding to 59' at the midheaven is 42' by these tables, and the eighth of it or an approximate 5' subtracted from Libra 29°42' gives 29°37'. This is corrected by subtracting a half of the diminishing 22' to the rising point at 52° north, to establish the horoscopic ascendant somewhat more precisely at Libra 29°26'.

If it is necessary to locate the house cusps of a horoscope for Oneonta, New York, at 2:00 P.M. on July 4, 1967, the procedure requires an additional adjustment that always is needed when birth is not on the prime meridian or at the 0° longitude of London. This of course is the usual case. Since Oneonta is situated almost precisely on the 75th west meridian, there is a time difference rounded to an even five hours from London to be taken into account. It will be found that the midheaven sidereal time at Oneonta is 49s later than for the same moment of the day in local mean time at London. What happens is the obvious fact that the sun must move in the zodiac during these five hours of time difference between 0° and 75° west longitude. The longitudinal adjustment becoming necessary is the unvarying correction of mean to sidereal time already employed in the preceding paragraphs for calculations at London when birth at that geographic point did not occur at the midnight or noon of the ephemeris. With the sun in its daily course rising in the east and setting in the west, time elapses progressively as horoscopic consideration is increasingly westward from London and the correction for this mean-time interval must obviously be added. Thus the midnight sidereal time at Greenwich can be used for Oneonta if the correction for the five hours of longitudinal difference or 50s approximately but 49.28s exactly is added into the computation as follows:

S.T., July 4, 1967:	18h	45m	16s		
Longitude correction:			49		
Time interval:	14	0	0		
Interval correction:		2	18		
	32	48	23	= 8h 48m 23s

The same result is obtained by the use of a noon-base ephemeris, thus:

S.T., July 4, 1967:	6h	47m	14s
Longitude correction:			49
Time interval:	2	0	0
Interval correction:			20
	8	48	23

Hence any astrological ephemeris for any particular year may be used for any combination of time and place in the year for which a horoscope is to be calculated. With the horoscope's individual midheaven or tenth house located, any Tables of Houses covering the geographic latitude of the place will show the zodiacal degrees and minutes for five more of the twelve house cusps. The six others lie precisely opposite, as seen in the example chart on page 312.

For a uniformity of horoscopic procedure that particularly helps a young student in an avoidance of error, calculation at all times is best from a previous midnight or noon, so that corrections here and at a later point in determining the planetary places at birth are always added. There is an important single exception, however, since in horoscopes for locations east of Greenwich the longitudinal adjustment would be cumbersome taken all around the globe as an extended west. Instead the distance east from the prime meridian is used to obtain the correction, which then is subtracted from rather than added to the midheaven sidereal time for midnight or noon given in the ephemeris.

Special Considerations

Daylight saving or summer or war time must always be corrected to standard, and then the standard hours and minutes must be changed to local mean time for the location of

319

the house cusps in zodiacal terms. If fifteen degress of geographical longitude correspond to an hour, each degree gives
a difference of four minutes. Thus New York City, 74° west,
uses eastern standard time that is correct in Oneonta in upper
New York State at 75° west. Local mean time in New York
City in consequence is always four minutes later than the
official indication of its clocks. Going to the east, standard time
is increased in the change to local mean since the sun arrives
there first and so makes it later while in moving to the west
it conversely is diminished, since the sun arrives later and the
time must be earlier.

If the horoscope is for southern latitudes, with only northern-hemisphere Tables of Houses available, twelve hours are
added to the midheaven in order to reverse the distortion in
the zodiacal correspondence to the houses. In such an operation the horoscopic cusps can be taken out of the tables if the
sign shown for each of them is replaced by its opposite. This
procedure first gains the proper relationship between the two
great heavenly circles for the particular time and place and
then recovers the correct zodiacal identification for the
houses. It can have illustration by a birth in Chile at Castro
which below the earth's equator has close to the exact situation of Oneonta in New York State above.[8] Again the event
is assumed for July 4, 1967, but at 3:00 P.M. in the Atlantic
standard time now used in Chile. This by mean local time is
the same as the 2:00 P.M. prevailing at Oneonta. The computation would be, using a Greenwich midnight ephemeris:

S.T., July 4, 1967:	18h	45m	16s	
Longitude correction:			49	
Time interval:	14	0	0	
Interval correction:		2	18	
To reverse distortion:	12	0	0	
	44	48	23	= 20h 48m 23s

[8] Castro, 42°30′ south and 74° west; Oneonta, 42°27′ north and
75°4′ west.

Referring to Dalton's Tables of Houses for northern latitudes, this locates the midheaven of the horoscope at approximately Aquarius 9°45' to represent Leo 9°45', and the ascendant somewhat more precisely at Gemini 4°44' to represent
Sagittarius 4°44'. Here is the parallel with the same Leo 9°45' for
Oneonta in the north, but the ascendant for the latter place
is located by direct computation for the sidereal time of 8h
48m 23s at Scorpio 2°42', or a difference of more than a whole
sign of the zodiac in the distortion of correspondence with the
house cusps.

The Calculation of Planetary Positions

To put the planets in the wheel-diagram or horoscopic
chart, as astrologers usually designate this part of the task, is
a different type of operation from the zodiacal location of the
twelve cusps. An ephemeris of the geocentric planetary
places in the heavens is almost universally calculated for the
prime meridian or 0° of terrestrial longitude, and to make use
of these tabulations the easiest procedure is to change the
mean local time into the time of the ephemeris of Greenwich
mean time customarily abbreviated as G.M.T. Once this is
done, the rest is simple proportion. Thus the horoscopic figure
for July 4th at 2:00 P.M. in London would show the planets
at the point to which they have moved either in fourteen out
of twenty-four hours, or seven-twelfths of the total movement
between the zero hours of July 4th and 5th in midnight-base
tables, or in one-twelfth of their daily motion when noon-base
tabulations are employed.

The use of fractions is easy for some astrologers, especially
in the occasionally simple case of the one-twelfth when using
the noon ephemeris for 2:00 P.M. G.M.T. Others however on
finding them difficult may employ a different method, and it
will be introduced shortly. Complex fractions can always be
handled readily enough by dividing them, as in the instance
of the fourteen hours to 2:00 P.M. from midnight. The planet's

movement can be taken as half the total from the zero hour of the 4th to the zero hour of the 5th, plus an extra sixth of that half. In other words the half is six-twelfths and the sixth of that as one of the twelfths makes the total seven-twelfths.

In all methods of calculation of planetary positions the geometrical proportion or rule of three is employed as follows:

$$\left. \begin{array}{l} \text{elapsed} \\ \text{hours} \end{array} \right\} : \quad 24\text{h} \quad : : \left\{ \begin{array}{l} \text{movement} \\ \text{required} \end{array} \right\} : \left\{ \begin{array}{l} \text{total} \\ \text{movement} \end{array} \right.$$

In the case of a 2:00 P.M. event at London on July 4, 1967, the position of the sun at 0^h on that day is Cancer 11°21′, and at 0^h on the 5th is Cancer 12°18′, or a total movement in the twenty-four hours of 57′. The proportion becomes:

$$14\text{h} \ : \ 24\text{h} \ : : \ x' \ : \ 57'$$

Since the product of the means is equal to the product of the extremes a missing mean number is obtained by dividing the product of the extremes by the known mean, thus:

$$14 \ \times \ 57 = 798$$
$$798 \ \div \ 24 = \ 33.25$$

This required movement is added to the position of the sun at 0^h Greenwich mean time to determine where the sun lies at 2:00 P.M. by the London clocks, or Cancer 11°21′ + 33′, giving Cancer 11°54′ for the sun's position in the horoscope.

The other procedure for calculating the planetary positions of only preliminary mention so far is by the use of logarithms. The logarithms of numbers to be multiplied can be added and their product gained by mere inspection of the tables. Division similarly is performed by subtraction. The operation just shown would be done in this fashion:

Logarithm of 14:	1461280
Add logarithm of 57:	7558749
	9020029
Subtract logarithm of 24:	3802118
	5217911

The resulting logarithm is found to be more than 5185139, the logarithm for 33, and less than 5314789, the one for 34, i.e., the 33.25 seen above. In this procedure one operation can be eliminated by the use of special diurnal proportional logarithms given in all ephemerides to four decimal places and readily available to five. The twenty-four hour factor is constant and so can be built into the structure of the logarithms themselves, whereupon it is not necessary to carry out the division by twenty-four hours but only to add the one for the elapsed hours to the one for the total movement:

Diurnal logarithm for 57′:	1.40249
Diurnal logarithm for 14h:	.23408
	1.63657

The result here is greater than 1.62688, for 34′, and less than 1.63985, for 33′, and the calculation is simplified considerably.

A Complete Example

The exact moment of the author's arrival at a hotel in Seattle on March 4, 1969, for a three-day literary retreat in which one particular objective was to rough out this revised or more up-to-date illustrative mathematical section of the appendix was 9:37 A.M. Pacific Standard Time. The city is located in Washington State at 47°37′ north latitude and 122°20′ west longitude, and so there is a time difference of nine minutes between the mean local and the standard times. Seattle is west of the standard-zone meridian, and consequently the local mean time is earlier or is 9:28 A.M.

Using a midnight-base ephemeris, the calculation of the sidereal time for the horoscopic midheaven is as follows:

S.T., March 4, 1969:	10h	46m	19s
Longitude correction:		1	20
Time interval:	9	28	
Interval correction:		1	33
	20	17	12

and with a noon-base ephemeris the computation will be:

S.T., March 3, 1969:	22h	44m	21s
Longitude correction:		1	20
Time interval:	21	28	
Interval correction:		3	32
	20	17	13

In Dalton's tabulation of houses for the horoscope the sidereal time of an even 2° of Aquarius on the midheaven is 20h 17m 3s, and in normal course the difference of ten-odd seconds of time is simply disregarded since it is seldom indeed that any event can be timed down to such a fine point of accuracy.[9]

Since Seattle does not lie on an even parallel of geographic

[9] Whenever there is a possibility of employment of the symbolized degrees of the zodiac, as presented in the author's *Sabian Symbols in Astrology,* Sabian Publishing Society, New York, 1953, a degree is rounded to the next full one no matter how small an increment may be. In this present instance however the testimony of the symbols themselves is the probable correctness of Aquarius 2° instead of Aquarius 3° since the issue was the unexpected storm of pyramiding interest in these texts and the practical problem of reprinting several of them prior to all expectation rather than exceptional challenge to persistence in the struggle with their creation.

latitude, an adjustment must be made at the ascendant. The zodiacal correspondence increases 70' from 47° north to 48° north, and a half plus a quarter of this for 37' of latitude north from 47° or 35' plus 9' or 44'-odd added to Taurus 29°31' locates the horoscopic first cusp at Gemini 0°15'. The minor cusps are then rounded to their next full degree as shown in the completed horoscopic chart.

In the Rice Tables of Houses the S.T. of the horoscope midheaven of 20h 17m 12-3s lies a fraction more than a minute of sidereal time beyond the 20h 16m 0s of a horoscopic midheaven of 1°45'1'' of Aquarius and hence is almost precisely Aquarius 2° with close confirmation of the ascendant determined in the Dalton tables.

When it comes to the location of the planetary positions in the horoscope for the author's several-day retreat, a G.M.T. of 5:37 P.M. established by the difference of 8h 9m may at a glance be seen as a close approximation to a simple quarter of a day after noon and so a half day plus a half of itself from the zero hour at midnight. The sun at this moment of the year and in 1969 is moving almost an exact sixty minutes in the twenty-four hours, or with a deviation of only five to six seconds of arc. A quarter of this sixty minutes adds fifteen to the sun's position in the noon-base ephemeris to correct Pisces 13° 44' to 13°59', and the half plus the half of itself adds forty-five minutes to the sun's position in the midnight-base ephemeris and corrects Pisces 13°14' also to Pisces 13°59'.

If the position of the moon in a nativity is desired to an appreciable preciseness the fractional method often is more trouble than an employment of the logarithms. Here the 5h 37m from noon taken as six hours in round terms is more than a twelfth of itself less than that. A quarter of the moon's daily motion on March 4th from noon or 13°9' is first 3° and then 17' or a total of 3°17' to be diminished by a twelfth of itself or 16' to become 13°1' to be added to Virgo 17°5' to locate it at Virgo 20°6' in the nativity. This varies by four or five minutes of arc from the results gained by logarithms and is a difference of little likely significance. The places of the slow-moving planets are easy to determine by a simple fraction. Jupiter's average daily motion is 12′ and normally a quarter would be 3′ but here in retrogradation it moves 7′ in the twenty-four hours and a quarter of 2′ would be insignificantly different. From Saturn on out the corrections are minor indeed.

As perhaps helpful example, the calculations by logarithms can be given from both noon-base and midnight-base ephemerides for placing five of the ten general significators in this horoscope. The result may be a somewhat greater preciseness. To be noted in that the logarithm for the elapsed time or here 5h 37m is used in each operation, and in consequence it is known familiarly to astrologers as the constant logarithm.

From Noon	Moon	Mercury	Sun	Venus	Mars
Daily motion	13° 9′	1°19′	1° 0′	28′	25′
Logarithm	.2613	1.2607	1.3802	1.7112	1.7604
Constant log.	.6307	.6307	.6307	.6307	.6307
Logarithm and	.8920	1.8914	2.0109	2.3419	2.3911
required motion	3° 5′	18′	14′	7′	6′
Position at noon	♍17° 5′	♒ 18°33′	♓ 13°44′	♈ 23°16′	♐ 3°11′
At 5:37 P.M.	♍20°10′	♒ 18°51′	♓ 13°58′	♈ 23°23′	♐ 3°17′

From Midnight	Moon	Mercury	Sun	Venus	Mars
Daily motion	13° 2′	1°18′	1° 0′	28′	26′
Logarithm	.2652	1.2663	1.3802	1.7112	1.7434
Constant log.	.1343	.1343	.1343	.1343	.1343
Logarithm and	.3995	1.4006	1.5145	1.8455	1.8777
required motion	9°34′	57′	44′	21′	19′
Position at 0h	♍10°37′	♒ 17°53′	♓ 13°14′	♈ 23° 2′	♐ 2°58′
At 5:37 P.M.	♍20°11′	♒ 18°50′	♓ 13°58′	♈ 23°23′	♐ 3°17′

How to Read a Horoscope

The materials in these example delineations are taken almost word for word from the paragraphs in Chapters Fourteen and Fifteen. No astrologer in practice would hold as literally as this to the thumbnail sketches given for the planetary positions. The indications blend into a wholeness of personality in exactly the same way as the features or form, the clothing, the acts and reactions of the native, when encountered in normal experience. Moreover, the present text is introductory in nature and scope, confining itself to the significance of the houses, signs and planets in their simple implication. There are important patterns of relationship formed among the planets, and many other ramifications of analysis, in any competent horoscopy.[1] Nonetheless a very interesting reading of the chart is possible with these elementary factors alone, and they remain the foundation of all astrological

---

[1] Prior reference to the planetary aspects has been made on page 236. The fundamental overview of the entire horoscope necessary in any complete delineation has been given a full if preliminary treatment in the author's smaller manual, *The Guide to Horoscope Interpretation*, Philadelphia, David McKay, 1941. A comprehensive outline of all natal technique is provided by the companion volume in the major series of astrological textbooks or the author's *Essentials of Astrological Analysis*, New York, Sabian Publishing Society, 1960.

delineation, no matter what else may be added, or given greater emphasis. The newcomer may proceed in the manner illustrated, at least until he has developed a greater skill and is enabled to present a more complete portrait of the native.

FRANKLIN DELANO ROOSEVELT

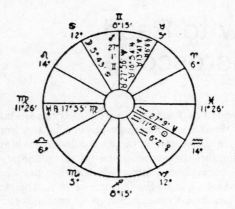

Hyde Park, New York, January 30, 1882, 7:46 P.M. local mean time.[2]

Vitality

$$(\odot : 5th, \approx\!\!\approx ; \ \mathcal{D} : 10th, \mathcal{S})$$

The practical focus of this life is the native's determination to flow out into every expression of selfhood. He has a conscious interest in the passing parade of events, and a tendency to make life an ever-varying carnival. He is able to bring a

[2] This chart has been obtained from Mr. Keye Lloyd, president of the American Federation of Astrologers, and is based on information given by Mr. Roosevelt's mother.

heightened enjoyment to himself, and everyone around him. Life for him must be purposeful, and he must be readily stimulated. He is high-visioned, optimistic, gregarious to a fault, and often gullible. He must be challenged to his best or he becomes dogmatic and jealous. He is a realist in minor things, a do-or-die idealist otherwise.

His personal experience is centered in public affairs, great or small, exaggerating his assimilation of himself to the group. His pleasure is in all large-scale and responsible act. He is able to further the interests of everyone with real success. His temperament is characteristically responsive to self-existence as an adventure, and he reacts to experience with a possessive and confident expectation. He is emotionally maternal, hence often patronizing, and always sympathetic in his own individual fashion. He is naïvely faithful in his affections, but devastatingly exacting of anything he cannot encompass.

Efficiency

(♂ : 10th, ♊ ; ♀ : 5th, ♒ ; ☿ : 6th, ♒)

Mr. Roosevelt has a type of initiative which primarily meets the needs of simple self-achievement or social recognition. He must have an everyday experience where group activity has an exceptional emphasis. He is able to demonstrate leadership or responsibility in every special field of effort. His characteristic inclination is to act with an enthusiastic acquiescence in anything projected by others, or by a momentary throwing of the self into every phase of familiar routine. He asserts himself in the petty details of life by taking more than his expected part in immediate affairs, destructively if he cannot do so otherwise, and by trying to be everywhere at once.

Any self-satisfaction is gained by him primarily thorugh a direct refinement and exhibition of individual skills. He must have a practical reward for effort which ultimately augments the channels for self-expression. He is able to dramatize himself most inspiringly. He shows a characteristic fondness for

329

life in its intellectual or ideal enthusiasms, and has a tendency to bring things to completion in response to a very deliberate notion. He makes himself comfortable under the everyday demands upon him by refusing to be involved in trivial matters, and by making everything around him significant in the light of his own personal ideas.

His mind or focus of awareness depends primarily, for self-orientation, upon a continual readjustment in human relations. His rational tendency is to think of everything as material for manipulation. He is able to solve any social dilemma. He has the type of mind which characteristically anchors itself in the idealized promise of life, and relies more upon its initial than its final insights. This means a mentality which is inspired rather than refined by experience, and so apt to overreach itself. The frame of reference in all its thinking is the pattern of values in which human vision is nurtured.

Motivation

$$(\text{♃} : 9\text{th}, \text{♉} ; \text{♄} : 9\text{th}, \text{♉})$$

The native's psychological orientation primarily seeks to keep life aligned to its own genius or heritage. The personal incentive is encouraged through an expanding intellectual discovery and insight. He is able to bring everyone to real wisdom. His consciousness is characteristically self-exploiting, and sure in its response to ideas. Its fundamental motivation arises from its own inexhaustible capacity for experience with inner implication. The native as a real personage is interested in making an effective contribution to the values of life, and his welfare requires a genuine role in human progress.

All personal motivation is centered in intellectual considerations or vicarious experience. He has a special sensitiveness to the particular competency of individual judgments. He is able to bring depth to every effort of men to understand themselves. His characteristic sensitiveness may lead him to an unnecessary agonizing over his deeper ideals. An inner dignity of self requires him to sustain a realization of some worthy destiny for himself. His basic personality is refined by the necessity that he translate his ideals into definite action, or in some way strengthen the *esprit de corps* of his own milieu.

Significance

(♅ : 1st, ♍ ; ♆ : 9th, ♉ ; ♇, 9th, ♉)

Any individuality in Mr. Roosevelt's case is encouraged most definitely by direct and intimate relationships. Any expression of independence is through some effective achievement by the self. He is able to bring new life to any situation in which he can develop an interest. His characteristic emphasis of individuality is through his gift for enhancing his own original usefulness in the commonplace functions he performs, and for bringing people into exceptionally practical relationship with each other. He is able to regrasp or master his destiny at any time by encouraging, organizing and utilizing various untried social potentialities of the given milieu.

His experience must remain intellectual or vicarious, and must eliminate all immediate attention to ideal realizations. He invites self-limitation through a vacillation or inconclusiveness of judgment. He is able to bring an illimitable scope to human thinking. He shows a characteristic conformity to his astrological generation, with its over-all culture of a new secular philosophy. He achieves his own desires fully when he shapes his action to general standards or idealized values.

His social perspective, which orients him to life as a whole, arises from the impact of science, religion and philosophy, enhancing his analytical interest in the competency of human knowledge. He is able to elevate the standards of any particular milieu in which he finds himself. He has an active interest in the practical integration of society, and is inclined to look upon life in utilitarian fashion, or with an extreme of psychological support for exploitation.

MARY BAKER GLOVER EDDY

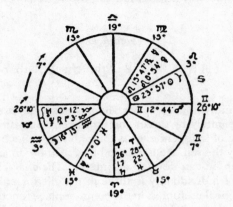

Bow, New Hampshire, July 16, 1821, 5:33 P.M. local mean time.[3]

Vitality

(☉: 7th, ♋; ☽: 2d, ♒)

The practical focus of this life is the native's determination to enjoy human relationships at every point of contact. She has a conscious flair for seeing an advantage or recognizing an opportunity, and is able to persuade all people to co-operate with whatever catches her interest. Life for her must be exciting, and she must be self-consummating. She is willful,

[3] This chart has been obtained from Mrs. Mabel Leslie Fleischer, president of the Astrologers' Guild of America, and is based on information gained by Evangeline Adams when she lived in New Hampshire, and was able to check on the data over a long period.

possessive, unhurried, and gifted with insight into the possibility of things. She is unpredictable, stubborn in whatever course she adopts, ever opportunistic or calculating, and self-centered.

Her personal experience is centered in a general sharing or utilization of human resources. She has an exaggerated sense of immediate possessiveness in every phase of life. She is able to bring a living significance to any event in which she participates. Her temperament is characteristically responsive to experience as the proving ground of self, and she reacts to everything on an idealistic or utilitarian pattern. She is emotionally overloaded with potentials of self-release which may be spilled out as sheer desire, used to buttress some pet cause, or stored up in high frustration. She is prodigal, but careful.

Efficiency

$$(\sigma : \text{6th}, \; \mathrm{I\!I} ; \; \varphi : \text{8th}, \; \Omega ; \; \xi : \text{8th}, \; \Omega)$$

Mrs. Eddy has a type of initiative which primarily meets the needs of simple adjustment in the social milieu. She must have an everyday experience where human inequalities and cross purposes are a problem. She is able to play the role of conciliator, thriving on the chance to reach high and low. Her characteristic inclination is to act with an enthusiastic acquiescence in anything projected by others, or with a momentary throwing of the self into every phase of familiar routine. She asserts herself in the petty details of life by taking more than her expected part in immediate affairs, destructively if she cannot do so otherwise, and by trying to be everywhere at once.

Any self-satisfaction is gained by her primarily through the recognition and use of purely social resources. She must have a practical reward for effort which ultimately will provide fresh cycles of experience. The native is able to call out new and constructive effort in every situation. She shows a characteristic fondness for life in its common or spontaneous dramatization of human values, and has a tendency to bring things to completion arbitrarily or in response to an inner and private consideration. She makes herself comfortable under the everyday demands upon her by ignoring her fellows, except as they show an effective respect for her accomplishments and her notions.

Her mind or focus of awareness depends primarily, for self-orientation, upon a conformity to the general social trend. Her rational tendency is to think of things as representing a greater reality than themselves. She is able to stimulate all people to a real accomplishment. She has the type of mind which characteristically anchors itself in the idealized reality of life, and which relies more upon its initial than its final insights. This means a mentality which is fundamentally stirred within itself rather than influenced by exterior relationships. The frame of reference in all its thinking is the significance of the self in the experience of the moment.

Motivation

$$(\text{♃} : 4\text{th}, \; \text{♈}; \; \text{♄} : 4\text{th}, \; \text{♈})$$

The native's psychological orientation primarily seeks some inner assurance for the self in every phase and turn of existence. The personal incentive is encouraged through success in stabilizing the immediate milieu of interest. She is able to help others achieve enduring fruits of experience. Her consciousness is characteristically self-sufficient, and quick in its response to new situations. Its fundamental motivation arises from its own unimpeachable sincerity in every issue of life. The native as a real personage is interested in adequate fields for her talents, and her welfare demands a continual and insistent personal challenge.

All personal motivation is centered in considerations of security or ease for the self and its own. She has a special sensitiveness to entrenched prerogatives and cloistered luxury as ends to be demanded or defended. She is able to bring depth to any place of retreat. Her characteristic sensitiveness may lead her to attempt too hurried a perfecting of her special potentialities. An inner dignity of self requires her to demand a more than normal recognition or encouragment from life at large. Her basic personality is refined by the necessity that she reconstitute and re-establish herself with every new development in her general situation.

Significance

(♅ : 1st, ♑ ; ♆ : 1st, ♑ ; ♇ : 3rd, ♓)

Any individuality in Mrs. Eddy's case is encouraged most definitely by direct and intimate relationships. Any expression of independence is through some effective achievement by the self. She is able to bring new life to any situation in which she can develop an interest. Her characteristic emphasis of individuality is through her gift for capitalizing upon the unexpected eventualities of experience, and so opening new avenues of self-expression to herself. She is able to regrasp or master her destiny at any time by gathering the scattered threads of any social milieu, weaving them together with a unique and fascinating effectiveness.

Her experience must remain naïve, and must eliminate all direct psychological support for the self. She invites self-limitation through a general indefiniteness of reaction to normal reality. She is able to rise for the moment to the most divergent of necessities. She shows a characteristic conformity to her astrological generation, with its over-all culture of political opportunism, sectional rivalry and personal ingenuity. She achieves her own desires fully when she capitalizes upon the community interest.

Her social perspective, which orients her to life as a whole, arises from her involvement in minor responsibility, enhancing her analytical interest in commonplace or neighborly relations. She is able to ferret out and capitalize upon the social capacities of everyone around her. She has universal aspirations, and is inclined to live easily, but always exercising herself over world-wide issues in a psychological encouragement for man's conquest of nature.

335

The Astrological Literature

Astrology has always had a voluminous literature. Dr. Charles Singer of London University points out, in an excellent although unfriendly article ("Astrology," *Encyclopedia of the Social Sciences,* New York, Macmillan, 1931), that the possible relation between man and the heavens was a chief object of scientific interest in Europe at the height of the Renaissance. Mrs. Ellen McCaffery, the New York astrologer, in her note on the library of William Lilly (*Astrology, Its History and Influence in the Modern World,* New York, Scribner's, 1942, page 396) notes that books on the stellar science were probably among the first to come off the newly invented printing presses. There is ample indication that the ancient civilizations of the Mesopotamian and Nile valleys had extensive writings on the subject. Much of this material, surviving into Grecian times, entered into the compilation by Claudius Ptolemy. The broad Stoic interest in astrological principles had its unquestionable reflection in Latin manuscripts without number. The Arabs were assiduous in collecting and copying treatises, in refining them and commenting upon them.

Except for the privately printed *Catalogue Raisonné of Works on the Occult Sciences, Volume II, Astrological Books,* by F. Leigh Gardner (London, 1911), no effort has been made to provide a critical list of the more important or most widely known writings. While he refers to over fourteen hundred works, these are largely limited to items possessed by the English astrologers within recent times. Bibliographies in older books and manuscripts are seldom extensive. Most of the documents that would be needed for a thorough account of natal horoscopy are buried hopelessly in old libraries, where they are victims of neglect, ignorance and prejudice with nearly all the source materials in an all-important early medieval period. The ancient records have probably survived, if at all, to the minimal extent common in other fields, and they may have suffered in special degree from a sheer unreasoning bigotry.

The historical accounts of astrology are few, and none possess a requisite critical competency. Most of them list the outstanding individuals of the past who have used or championed horoscopy—in an unblushing compilation of testimonials—otherwise merely repeating the traditional accounts of increase or recession in astrological interest. If the stellar science is not dismissed as a surviving superstition by its critics, it is apt to be exalted as a divine art, or given a magical sponsorship by its devotees. There is no attempt whatever to trace out the evolution of idea represented by its development, or to find the roots of the many and widely varying horoscopic techniques. Manly Palmer Hall's *The Story of Astrology* (1933; new edition, Philadelphia, McKay, 1943) presents a simple and very general survey. Mrs. McCaffery's book, to which reference has been made, is a pioneer effort to introduce the science on the basis of actual source materials.

A history, to be critically adequate, would have to give major attention to the changing milieu in which the judicial art has functioned, and to the varying implication of the horoscopic factors in highly discrete ages or cultures. The existing narratives never seem aware of the psychological fallacy arising whenever a contemporary conception of planetary correspondences is carried back into earlier times, or into alien modes of life, and then read into words that are part of an entirely different language of experience. No distinction is ever made between Assyrian and Hellenistic, or Greco-Roman and medieval periods. Astrology is revealed, in its real contribution to a given age, as much by the individuals and groups who will have none of it as by those who are its proponents. Any divination or technique of measurement, whether a science or pure intuition, is always a creature of the special world in which it functions. Horoscopy does not exist in a vacuum, insulated from a universe characterized by change and growth. The real question is not what has happened to the stellar art as a belief—that is, a sort of religious faith, or sacred practice, such as is supposed to have come down through the ages in a perpetual or innate perfection—but rather what has forged this or that aspect of astrological procedure, and in what way has man been able to know himself better, or to handle his affairs more effectively, by developing this means for patterning himself in the stars.

Judicial astrology has undoubtedly been derived from Mesopotamian lands, reaching historical notice through the Sumerians, Assyrians and Babylonians, whatever its actual roots may have been. In its development it has obviously paralleled natural astrology, or the investigations of weather and climate upon which the very existence of these early peoples depended. Apparently men felt themselves in partnership with their cosmos, however they may have expressed this idea, and the source of the horoscope may well have been their wish to divine those conditions under which the individual could best adjust himself to the necessities of his existence, and their effort to measure these in time and persistency. The original psychology was probably fatalistic, or what any modern view would regard as defeatist. However, the sense of a touch with the totality of all existence—a universal oversoul, a purpose or plan of greater compass than mere personal luck or ill-fortune—was a step forward from the species of animism which would have preceded it. Turning away from the sense of a need to propitiate the spirit in everything, from the rock in the path to the threshold of the house, was a move towards science, and away from superstition, no matter how feeble it might have been. This initial role would make astrology a psychological tool of the intelligent and educated classes, who may be presumed to have been the ones perfecting its general techniques.

With the rise of a true physics among the Greeks, and their stress of a high individualism, the judicial art would naturally appear in evil guise. It would seem to be an effort at cosmic appeasement, or animism on a larger scale. In its natural degeneracy among the illiterate masses, it obviously was an abject surrender to the inevitable in events. The Grecian thinkers on the whole would have nothing of it, and there is little evidence of any great interest in the horoscope through the great Hellenistic ferment. There are references in Hesiod, and in the *Hippocratic Collection* of the fifth century B.C. Plato provides a mention in the *Timaeus*, a phase of his work left incomplete and unrefined. In view of the tremendous impact of so large a part of the Babylonian culture on the Greeks otherwise, the lack of interest in astrology becomes highly significant. If before this it had been the channel for an escape from superstition, now it appears as one of the most debased forms of pseudo-divination. Christianity, with its doctrine of an unimpeachable free will, fought the stellar art from the days of the Church Fathers, on into the modern era, and only in very scattered instances has the Christian religion been willing to have any commerce with its techniques.

Meanwhile there was one segment of Greek thought which rose to dominate the Roman intellectual world for several centuries. Stoic philosophy found a ready instrumentation for its belief in a world of over-all ordering—that is, the idea of man as a microcosm which lives in a precise conformity to the will held for it by a macrocosmic universe—and it was these thinkers who contributed a real rational competence in the recrudescence and more thorough refinement of judicial astrology. Here is the turn in events responsible for such references as may be found in Cicero's *Dream of Scipio,* or in the *Meditations* of Marcus Aurelius Antoninus. Probably the oldest known actual work of consequence on horoscopy is the poem *Astronomica,* in five books, by the Stoic poet Manilius. This is not quoted in antiquity and, while a composition of great erudition, was never completed. There are editions by Regiomontanus (Johann Mueller) in 1472 and Joseph Scaliger in 1579, two of the outstanding scholars of the Renaissance, and a translation with introduction by A. E. Housman (London, 1903). It was a Greek at Alexandria in the second century A.D., Claudius Ptolemy, who summarized and preserved the astrological techniques of this Stoic period. His *Tetrabiblos,* or four books concerning the influences of the stars, established him as the real father of European, modern or western judicial art. The translation of this work by James Wilson (London, 1820), and a better one by J. M. Ashmand (London, 1822), have been familiar to English-speaking astrologers for the past century.

Astrology in Europe went into decline with the fall of the Roman Empire. As was true of all learning, fragments of varying merit survived here and there, and a ferment of creative thought was at work throughout the Dark Ages. However, the new impetus was to come from the outside and, in the case of horoscopic analysis, through the Arabian influence. Much of the Renaissance spirit came from the Greeks when Byzantium was engulfed by the Moslem tide, but everything astrological seems to have been mediated by Moslem thinkers. In this stage of things the stellar science offered an instrumentation for the idea of an impersonal law operating in the universe, as opposed to the notion of a divine will which had no guiding principle but its own caprice. Astrology thereby came to express, paradoxically enough, the operation of freedom and chance rather than fatality. In other words, to the extent that man could find out the dependable course of events, or could estimate any particular tendency as a predictable constant in some given case, he was able to make a free choice and establish a measure of guidance for his own affairs. The church, meanwhile, had taken over the Stoic conception of micro-macrocosm, and made of it an immutable cosmic plan moving on to its own absolutely certain conclusion, with no hope for anyone except as he accepted the preordained design in his own case, i.e., the ancient defeatism in a new set of terms.

Astrology might have anticipated its present development and progress by a good six to seven hundred years had not the philosophical turn of the later Renaissance, by taking man out of nature and considering him a spiritualistic being—that is, a visitor from another world of reality sojourning in this one—left no real connection between the true person and the actual universe. Because horoscopic insights fundamentally deny this separation of the native and his milieu of tangible events, the rising metaphysical and psychological fallacies of the seventeenth and eighteenth centuries conspired to push the stellar art back into the role it had filled with the Stoics, that is, the measurement of fatality or compulsion rather than freedom. The literature, in consequence—as far as the underlying assumptions are concerned—picks up just where Ptolemy left off, with little to show for the intervening centuries. There were many writers, as Lucas Gauricus (1476–1558), the astrologer of Catherine d'Medici—whose personal security enabled them to do the careful work which would gain broad circulation or win high esteem—or as Michel Nostradamus (1503–1566)—who, while not making any direct contribution to astrology as such, were yet famous enough in their own day or after to give considerable weight to judicial practice—but of those who have had any direct influence upon the growth of horoscopy in English-speaking countries, only a relatively small number have been at all significant.

The men directly responsible for the survival of astrology, as established in the modern world, were for the major part scientifically *declassé* enthusiasts. Because they were deprived of all co-operative fellowship with the men engaged most outstandingly in astronomical, medical and psychological research, they suffered from a cultural lag for which they should not be condemned. In the same way that isolated ethnic groups have tended to preserve archaic languages and customs all over the globe, the highly insulated astrologers clung curiously but characteristically to an earlier and outmoded scientific view. This was an intellectual framework which developed in the eleventh to fifteenth centuries primarily and which, none too happily on the whole, lost all respectability with the seventeenth century's materialistic synthesis. The marks of this astrological crystallization are to be noted in (1) an unreasoning veneration for old books, (2) a deference to the fathers of the art as beyond error, and (3) the idea that the real nature and powers of the horoscope were determined for once and all in a dim antiquity, if indeed these did not come direct from the gods, so that (4) interpretive skill would depend on spiritual merit or divine favor. Here is the basic explanation for the fact that so much astrological literature consists of materials copied without change from those who have gone before.

William Lilly's *Christian Astrology* (London, 1647) is the most important pioneer work in the modern development. In this the author culled freely from the sources to which he had access, and of which he printed a complete catalogue. Richard James Morrison, the first to use the pseudonym Zadkiel, selected and edited an *Introduction to Astrology by William Lilly* in 1852, which, combined with Morrison's own *Grammar of Astrology*, written in 1833, has been incorporated in Bohn's Scientific Library (London, 1865). Lilly's pupil, John Gadbury, provided an all-important clarification of natal practice, as far as horoscopy in British practice is concerned, with his *Doctrine of Nativities* (London, 1658) and his *Collection of Nativities* (London, 1662). Henry Coley, Lilly's adopted son and secretary, wrote in this period. William Salmon issued his works of possible significance in 1671–9, and John Partridge, Gadbury's pupil and victim of Jonathan Swift's rapier wit, published his *Mikropanastron* in 1679.

Meanwhile the *Tabulae Rudolphinae* Of Tycho Brahe and Johannes Kepler appeared at Ulm in 1627. Of signal importance on the mathematics side was the work of Didacus Placidus de Titus, the *Primum Mobile* (Padua, 1657) which, translated by John Cooper (London, 1820?) has ranked with Ptolemy's *Tetrabiblos* in its general influence on modern methods. No other figures on the continent made any appreciable impact on England's astrologers, however, and the only British writer of any appreciable originality, until well into the last century, was William Joseph Simmonite, whose *Complete Arcana* appeared in 1844, and whose *Horary Astrology* was published about 1851.

The beginning of a true modern astrology dates from the publication of James Wilson's *A Complete Dictionary of Astrology* (London, 1819; reprinted at Boston, 1885). Robert Smith, the first Raphael, began the real flood of new books with his *Manual of Astrology* (London, 1828). When he founded his *Prophetic Messenger*, in 1826, he launched the wave of periodicals. The sixth of those to take the name Raphael, Robert Cross, became the pioneer popularizer of astrology in the world of today. His handbooks, *The Guide to Astrology* (London, 1877–79; revised in America as *Raphael's Key to Astrology*, new edition, Philadelphia, McKay, 1943), *Horary Astrology* (London, 1883), and several others of lesser importance, were for long indispensable for students unable to obtain the older and usually rare items. Alfred J. Pearce took over the almanac and name of Zadkiel a year after the death of Morrison in 1874, and in 1879–89 published what remained for many years the most scholarly work available on horoscopy, *The Textbook of Astrology*.

Of the English writers, two more of wide popularity made outstanding contributions to the literature at the turn of the century. Walter Gorn Old, writing under the name Sepharial, provided a valuable volume in his *The New Manual of Astrology* (London, 1898). Alan Leo with his *Modern Astrology* (a periodical started as *The Astrologer's Magazine* in 1890), his *Practical Astrology* (London, 1902?; new edition, Philadelphia, McKay, 1944), his seven large textbooks (London, 1903–5), his fourteen manuals (London, 1901–12) his dictionary and other books and pamphlets, completely revolutionized astrological literature. Among British astrologers of recent importance, Vivian E. Robson and Charles E. O. Carter are competent writers. In France and Germany the contemporary development in astrology has been a stress upon statistical research and mathematical theory. The Oriental world has a long-established tradition of considerable originality and importance, but little is known of its content, methods or history in Western lands. Walter Gorn Old greatly stimulated the current interest in the Hindu system, and Robert DeLuce, an American astrologer of ability, is at work upon a complete description and account of East Indian practice.

Astrology in the United States has had a long and hard struggle. L. D. Broughton published *The Elements of Astrology* at New York about 1898; and this was long the New World's only textbook (*The Primer of Astrology* by W. H. Chaney, Broughton's pupil, Boston, 1890, had little to recommend it beyond its tables). The *Astrological Bulletina,* oldest of the American magazines still in circulation, was launched by Llewellyn George in 1908, and his *A to Z Horoscope Delineator* (Portland, Oregon, 1910), exceedingly modest in its first edition, represented the actual start of a new nonperiodical literature on this side of the Atlantic. Catherine H. Thompson, who was taught by Dr. Broughton in New York, started her magazine, *The Sphinx*, in Boston in 1901, and began to command a more respectable hearing for the stellar art. However, not until her pupil, Evangeline Adams, was able to get a much broader and more continuous publicity, based upon a practice in which the most prominent figures of her day were conspicuous, and so justifying the publication of her first book by Dodd-Mead (*The Bowl of Heaven,* New York, 1926), was there any development to parallel the large-scale promotion of horoscopy in London.

The full story of American astrology has yet to be put into print. Mrs. McCaffery gives an interesting but incomplete account, frankly stating her difficulties and hoping that many will take up the task for which she has pointed the way. Manly Palmer Hall is gathering, in the library of the Philosophical Research Society in Los Angeles, what promises to become the finest collection of actual source materials in the world, and eventually he will complete an ambitious, large-scale and documented narrative to follow his own earlier outline. George J. McCormack, president of the American Academy of Astrologians, has been adding to the records accumulated for a generation by Oliver Hazelrigg—aided by his brother, John Hazelrigg, one of the first American astrologers to bring a real social prestige to his calling—and is planning to bring out a vastly expanded bibliography of astrological books, replacing the limited listings by F. Leigh Gardner. His work will provide very needed information on the outstanding individuals of the field in the United States.

The first astrological periodical in America was Hague's *United States Horoscope and Scientific and Literary Messenger,* published in Philadelphia from 1840 to 1848, Broughton's *Monthly Horoscope* following in 1849. The *Star of the Magi,* published in Chicago around 1900, was the most prominent early periodical. The newsstand type of popular monthly was pioneered by Paul G. Clancy, whose *American Astrology Magazine* appeared on the stands with country-wide distribution in March, 1933. (Actually Mr. Clancy launched his publishing venture with the *Astrological Bulletin*—later *Popular Astrology*—on May 20, 1931, circulating these nationally through bookstores from Detroit, then moving to New York and continuing the original editorial plan under the broader distribution which had not been achieved before by astrological publications.)

Of importance in American astrological history has been the encouragement of study groups and correspondence work by Max Heindel's Rosicrucian Fellowship and Elbert Benjamine's Brotherhood of Light (now Church of Light). Until very recent times the really vital contribution of books on the stellar art from the United States has been in the realm of mathematics with the publication of *The Spherical Basis of Astrology* by Joseph G. Dalton (Boston, 1893; seventh edition, New York, Macoy, 1942), and the *American Astrology Tables of Houses* by Hugh S. Rice (Philadelphia, McKay, 1944), both men of standing in the astronomical field.

This index is arranged primarily for students and teachers of astrology. The terms listed are those most apt to enter the mind when referring to some one or another phase of horoscope theory and technique. Thus all proper names are included (other than the fictitious ones), but only familiar book titles. There is no general tabulation of house, sign and planetary meanings here, since the index does not duplicate the tables, and omits all obscure implications, or those which would be too general, or too ambiguous out of context. Only general references are made to Chapters Fourteen and Fifteen, and to Appendix B. The additional astrological meanings are given to facilitate the use of the text in horoscopic delineation.

INDEX

Descriptive List of Chapter Sections

The Tables of Relations, Meanings and Keywords

Fundamental Terms Defined and Described

TECHNICAL TERMS AND KEYWORDS

351

Proper Names and Book Titles

Additional General References

Additional Astrological Meanings

Horoscopes and Their Calculation

Common Abbreviations

A.C.D. adjusted calculation date (artificial birthday for computing directions)
E.S.T. eastern standard time (and similarly for other zones)
G.M.T. Greenwich mean time
I.C. *imum coeli* or nadir
L.M.T. local mean time

M.C. *medium coeli* or midheaven
M.M. moon's daily movement
P.M.T. Philadelphia mean time
R.A. right ascension
S.T. sidereal time (sometimes standard time)

*Some other books published by Penguin
are described on the following pages.*

*Some other books published by Penguin
are described on the following pages.*

THE PRACTICE OF ASTROLOGY

Dane Rudhyar

Here is a new, step-by-step approach to astrology. The basic facts and methods are reviewed, as well as essential preliminaries often overlooked by both student and practicing astrologer. All the important elements of the birth chart are explained in terms of how they work together in prediction and interpretation. Finally the author shows how these techniques can be used to reach astrology's highest goal: human understanding. Dane Rudhyar has been a leading figure in international astrology for almost forty years.

THE BOOK OF MIRDAD

Mikhail Naimy

A penetrating look at the age-old problem of the *whence, whither,* and *wherefore* of man. Blending legend, mysticism, philosophy, and poetry, the author, a Lebanese mystic, seeks and finds answers in man himself. His aim is to uncover God in man by dissolving man's sense of duality—the *I* and the *non-I*. The *non-I* he calls a shadow, which must be cast away in order that man may realize the *Perfect Balance*. "Spread out," says Mirdad, the book's central figure, "spread out until the whole world be wherever you may chance to be." To read *The Book of Mirdad* is to expand one's consciousness beyond all dualities and to reach that Holy Understanding which alone is a lighthouse and a haven. Widely read throughout the Arab world, Mikhail Naimy's works include drama, poetry, criticism, short stories, biography, autobiography, and essays on the deeper meanings of human existence.

MAGIC AND MYSTERY IN TIBET

Alexandra David-Neel

A unique account of strange experiences in a mysterious and forbidden land. The author spent fourteen years exploring Tibet and spoke all of the Tibetan dialects fluently. Among much else, she reveals how Tibetan mystics are able to live naked in zero temperatures by generating a protective body heat; how they can run incredibly long distances without rest, food, or drink; how they talk to each other by a sort of telepathy; how they learn to float in air and walk on water; and how they can actually create animate objects by thinking them into existence. Alexandra David-Neel was the only European woman given the rank of Lama. At the time of her death in 1969, she was regarded as one of the world's foremost explorers.

B DAYS

PEGGY (KIMBERLIN)
          BAGGET

12:45 PM
1 AUG 41
Front Royal, Va